CHRISTIANITY
AND THE SOUL OF THE
UNIVERSITY

CHRISTIANITY
AND THE SOUL OF THE
UNIVERSITY

FAITH AS A FOUNDATION
FOR INTELLECTUAL COMMUNITY

Edited by

Douglas V. Henry and Michael D. Beaty

Baker Academic
Grand Rapids, Michigan

© 2006 by Douglas V. Henry and Michael D. Beaty

Published by Baker Academic
a division of Baker Publishing Group
P.O. Box 6287, Grand Rapids, MI 49516-6287
www.bakeracademic.com

Printed in the United States of America

Library of Congress Cataloging-in-Publication Data
Christianity and the soul of the university : faith as a foundation for intellectual community / edited by Douglas V. Henry and Michael D. Beaty.
    p. cm.
    Includes bibliographical references and index.
    ISBN 10: 0-8010-2794-2 (pbk.)
    ISBN 978-0-8010-2794-9 (pbk.)
    1. College students—Religious life. 2. Universities and colleges—Religion.
I. Henry, Douglas V. II. Beaty, Michael D.
BV639.C6C47 2006
261.5—dc22
                                                  2005036688

CONTENTS

Acknowledgments

We owe a debt of gratitude to a number of colleagues who shared in bringing this volume to fruition. In the first instance, since the book represents a sustained conversation initiated in connection with a March 2004 conference at Baylor University, words of thanks are due to several individuals involved in the planning and administration of that conference. They include senior colleagues at Baylor: David Jeffrey, Stephen Evans, and David Brooks; members of the board of directors of the Institute for Advanced Christian Studies (IFACS), which significantly underwrote conference costs: Elving Anderson, Judith Dean, Robert Frykenberg, Arthur Holmes, Lamin Sanneh, Rodney Stiling, and Keith Yandell; various colleagues on the executive committee of the Council of Christian Scholarly Societies, which cosponsored the conference: Amy Black, Russell Howell, and Don Munro; and staff members of Baylor University's Institute for Faith and Learning: Vickie Dunnam, Ronny Fritz, and Wynne Vinueza. In addition, we recall with appreciation the enthusiastic involvement in the conference of more than two dozen associations, centers, and scholarly societies with a common stake in the theme of "Christianity and the Soul of the University: Faith as a Foundation for Intellectual Community." While too numerous to list by name here, en masse they provide encouragement to believe that renaissance and not retrenchment is the order of the day for the Christian academy.

In completion of the book itself, we express genuine indebtedness to the contributors who have collaborated with us: Joel Carpenter, Jean Elshtain, Susan Felch, Aurelie Hagstrom, Steven Harmon, Richard Hays, David Jeffrey, John Polkinghorne, Daniel Russ, Mark Sargent, and Daniel Williams. In the Christian diaspora twenty centuries after Jesus of Nazareth, they represent the flesh-and-blood virtues of Christian intellectual community, even when widely scattered over space, and to them we offer thankfulness for their conscientious reflection and patient work with us along the way. Our graduate assistant, Travis Pardo, devoted considerable energies to tracking down details, confirming citations, and offering advice about content. Not least of all, we express appreciation to Baker Academic, especially to Jim Kinney, for offering generous support on behalf of the Baylor conference, expressing enthusiasm for publishing a book on the subject, and working diligently with us to bring the project to completion.

We owe one final word of particular appreciation to Robert B. Sloan Jr. Under his presidency—and now chancellorship—of Baylor University, we have witnessed the flowering of a Christian intellectual community beyond all expectation. Among many others near and far, we have benefited extraordinarily from his relentless effort to join together accomplished scholars who embrace the scandal of the gospel of Jesus Christ. Inasmuch as his vision and leadership played a role in our efforts with this project, we offer sincere thanks, along with hopeful prayers that springtime for Baylor will tarry long. *In nomine Jesu et soli Deo gloria.*

INTRODUCTION

THIS BOOK EXPLORES THE ROLE that reflective Christian faith can play in unifying the intellectual life of the university. In the midst of a larger academic culture prone to confusion, fragmentation, and ideological strife, its multiple authors call Christian scholars to an ever ancient and always new faith that heralds clarity, unity, and accord, not least of all for the life of the mind that the university prizes. They thereby underscore the central place that Christian faith holds as scholars consider how they are called to intellectual labor and how they regard their disciplines. By so doing, they offer a compelling and provocative alternative to business as usual within higher education and the scholarly guilds.

Growing out of a conference held at Baylor University in March 2004, the book more particularly features theologically grounded reflection on the relation of Christian faith to the church-related university's aspiration for intellectual *community*. It offers a rallying call to all those who, committed to the unity of truth in the Triune Godhead, long for a community vitalized by faith formed by intelligent inquiry and characterized by the kindled flame of friendship which, as St. Augustine once professed of his own intellectual community, "fused our very souls and of many made us one."[1]

The prosaic, predictable routine of lamenting the loss of "community" and urging its renewal typifies postmodern American culture. Especially since Robert Putnam's much-publicized book of a few years ago, *Bowling Alone*, everyone seems to have a theory about the collapse and revival of American community.[2] Putnam, following the lead of such social theorists as Jane Jacobs, James Coleman, and Glenn Loury, appropriates the notion of "social capital" to make sense of "the features of social organization such as networks, norms, and social trust that

---

1. Augustine, *Confessions*, trans. F. J. Sheed (Indianapolis: Hackett, 1993), 4.8.
2. See Robert D. Putnam, *Bowling Alone: The Collapse and Revival of American Community* (New York: Simon & Schuster, 2000).

9

facilitate coordination and cooperation for mutual benefit."[3] Whether one may fruitfully reduce the good of human community to an essentially economic concept is, in our judgment, questionable. Yet whatever else might be said about the merits or limitations of Putnam's account (and those like it), he surely is right about two things: we live in a period in which anything approximating genuine community is in short supply, and the breakdown of community represents a phenomenon long in the making and for which there can be no quick fix.

To make matters worse—at least for all who are abidingly convinced of the virtues of families, friendships, and communities—many evidently prefer lives of personal autonomy that are relatively unconstrained by the burden of relationship with others. Far from mourning the waning of the bonds of community, they embrace the independence and fulsome range of free choice opened up for them in an individualistic culture. Some see themselves "not primarily as social and relational beings who need others in order to develop and flourish but as essentially private, solitary, and autonomous individuals for whom relationships are more likely an unwanted restriction than the key to our humanization."[4] Thus, for them, the present age's privileging of individuals over communities constitutes assured progress rather than mournful decline.

Disappointingly, at precisely the point where church-related colleges and universities ought to display a countercultural communitarian impulse, they generally mirror the radically individualistic tendencies of the rest of American culture. Thus, they do not realize in any exceptional way the kind of peaceable polity described by St. Augustine: "a perfectly ordered and perfectly harmonious fellowship in the enjoyment of God, and of one another in God."[5] Irrespective of their rhetoric, Christian colleges and universities in practice seldom if ever resemble anything like the commonwealth of which St. Augustine speaks, wherein all are "united in fellowship by common agreement as to what is right and by a community of interest."[6] To the contrary, on these matters church-related colleges and universities all too easily reflect the character of the wider culture and thus fail to embody imaginative, faithful alternatives in which community simpliciter, and Christian intellectual community in particular, are in evidence. The familiar results include hyperspecialization that is not only content with but also prides itself on interdisciplinary

3. Robert D. Putnam, "Bowling Alone: America's Declining Social Capital," *Journal of Democracy* 6, no. 1 (January 1995): 67.

4. Paul J. Wadell, *Becoming Friends: Worship, Justice, and the Practice of Christian Friendship* (Grand Rapids: Brazos, 2002), 44.

5. Augustine, *City of God*, ed. and trans. R. W. Dyson (New York: Cambridge University Press, 1998), 19.17.

6. Ibid., 19.21.

irrelevance and inaccessibility; fragmentation of the curriculum; faculty disinclined toward conversation about common educative aims and curricular priorities; and students confirmed in their untutored, careerist, and consumerist impulses. In short, Christian educational institutions exhibit a failure to acknowledge and cherish our mutual interdependence, an aversion toward the hard work of finding common ground and arguing contested points, and resignation to lives and ideas torn asunder from the joys of serving a shared, mutually enriching good.

Still, the contributors to this volume stand in hopeful solidarity, convinced that Christian colleges and universities can and must point to a better way. From a variety of denominational perspectives and disciplinary vantage points, they seek to give articulate expression to the character of Christian learning at its best. In doing so, they give thoughtful attention to the properly communitarian character of the well-formed Christian college or university, along with the range of virtues integral to such a community. In the best of circumstances, church-related higher education instantiates an existentially committed way of Christian life in community, grounded in dependence on others and on a range of theologically shaped practices and virtues necessary for its flourishing, and in all such respects finding its *telos* in the Triune God. Moreover, when Christian communities of learning fulfill their potential, they are far from being the moribund enterprises supposed by some in the secular academy: they provide the most interesting and enlarging kind of education possible.

As becomes clear in the conversation that follows, Christian education ideally takes shape within the freeing bonds of community both because of the character of knowledge, and also because of our character as human beings formed by God for *koinōnia*. On the one hand, the vision of Christian faith as a comprehensive, unsurpassable, and central narrative about our place in relation to God and the rest of the world[7] bespeaks the need for self-transcending academic disciplines, and thus the need for communities of scholars responsive one to another across academic fields. We simply cannot do without the resources of an intellectual and spiritual community if we aspire to comprehend the all-encompassing Christian vision of life. On the other hand, an essential part of accepting God's graceful initiative in redeeming us through Christ involves our incorporation into the church, Christ's body, and thus involves locating ourselves in relation to and dependence on other members of the church. Whether in Richard Hays's refreshing exegetical reflection on

---

7. See Paul Griffiths's characterization of Christian faith in these terms in *Religious Reading: The Place of Reading in the Practice of Religion* (New York: Oxford University Press, 1999), 6–13.

1 John's implications for intellectual community, or in Joel Carpenter's rousing call for engagement with the new Christian universities of the two-thirds world, the human vocation of communal responsibility is in evidence below.

Organizationally, chapters in the first part of the book survey the fundamental issues that bear on the notion of Christian intellectual community. In a series of elegantly crafted reflections, Richard Hays, Jean Elshtain, John Polkinghorne, Joel Carpenter, and David Jeffrey give attention respectively to some of the biblical resources, principal interlocutors, conceptual challenges, global concerns, and tradition-bound features of faithfully Christian university life. In the second section of the book, contributors consider a range of practices integral both to understanding and to realizing the ideal of a Christian academic community. Here, a lively discussion of the nature of doubt and delight, tolerance and hospitality, worship, moral imagination, and vocation takes place, featuring thoughtful efforts by Susan Felch, Aurelie Hagstrom, Steven Harmon, Daniel Russ, and Mark Sargent, as well as Daniel Williams.

More particularly, Richard Hays explores the qualities of true human community by tapping the roots of Christian tradition in Scripture, setting his sights primarily on John's first epistle. Arguing that all true community depends on the Logos embodied in Jesus Christ, he skillfully draws out the implications of the "palpable Word" for *intellectual* communities. Christian intellectual communities reflect a morally attuned "epistemology of love," constitute bodies of truth-telling sinners under divine grace, discerningly test the larger culture, locate themselves within a narrative formed by God's gracious initiative, and await in humble and expectant hope for a future transformation that we cannot yet see.

With a line from Robert Bolt's play about Sir Thomas More for her title, Jean Elshtain exemplifies witty service to God in the tangle of her own intellectual and spiritual pilgrimage. Recounting her experience in a culture that regards Christianity as either peripheral or counter to its fundamental commitments, she endorses reasoned faith and respectful discourse as a principal mode of Christian engagement. Such a quality of faith and discourse demands a vital community of critical interlocutors. In recognition of this, Elshtain shows what and how she has learned from a diverse community of thinkers, including Camus, Freud, Arendt, Bonhoeffer, Pope John Paul II, and St. Augustine.

Within a common scholarly community, Christian universities seek a unity that embraces and integrates the diversity of its specialties, contends John Polkinghorne. Such a quest, however, constitutes a different project from modernity's ambition for a single, universal rationality that, Procrustean-like, reduces everything to the measure of the human mind. Instead, Christian interdisciplinarity—informed by trinitarian theology—acknowledges that unity is not the same thing as homogeneity; that varied forms of rational expression are needed to express the complexities of reality; and that the only adequate theory of everything we have may be found, not in science alone, but rather in the Triune God revealed to Israel, incarnate in Jesus Christ, and present amid the church's continuing life, witness, and unfolding understanding of truth.

Joel Carpenter compellingly argues that talk of Christian intellectual community, without attention to the global character of the twenty-first-century church, risks distortion of the evangelical and catholic vision of Christianity. Attending to the southward and eastward demographic shifts in world Christianity, he cites the emergence of new leaders, lines of thought, lines of action, and centers of learning giving evidence of the global church's vigor. And responsive to these developments, Carpenter spells out a provocative set of new mandates for Christian scholarship in the West, for the sake of the global Christian intellectual community to which we belong.

Two recently dominant educational strategies, retreat and accommodation, fall short of the kind of Christian intellectual community worth pursuing. Invoking the mighty yet scattered voices standing behind the tradition of the Christian university, David Jeffrey examines the necessary conditions for founding a fully satisfactory exemplar of the Christian university today. He identifies deep understanding of the scriptural narrative, intellectually and spiritually authoritative theological leadership, the worshipful practices of the gathered church, and self-effacing Christian freedom, inter alia, as central to the faith, fortitude, and future of the intellectual community to which Christians must aspire.

Delight rather than doubt stands at the heart of Christian intellectual community, Susan Felch argues. Though faith may wend its way across the landscape of either doubt or delight, delight provides the richer aesthetic and moral landscape through which to chart our course as faithful scholars and teachers. Delight—an essential attribute of Christian intellectual community—conveys the plenitude that is the soul of Christian witness about God, the world, and ourselves; it expresses a deepness of understanding and community that educates the mind and heart toward maturity.

Challenging a fundamental presupposition of modern intellectual life, Aurelie Hagstrom insists that hospitality, not tolerance, ought to govern Christian intellectual community. While tolerance tends to falter in times of crisis and to trivialize deep disagreement, hospitality—modeled on the self-giving, loving character of the incarnate Word—welcomes the stranger into a fellowship that does not compromise Christian conviction, celebrate thin platitudes about diversity, or compel conversion. Hospitality instead risks the mutuality of dialogue grounded in committed Christian love; it thereby helps frame a theologically supple understanding of such matters, among others, as academic freedom, hiring policies, and student-life expectations within Christian intellectual communities.

Christian intellectual community constitutes an ideal more easily discussed abstractly than realized concretely, for serious engagement can prompt conflict over theologically significant ideas. However, Steven Harmon maintains that such disagreements are integral to vital church-related higher education. Following Alasdair MacIntyre, he points to the contested nature of living traditions as "continuities of conflict," and then he identifies a common ground for Christian intellectual community in the foundational narratives of the canonical Scriptures, the ancient rule of faith, and the practices of the church. Among the practices important for the Christian university, Harmon singles out worship as indispensable, for worship is inescapably formative and normative for theological reflection.

Imaginative obedience to the moral vision of the New Testament, Richard Hays maintains, constitutes a paramount ethical challenge for Christians. Informed by Hays's insight, Daniel Russ and Mark Sargent question whether and how church-related colleges and universities cultivate the moral imagination requisite for faithfully Christian intellectual community. They begin by critiquing the primacy of moral ideology over moral imagination within evangelical Christian life. Subsequently, they propose a variety of discipline-based practices that hold promise for richer spiritual life and socially attuned responsiveness to the moral demands that life in Christian community presents.

In the concluding chapter, Daniel Williams strives to recapture a theologically stout conception of vocation for the Christian university. With clear-eyed awareness of liberal Protestantism's program for pedagogical reform under the banner of vocation in the last century, he rejects any theology or practice of vocation that devolves into banalities about civic and moral education. To the contrary, he argues, any institution wishing to preserve its identity as a Christian intellectual community within a pluralist, American context must embrace a confessional outlook that unapologetically espouses basic propositions pertaining to the core of Christian identity.

The contributing authors of this volume, in short, hold that theological reflection and practice are not peripheral to the academic life of church-related universities, but rather constitute a fundamental feature of education in its fullest sense. Furthermore, because Christian faith and life always call us up and beyond ourselves, intellectual *community* cannot merely stand as an abstract ideal or rhetorically honored desideratum for Christian academics. It forms a sine qua non for the essential character of the church-related university. No less a Christian mind than

Thomas Aquinas recognized, "A man needs the help of friends in order to act well, the deeds of the active life as well as those of the contemplative."[8] Let faith in the risen Lord therefore serve as the firm foundation that grounds and guides the work of all who labor together in Christian intellectual community, "because you know that in the Lord your labor is not in vain" (1 Cor. 15:58).

8. Thomas Aquinas, *Summa theologia* I–II, qu. 4, art. 8, in *Thomas Aquinas: Selected Writings*, ed. and trans. Ralph McInerny (New York: Penguin, 1998), 536.

PART 1

BASIC ISSUES

1

THE PALPABLE WORD
AS GROUND OF *KOINŌNIA*

Richard B. Hays

Eruditio et Religio?

In the center of the main quadrangle of the West Campus of Duke University stands a bronze plaque, amid the university's imposing neo-Gothic buildings. On the plaque are inscribed the following words:

> The aims of Duke University are to assert faith in the eternal union of knowledge and religion set forth in the teaching and character of Jesus Christ, the Son of God, to advance learning in all lines of truth, to defend scholarship against all false notions and ideals, to develop a Christian love of freedom and truth, to promote a sincere spirit of tolerance, to discourage all partisan and sectarian strife, and to render the largest permanent service to the individual, the state, the nation, and the church. Unto these ends should the affairs of this university always be administered.

These words—written by President John Kilgo—were adopted in 1924, at the founding of Duke University, as article 1 of the university's bylaws.[1]

---

1. The words were composed originally in 1903 by Kilgo, who was then president of Trinity College, Duke's precursor institution. The language became part of Trinity College's

One might quibble with some details of the formulation—Kilgo was not a theologian—but the statement expresses a clear intention that Duke be a *Christian* university whose affairs are consciously ordered toward the end of promoting a harmonious synthesis of faith and learning: as the university's motto puts it, *Eruditio et Religio.*

Yet today, eighty years later, students and faculty pass by this plaque with scarcely a glance, and the university, which has forged ahead ambitiously to become a major research institution in a post-Christian culture, is governed by values far removed from President Kilgo's concern for "the eternal union of knowledge and religion set forth in the teaching and character of Jesus Christ, the Son of God." To be sure, Duke has a towering chapel and a fine divinity school, which trains students for leadership in the church, but the university as a whole has become pluralistic and secular. It is a standard quip that we should change the motto to read *Eruditio et Basketballio.* In this secular ethos, no tenure review committee in the literature department will ever ask whether the candidate's work has promoted "Christian love of freedom and truth." Any unwary junior faculty member venturing to ask the faculty's Academic Council whether the present undergraduate curriculum is fulfilling the mandate to "assert faith in the eternal union of knowledge and religion set forth in the teaching and character of Jesus Christ" would probably be laughed out of the room. Yet just beneath the glossy surface of brochures that tout successful capital campaigns and high rankings in *U.S. News & World Report* lurks the deep intellectual crisis of the postmodern university: the crisis that the university, having allowed Kilgo's words to recede into its past, finds itself intellectually incoherent and therefore captive to market forces that threaten to distort its mission beyond all recognition.

Similar stories have been played out across the spectrum of American higher education. George Marsden has chronicled the way in which many colleges and universities have undergone a slow cultural conversion from Christian beginnings to secular ends.[2] In this respect, Duke is no exception. Because, however, it has so rapidly developed from pious Methodist college to aggressively secular Top Ten university, it offers a useful focal instance for the issues at hand. Can or should faith offer a

---

bylaws and twenty-one years later was adopted by the nascent university. The plaque was placed on the quadrangle in 1942. The university's bylaws are available on the Duke University website at http://www.duke.edu/web/ous/bylaws00.htm.

2. George M. Marsden, *The Soul of the American University: From Protestant Establishment to Established Nonbelief* (New York: Oxford University Press, 1994). See also James Tunstead Burtchaell, *The Dying of the Light: The Disengagement of Colleges and Universities from Their Christian Churches* (Grand Rapids: Eerdmans, 1998).

foundation for intellectual community? Or, as I prefer to cast the question: Can there be intellectual community apart from faith?

Even in the Divinity School, one encounters the fallout of the cultural situation that I am describing. At a recent faculty meeting, we were debating a report on a proposed new curriculum. The report offered an opening section called "The Goal of Our Instruction," seeking to describe the qualities and abilities that we hope to nurture in our graduates. It delineated these qualities in a bulleted list of things such as these:

- The ability to read Scripture and the great texts of the Christian tradition with attentiveness, nuanced understanding, humility, and a lively imagination.
- The ability to think theologically, in a way that is both faithful to the tradition and responsive to the challenges of our time.
- The ability to think critically, both about the practices of the church and about the world in which the church finds itself.

And so forth. For the most part, this list was well received. But one item on the list sparked immediate controversy:

- A commitment to living a life ordered toward holiness, justice, peace, and reconciliation.

Some members of the faculty objected to this item because they feared it implied a "Pelagian" theology. (As you might guess, this objection did not come from among my Methodist colleagues!) Others, however, had a different sort of objection. They did not necessarily disapprove of holiness, justice, peace, and reconciliation; they just questioned whether it was the job of a *university divinity school* to inculcate a commitment to such things. As one of our theologians put it, the committee's list of goals mixed together intellectual aims with moral and religious ones in a way that he found problematic; better to stick to purely intellectual goals and leave the moral and religious elements out of it.

Despite my great respect for the colleagues who raised this objection, I believe that their comments are symptomatic of the church's loss of its own proper intellectual tradition, and at the same time symptomatic of the spiritual captivity of the modern university. The truth is that we cannot divide the intellectual from the moral and religious. Or if we do, we will have created universities that are—paradoxically—no longer "intellectual *communities.*"

To reflect more deeply about the formation of intellectual community, I propose to go back to the roots of our tradition in Scripture. After all, the university as an institution is the fruit of Christian culture. Perhaps if we return to the rich original soil from which that culture grew, we will find fresh nourishment for the spiritually desiccated university of the twenty-first century. The particular text that I want to consider is a somewhat unlikely choice: the First Epistle of John.

Few interpreters of the New Testament would immediately think of 1 John as a key text for reflection about the foundations of intellectual community. Its author wrote in an artless style. Because its diction and syntax are simple, this little epistle is a favorite text for first-year courses in New Testament Greek. After learning just a little grammar, beginning students can work their way through 1 John without much difficulty. But although its syntax is clean, its overall structure seems aimless and repetitious, lacking both the rigorous theological dialectics of Paul's letters and the rhetorical polish of the Letter to the Hebrews. This is not a piece of high-culture writing. It seems to be a homely homily—indeed, a homily that would benefit from some critical editing by a good homiletics professor.

Further, its message is widely regarded as insular and sectarian. Within the New Testament, the Johannine Epistles are exhibit A for the fissiparousness of early Christianity. This text appears to be the product of a marginalized community that had its own quite distinctive version of the traditions about Jesus. Its community has suffered splintering and defections, with the result that those who have left the fold to form a new church are now anathematized by the author as liars and bearers of the spirit of antichrist. In short, 1 John seems to come from an embattled sectarian enclave—or so distinguished New Testament critics such as Raymond Brown interpret it.[3] A vivid statement in the letter's final paragraph encapsulates its stance toward the rest of the world: "We know that we are God's children, and that the whole world lies under the power of the evil one" (1 John 5:19). In his classic book *Christ and Culture*, H. Richard Niebuhr chose 1 John as his parade-leading example of the "Christ-against-culture" type of Christian faith, followed by Tertullian and Tolstoy.[4]

For this reason, 1 John seems to represent the antithesis of the (post)modern university's aspiration to create an ecumenical discourse that is both sophisticated and pluralistic. In sharp contrast to the writings of Friedrich Schleiermacher or John Henry Newman's *The Idea of a University*, the simple First Epistle of John looks like a distinctly unpromising place to begin reflection about "Christianity and the Soul

---

3. See Raymond E. Brown, *The Community of the Beloved Disciple* (New York: Paulist Press, 1979); idem, *The Epistles of John*, Anchor Bible 30 (Garden City, NY: Doubleday, 1982).

4. H. Richard Niebuhr, *Christ and Culture* (New York: Harper & Row, 1951), 45–49.

of the University." Nonetheless, if it is intellectual *community* that we seek, we might do well to ponder 1 John, for the theme of *koinōnia* is at its heart. According to 1 John, all true community is grounded in the Word that became palpable: the coherence of human community depends on the Logos embodied in Jesus Christ. The author of this epistle is not writing about universities. Nonetheless, if his claims are true, they have implications for all communities, including those that aspire to be intellectual communities.

What follows, then, explores 1 John's vision of community, giving attention to its trenchant critique of the practices of self-deception that impede knowledge of the truth. It also gives some attention to the dangers and the limitations of 1 John's vision and recognizes some of the other voices in the New Testament canon that amplify and correct the Johannine picture. Finally, this chapter asks how these all-too-brief soundings in the New Testament might inform our thought about the life of the university at the beginning of the twenty-first century.[5]

The Vision of Community in 1 John

Incarnation as Ground of Koinōnia (1 John 1:1–4)

Contrary to the impression created by some English translations, the First Letter of John does not open with "We declare . . ." The main verb of the sentence, of which the mortal "we" is the subject, does not appear until verse 3. Instead, the letter opens with a description of the Word of life, in language that echoes Genesis 1 and the beginning of the Gospel of John: "That which was from the beginning . . ." The Greek syntax subtly suggests that this Word whom we proclaim *precedes* our hearing and proclaiming. This Word is not an invention of our ingenuity or our need, but it is "revealed" to us (1:2).

In contrast to the prologue of the Fourth Gospel, which takes fourteen verses to build up to the mystery of the incarnation of the Word, 1 John presses its astounding claim upon us immediately in its opening sentence: the Word of life is not merely a proclamation that we hear; it is also "that which we have seen with our eyes, that which we have looked at and touched with our hands" (1:1 author's translation). This Word is a *palpable* Word, a Word that has become embodied and has

5. I want to acknowledge with gratitude the inspiration and assistance of George Hobson, the canon theologian of the American Cathedral in Paris, and his wife, Victoria. An extended conversation with them over dinner clarified my thoughts about the themes of this essay; their friendship over the years has embodied the *koinōnia* about which 1 John speaks.

given itself to be felt, concretely and physically, by our clumsy fingers.[6] To know this Word rightly, we do not have to ascend to heaven, we do not have to escape our time and space, we do not move in Platonic fashion from illusory physical appearances to disembodied reality. Rather, we see and touch this Word with our hands. We are perhaps meant to recall the risen Lord's invitation to Thomas to place his fingers in the marks where the nails had been (John 20:27).

Whether Thomas accepted the invitation or not (the Gospel does not tell us), the author of 1 John (unnamed in the text) makes the mind-altering claim that *he* is among the company of those who have *tactile* experience of the Word of life, the eternal life that was with God the Father and has now been revealed. One might suppose that this would be the climax of his message—how do you top that?—but it is not so. There is another *telos* in view here; the news of this palpable Word is proclaimed "so that you also might have *koinōnia* with us; and truly our *koinōnia* is with the Father and with his Son Jesus Christ" (1:3 author's translation). It is difficult to preserve the nuance of the Greek word *koinōnia* just right in English translation; it suggests sharing, commonality, fellowship, *community*. It is not just a matter of friendly social relations (as "fellowship" might suggest), but a matter of a deep bond of common interest and commitment.

Let us pause over this just a moment. The purpose of the proclamation of God's revelation is not (as modern evangelical convention might expect) "so that you might be saved," or "so that you might go to heaven when you die," or some such. Rather, in 1 John's forceful purpose clause, the message is proclaimed so that "you" might enter into *community* with "us." The aim of the incarnation is the formation of *koinōnia* (community), a familial community that includes us in direct relation with the Father and the Son. The coming of the palpable Word into the world creates a new bond of solidarity that links human beings together in love precisely by incorporating them into the life of the Triune God.

This leads on to the final verse in this opening paragraph: "We are writing these things so that our joy may be filled up" (1:4 author's translation). The *written* proclamation about the palpable Word leads to the inclusion of the believing reader in the new community that the Word creates, and the end result of this community-formation is joy, a joy that both reader and writer share with the Father and the Son.

All of this is directly pertinent to our question about what it might mean to think about intellectual community. The opening verses of 1 John

---

6. My use of the expression "palpable Word" is inspired in part by the title of one of Reynolds Price's early reflections on the New Testament, *A Palpable God: Thirty Stories Translated from the Bible: With an Essay on the Origins and Life of Narrative* (1978; repr., San Francisco: North Point, 1985).

tell us that the *telos* of the incarnation of the Word is forming loving community that links us as human receivers of revelation in joyful *koinōnia* with God the Father and his Son Jesus Christ. Further, the suggestion is made implicitly that *only* through the revealed Word can such community take shape. Apart from such union in Christ, human beings remain strangers to one another and to the life that animates creation.

In a recent essay titled "Alone in the Academy," Eric Miller articulates a devastating critique of the wistful but doomed desire of the social critic Christopher Lasch for the recovery of authentic human community:

> Despite the acuity of his vision, Lasch seemed unable to accept one ominous historical reality: due to the modern rejection of a world governed by a "spiritual order" and the affirmation instead of "the creation of value and meaning by autonomous human subjects," the sort of community for which Lasch and so many others yearned—whether they were on the left, center, or right—was impossible. . . . Americans were, constitutionally, "a people bound together only by a belief in their inalienable right not to be bound together to anything."[7]

In contrast to this radical individualism, 1 John envisions a *koinōnia* in which we are bound together joyfully in the Word.

Walking in the Light, Doing the Truth (1:5–10)

One component of being bound together in such a community is that we are drawn into a community of truthful speech and action. Few persons need the testimony of an expert to tell them that universities are full of pretentious people who are skilled at complex defenses of their own impeccability. But in 1 John's vision of community, rather than hiding our sins and weaknesses behind a façade of intellectual brilliance, we enter into *koinōnia* with God and one another only when we "walk in the light" by confessing our sins. "If we walk in the light as he himself is in the light, we have . . . [*koinōnia*] with one another, and the blood of Jesus his Son cleanses us from all sin. . . . If we say that we have not sinned, we make him a liar, and his word is not in us" (1:7, 10). Rationalization cannot be the ground of *koinōnia*. Without confession and forgiveness, there is only the endless play of keeping up appearances, which ultimately separates us from one another. In his book *Life Together*, Dietrich Bonhoeffer penetratingly describes our situation:

7. Eric Miller, "Alone in the Academy," *First Things* 140 (February 2004): 30. Miller is summarizing the critique of Lasch offered in Christopher Shannon, *Conspicuous Criticism: Tradition, the Individual, and Culture in American Social Thought, from Veblen to Mills* (Baltimore: Johns Hopkins University Press, 1996).

He who is alone with his sin is utterly alone. . . . The pious fellowship permits no one to be a sinner. So everybody must conceal his sin from himself and from the fellowship. . . . Many Christians are unthinkably horrified when a real sinner is suddenly discovered among the righteous. So we remain alone with our sin, living in lies and hypocrisy. . . . But it is the grace of the Gospel, which is so hard for the pious to understand, that it confronts us with the truth and says: You are a sinner, a great desperate sinner; now come, as the sinner that you are, to God who loves you. . . . In confession the break-through to community takes place.[8]

So 1 John offers us a vision of community in which we come into the light with one another, knowing one another as sinners.

Such a vision of our human condition may also give us insight that will make us sharper and wiser interpreters of the fields we study. In a recent book on the American civil rights movements, David Chappell argues that Martin Luther King Jr. "had a more accurate view of political realities than his more secular liberal allies because he could draw on biblical wisdom about [sinful] human nature. Religion didn't just make civil-rights leaders stronger—it made them smarter."[9] A similar point could be made about scholars in the academy. If we study human behavior—whether in psychology or history or literature—we may find that the wisdom of the Christian tradition will give us a more mature and balanced picture of who we are as God's creatures in the world. If so, our studies may be illumined—and our aspirations tempered—by such wisdom. If we truly know ourselves to be sinners, will we plunge quite so eagerly into such perilous initiatives as the Human Genome Project?

But I digress. To return to the main line of our reflection, why is walking in the light necessarily important for the formation of *intellectual community*? Because the alternative to walking in the light is living in deception. As Nicholas Lash has observed, the first casualty of sin is truthfulness of speech.[10] Intellectual community depends on a free seeking and naming of the truth. But when we begin to hide from one another, as Adam and Eve did in the garden, we begin to tell lies to

8. Dietrich Bonhoeffer, *Life Together* (New York: Harper & Row, 1954), 110–12.

9. David Brooks, "One Nation, Enriched by Biblical Wisdom," *New York Times*, March 23, 2004, commenting on David L. Chappell, *A Stone of Hope: Prophetic Religion and the Death of Jim Crow* (Chapel Hill: University of North Carolina Press, 2004).

10. "Commissioned as ministers of God's redemptive Word, we are required, in politics and in private life, in work and play, in commerce and scholarship, to practice and foster that philology, that word-caring, that meticulous and conscientious concern for the quality of conversation and the truthfulness of memory, which is the first casualty of sin. The church, accordingly, is or should be a school of philology, an academy of word-care" (Nicholas Lash, "Ministry of the Word or Comedy and Philology," *New Blackfriars* 68 [1987]: 477).

God and to ourselves. (The most primitive of these lies is the delusion that we can be like gods, knowing good and evil.) Consequently, we fall into habits of posturing and dishonesty that corrupt our academic work, right along with all the other parts of our lives. I do not necessarily mean that we will commit plagiarism or falsify data or cover up wrongdoing (although God knows such things are more widespread than we would like to admit). I mean, rather, that we will fall into untruthful and artificial ways of seeing the subjects that we study, and we will become blind to what is before us. (For example, in my own field of biblical studies, many interpreters evade the challenge of finding themselves addressed by the text by focusing on the allegedly oppressive social power relations encoded in the texts. Assuming a posture of moral superiority over the biblical texts, they talk endlessly about the politics of interpretation, but lose the power to perform constructive interpretations for the community of faith.)[11] This blindness in turn will corrupt our actions. First John is intensely attuned to the dangers of self-deception and dishonesty: "If we say that we have *koinōnia* with him while we are walking in darkness, we lie, and we do not *do the truth*" (1:6; see also 2:3–6, 9–11).

English translations usually do not literally render the expression *do the truth*.[12] But this striking turn of phrase is not incidental. For 1 John, the truth must always be embodied, just as the Word became flesh. To speak of knowing the truth in isolation from action is not only fallacious but also deeply dishonest. If we know God authentically, active obedience will follow. Or to put it in a way more faithful to 1 John's vision, there is no authentic knowledge of God apart from active obedience.[13]

This point is devastating to Western accounts of *Wissenschaft* that divorce theory from practice. To the extent that arts and sciences faculties disdain the practical applied knowledge that is central to the work of fields such as engineering, law, medicine, nursing, and ministry, they are living in a state of artificial alienation from the palpable Word. If we are guided by 1 John in our vision of intellectual community, we will insist that such applied disciplines are pursuing the proper goal of all knowledge: to put the truth into practice. We must do the truth, not just conceptualize it. "Whoever says, 'I have come to know him,' but does

11. For a critique of this approach, see Richard B. Hays, "Salvation by Trust? Reading the Bible Faithfully," *Christian Century* 114, no. 6 (February 26, 1997): 218–23. For a programmatic proposal of a more fruitful approach to biblical interpretation, see Ellen F. Davis and Richard B. Hays, eds., *The Art of Reading Scripture* (Grand Rapids: Eerdmans, 2003).

12. It appears elsewhere in the New Testament only in John 3:21, in a similar context about deception and hiding from the light.

13. See R. W. L. Moberly, "How Can We Know the Truth? A Study of John 7:14–18," in *Art of Reading Scripture*, 239–57.

not obey his commandments, is a liar, and in such a person the truth does not exist" (2:4).

The doing of the truth also requires that we do justice (*poiein dikaiosynēn*), an expression that occurs three times in this letter (2:29; 3:7, 10). This is usually translated in English by some weaker phrase such as "do what is right," but in 1 John the single outstanding example of such behavior pertains to just sharing of economic resources: "How does God's love abide in anyone who has the world's goods and sees a brother or sister in need and yet refuses help? Little children, let us love, not in word or speech, but in truth and action" (3:17–18). For 1 John, the truth is the truth of God's embodied love for the world; thus, truth can never be separated from concrete acts of love and mercy.

By way of contrast, the alternative to active obedience can be described not only as "sin" but also as "lawlessness" (*anomia*, 3:4). The word *anomia* suggests living in a state of loose nonaccountability, precisely in the state of asserting one's inalienable right not to be bound by anything. First John's term offers a chillingly accurate diagnosis of our disintegrating late-modern cultures, in which anything goes but nothing is any longer *true*, because we find ourselves alienated from the palpable, binding Word that gives order to our lives.

The Danger of Idolatry (5:21; 2:15–17)

Finding ourselves in such a state of alienation, we will always be tempted to seek quick-fix solutions by turning to false gods. It is not merely random that 1 John ends with this abrupt warning: "Little children, keep yourselves from idols" (5:21). The idols against which the author warns are closely linked with the illusory desires enumerated in one of the most stringently "sectarian" passages in 1 John (2:15–17):

> Do not love the world or the things in the world. The love of the Father is not in those who love the world; for all that is in the world—the desire of the flesh, the desire of the eyes, the pride in riches—comes not from the Father but from the world. And the world and its desires are passing away, but those who do the will of God live forever.

At first hearing, this command not to love the world sounds antithetical to the message of Jesus and to most of the rest of the New Testament, which consistently summons Jesus's followers to love even their enemies and to practice costly acts of loving self-sacrifice for the sake of the world. Yet we should not be too hasty to brush this text aside as evidence of a pathological rejection of God's good creation. The lust and materialism against which 1 John warns us are actually ever-present dangers for us all. John poses a stern challenge not to set our desires and hopes on ephemeral idols in a world that is "passing away" (2:17).

We in the university are hardly immune to the desire of the flesh and the lure of riches, but perhaps for our particular *Sitz im Leben,* 1 John's list of the world's temptations and false gods should be expanded a bit: all that is in the world—the ambition for fame, the desire of tenure, the boastfulness in distinguished chairs—comes not from the Father but from the world. So we must be vigilant and self-critical of our own devices and desires, of the self-aggrandizement that sets us in a competitive relation to our colleagues.

At the end of the day, though, in 1 John's vision the danger of idolatry is overcome not by our own vigilance, but by the triumph of God. God has sent his Son as "the Savior of the world" (4:14), and those who place their trust in him will also find these hostile powers and temptations subdued, for "whatever is born of God conquers the world" (5:4). Such a claim makes sense only within the larger narrative framework of the Fourth Gospel, in which Jesus, on his way to the cross, declares, "Take courage; I have conquered the world!" (John 16:33). For that reason, and that reason alone, the world and its desires are passing away.

Testing the Spirits (4:1–6)

Still, even though Jesus is triumphant over the powers and idols of the world, the author of 1 John assigns us the task of critical discernment, to test the spirits and distinguish false prophets from true ones (4:1–6). At last, we say, this sounds more like the sort of job description we are familiar with. We in the university may not be so good at confessing our sins or putting truth into action, but critical discernment is precisely what we know how to do: examine the evidence, weigh the reliability of sources, decide who is right and who is wrong. Yet rather than affirming our usual battery of analytical devices, 1 John proposes two disconcertingly simple criteria to distinguish false spirits from true ones.

First, "every spirit that confesses that Jesus Christ has come in the flesh is from God, and every spirit that does not confess Jesus is not from God" (4:2–3). The critical test on which claims about the identity of Jesus must stand or fall is the incarnation. The true Word is the palpable Word. Every docetic Christology is a deception. (Parenthetically, I cannot resist the observation that this criterion skewers the neognostic images of Jesus that are so titillating to *Time* magazine and the book buyers in the religion section at Barnes & Noble.) Further, I would suggest that a Christology of the palpable Word implies more broadly that truth must be sought and grasped in its concrete particularity—not only in Christology but also in all our efforts to understand the created world, in all academic disciplines.

Nevertheless, 1 John proffers a second equally definite and no less disconcerting criterion for critical discernment: "We are from God. Whoever knows God listens to us, and whoever is not from God does not listen to us. From this we know the spirit of truth and the spirit of error" (4:6). *Quod erat demonstrandum!* (This is precisely what I always tell my students: everyone who does not listen to me is led astray by the spirit of error.) On the face of it, this criterion appears absurdly circular. In a sense, there is no escaping this circle. But two observations will help us to interpret the criterion in a more nuanced way.

First, the "we" that makes this self-validating claim is the same "we" that has heard and seen and touched the Word of life. Thus, the author is not arbitrarily privileging his private opinions and sentiments; rather, he is bearing witness to the revelation of God that came to us in embodied form. Consequently, the second criterion noted above is closely linked to the first: the authority of the community's testimony is indissolubly bound to the truth that Jesus Christ has come in the flesh. These two claims stand or fall together.

The second observation is this: when the author says, "Whoever knows God listens to us," he is speaking—as we have repeatedly insisted—not merely of intellectual assent but especially also of adherence to a community of love. That is why the very next verse shifts to exhort the readers to participate in such a community: "Beloved, let us love one another, because love is from God; everyone who loves is born of God and knows God. Whoever does not love does not know God" (4:7–8). This is a recurrent theme of the letter. First John posits what we might call an epistemology of love. Love is both the instrument and the object of true knowledge. Apart from love, we remain in ignorance and death. Thus, testing the spirit of truth and error on the basis of adherence to the message of a community whose identity is defined in just *this* way turns out to be something very different from a power play or an act of self-assertion. Indeed, truly understood, such critical testing constantly calls believers to serious self-scrutiny: "Those who say 'I love God,' and hate their brothers or sisters are liars; for those who do not love a brother or sister whom they have seen, cannot love God whom they have not seen" (4:20). Again, the test of concrete practical action is the criterion for truth and error. Those who know and do the truth will remain in loving unity with God's people.

Eschatological Transformation (2:28–3:2)

One final element in 1 John's vision of community finds only brief expression in the letter, but it is of crucial importance: in the present time the *koinōnia* we share with God and with one another remains incomplete. We look to the eschatological future for the completion of the transforming power of the palpable Word. "Beloved, we are God's children now; what we will be has not yet been revealed. What we do know is this: when he is revealed, we will be like him, for we shall see him as he is" (3:2). This conviction is also crucial for the formation of intellectual community because it allows us simultaneously to affirm the sure ground of our knowledge (5:20: "And we know that the Son of God has come and given us understanding so that we may know him who is true") and the radical incompleteness of our understanding of the knowledge we have been given. The palpable Word both reveals the truth and eludes our final comprehension. Analogously, God's revelatory action has claimed us as a people and begun to reshape our lives, but it does not yet appear what we shall be. Therefore, an intellectual community grounded on this Word will remain expectantly open to the future and to surprises.

The Danger of Schism and the Corrective Witness of the Canon

The Danger of Sectarianism and Partisan Strife

There is one great danger that attends my proposal to take 1 John as a witness concerning faith as a foundation for intellectual community. It is the one dominant and abiding danger of this luminous little epistle, a danger that has no doubt loomed large in the minds of many of you from the moment you began to read this chapter: the danger of "sectarianism." Does 1 John not articulate a narrow particularism that seeks to exclude or invalidate all other voices? This is a text that castigates its opponents as "antichrists" and limits the possession of true knowledge to those who participate in a tiny in-group of those who share its sharply distinctive confessional stance. Yet this is precisely the way *all* Christians are now perceived by many opinion-makers in post-Christian secular culture. Precisely for that reason, these potentially dangerous aspects of 1 John's vision need to be seriously reckoned with. Is it true, as some critics fear, that the Johannine claims about special revelation and privileged knowledge will inevitably lead to schism, hostility, and even violence?

My remarks (above) about the Johannine community as a community ordered by the love of God go some distance toward addressing the issue, but they do not yet constitute a fully adequate response. After all, 2 and 3 John seem to provide direct evidence that the fears of 1 John's detractors are justified: the community seems to have lapsed into name-calling and exclusion of other Christians (e.g., 2 John 10–11; 3 John 9–10). Is this where the theology of 1 John inevitably leads? This sounds like precisely the sort of "partisan and sectarian strife" that, according to Duke's bylaws, the university should discourage. With respect to its vision of the relation between the community of faith and the unbelieving world, the First Letter of John stands at one extreme end of the spectrum among the New Testament witnesses—as Niebuhr rightly observed. Precisely for that reason, its testimony brings some important matters into sharp focus; however, precisely for the same reason, its testimony needs to be supplemented and counterbalanced by other witnesses.

The scope of this essay permits only a hasty sketch, but I want at least to mention some of the other New Testament texts that might play a role in shaping our thought about faith as a foundation for intellectual community. Three other New Testament witnesses are especially pertinent: Paul, Luke, and 1 Peter.

Paul: Be Transformed by the Renewing of Your Minds

In his role as a missionary, Paul is pervasively concerned with the building of community, and he is convinced that the gospel's community-forming power creates a new world of discourse that confounds "the wisdom of the world" (1 Cor. 1:18–2:5). The faith that is the foundation of true community proclaims "the foolishness of the cross," which summons believers to a cruciform life of self-emptying service (Phil. 2:1–13). For that reason, Paul champions an epistemology of humility. He is constantly admonishing his communities not to think of themselves as wiser than they are, but to recognize both the limitations of their own understanding and the ultimately reconciling purposes of God. Even when Paul uses military metaphors such as "taking every thought captive for the obedience of Christ," he is careful to stipulate that the warfare to which he refers is not "according to the flesh" (2 Cor. 10:3–5 author's translation). Rather, he is speaking of a world transformed by the death of Christ, a world in which the reconciling power of "new creation" is already appearing and claiming sovereignty over all things (2 Cor. 5:16–21). To catch the vision of this new creation is to glimpse a vision for a new kind of community—including intellectual community: "Do not be conformed to this world, but be transformed by the renewing of your minds, so that you may discern what is the will of God—what is good and acceptable and perfect" (Rom. 12:2). A community transformed to share the mind of Christ can never be exclusivist or violent; rather, it must foreshadow the eschatological hope of a reconciled humanity praising God together.

Luke: Turning the World Upside Down

Like Paul, Luke has a wide-ranging view of God's redemptive purpose, which he characterizes as "the plan of God." His two-volume work shows how God has worked through the long story of Israel to bring into being "a people prepared for the Lord" (Luke 1:17). In accordance with Israel's prophetic tradition, Luke forthrightly declares that God's work of election and revelation entails judgment on the disobedient; at the same time, however, Luke's vision is soteriologically expansive. The good news is not an esoteric word for a tiny in-group: "The promise is for you, for your children, and for all who are far away, everyone whom the Lord our God calls to him" (Acts 2:39). One of the major motifs of Luke's two-part epic is the inclusion of the Gentiles within God's mercy. Thus, Luke has a broadly inclusive view of Christian community as a community in which different ethnic and cultural communities are brought together by the gospel.

What sort of foundation for *intellectual* community does Luke offer? In the Acts of the Apostles, we find the apostles engaged in an impressive range of debates and deliberations, engaging dialogue partners from Jerusalem to Athens to Rome, seeking to show how the gospel addresses their worldviews. Yet it is always clear that the gospel has the effect of "turning the world upside down" (Acts 17:6). In Luke's account, the church is a community of vigorous debate, propounding strong revisionary readings of Israel's Scriptures and joining intellectual battle with all comers in the public square of Greco-Roman antiquity. Yet when all is taken into account, the foundation for this intellectual enterprise lies in the community's rich shared life of apostolic teaching, prayer, table fellowship, and sharing of goods (2:42–47). This community life enables the apostles' proclamation of the resurrection to go forth in power (4:32–35). Thus, for Luke, the coherence of intellectual community rests ultimately on the gracious power of the God who has gathered the *ekklēsia* (church) as a community of praise, as well as a community of interpretation.

1 Peter: Soft Difference

Finally, 1 Peter presents an image of the community of faith engaged in outward-looking conversation with the pagan world: "Always be ready to make your defense to anyone who demands from you an accounting for the hope that is in you; yet do it with gentleness and reverence" (1 Pet. 3:15–16). This advice is offered to the community of faith in a context suggesting that the community may be the target of intimidation and persecution at the hands of outsiders (4:12–19; 5:6–11). Outsiders hold the power, and the Christian church offers its testimony from a minority position as "aliens and exiles" (2:11). Yet unlike 1 John, which paints a grimly dualistic picture of the church facing an evil world, 1 Peter offers a modestly hopeful vision of the church as a contrast society that may effectively commend the gospel to the world by its peaceful, dignified, and holy common life: "Conduct yourselves honorably among the Gentiles, so that, though they malign you as evildoers, they may see your honorable deeds and glorify God when he comes to judge" (2:12). As Miroslav Volf has observed, the relation of the church to the surrounding culture, according to 1 Peter, is one of "soft difference": the church is a diaspora community, aware of its own distinctive identity and calling, but still seeking to live constructively within the majority culture and to commend its message to that culture.[14] It is less clear for 1 Peter than for Paul and Luke that the church might be the nucleus of an *intellectual* community; nonetheless, 1 Peter emphasizes the crucial importance of providing an *apologia* to outsiders. This suggests that some part of the community's mission is to order its self-interpretation in a way that is publicly appealing and defensible. Herein lies one possible seed of the particular vocation of the Christian university.

This brief survey of Paul, Luke, and 1 Peter indicates that the New Testament provides varying models for thinking about the faith as the foundation of intellectual community, and also about the relation of the Christian community to a pluralistic culture. My point is that 1 John should hardly stand as our only model for thinking about these matters; we must read the apparent sectarianism of 1 John as in conversation with other voices in the New Testament canon. In some ways, these other voices speak in counterpoint to 1 John. They all deserve to be weighed carefully. Yet there is also significant common ground. In all of the examples we have considered, the gospel of Jesus Christ is the foundational truth, the story within which all other stories and claims must find their place. Further, all of these New Testament witnesses agree that the gospel message is necessarily enfleshed in communities whose life then becomes both the instrument of the Word and the living evidence of its truth. Thus, Paul, Luke, and 1 Peter, in their differing ways, all reinforce 1 John's claim that the incarnate Word is the ground of authentic community.

The Palpable Word as Ground of *Koinōnia*: Implications for the University

What are the implications of these observations for Christians who seek to shape universities in our time? Or for Christians who seek to live out scholarly vocations within secular universities? (The two questions are very different.) To explore these questions adequately would require another essay longer than this one. But by way of conclusion, I

14. See Miroslav Volf, "Soft Difference: Theological Reflections on the Relation between Church and Culture in 1 Peter," *Ex auditu* 10 (1994): 15–30.

offer just a few reflections and proposals based on what we have heard and seen in 1 John.

First, an intellectual community grounded in the palpable Word will value concreteness over abstraction, particularity over generality, engagement over objectivity. The "epistemology of love" suggests that we know best and most truly by loving and by forming committed relationships with the community in which we are engaged in service. This runs counter to Enlightenment assumptions about the objectivity of knowledge, the task of *Wissenschaft.* That is why I believe that in our curriculum at Duke Divinity School we should seek, precisely as part of our *educational* task, to form our students in lives ordered toward holiness, justice, peace, and reconciliation.[15] We should seek to teach our students to do the truth. Inculcating such commitments and character formation should be the aim of all Christian institutions, not just seminaries.

Second, an intellectual community grounded in the palpable Word will be a community that tells the truth, confesses its sins and weaknesses, lives without pretense, bears one another's burdens. (This is a hard act for us!) It will be a community of those who know themselves to be sinners under grace. Precisely for that reason, it will also be a community in which there is a meeting of *persons,* not of disembodied intellects. It will be a *koinōnia,* not just an institution.

Third, an intellectual community grounded in the palpable Word will be a community wary of the power of idols and the lure of the world's idol-makers. Such a community would be discerning and critical of the culture in which it finds itself, testing the spirits to see whether they are from God.

Fourth, the revelation of the palpable Word is the culmination of the *story* of God's gracious initiative. Therefore, a university that seeks to ground its common life in this Word is necessarily locating itself within the highly particular story of the people Israel, to whom God chose to reveal himself distinctively. In the first instance, this means that the university's programs and curricula should honor this historical rootage. (A plaque on the quad is hardly sufficient unless it corresponds to the reality of the university's administration of its affairs.) But there is still a further implication. It is not sufficient simply to acknowledge the university's cultural history; rather, the university must reckon with the fact that it lives and moves within a story in which the God disclosed in Scripture is still actively at work. An intellectual community grounded in the palpable Word is not simply a political society based on a shifting equilibrium of competing interests and power games; instead, it

---

15. I am happy to report that our faculty did, in the end, vote in favor of keeping this language in the text of our new curriculum document.

is a manifestation of the life of God in the world, and its effectiveness depends on its receiving the gift of the embodied Word.

The alternative is that a "pluralistic" university will seek to live apart from any story and will therefore be, quite literally, incoherent: with no story, it has nothing holding it together.[16] In such cases, the university will surely be co-opted into the story of Western capitalist "progress" and human autonomy, in short, into the Enlightenment metanarrative, which has had such destructive consequences for human wholeness.[17]

Fifth, an intellectual community grounded in the palpable Word will be intellectually charitable, loving one another, and receiving the work and ideas of others with generosity of spirit.[18] (This means, by the way, that, in contrast to the schismatic impulse displayed in 2 and 3 John, a university grounded in the palpable Word will not apply exclusionary confessional tests for membership in its faculty or student body. It will welcome members of other confessional communities as voices that enrich the university's conversation.) Such a community, having been called into existence by an astounding God who summoned them to handle the Word of life, will continue to await the surprises and paradoxes of grace. It will also be ordered toward a future transformation that we cannot yet see. Therefore, it will acknowledge what it does not know and confess its ignorance without embarrassment. "It does not yet appear what we shall be" (1 John 3:2 author's translation).

But one thing we do know: in the eschatological transformation, in which we will be shaped to become like Christ, we will not be alone but in community. The community we have now is a foretaste of that final celebration. The point is voiced simply and gracefully by T. S. Eliot:

> What life have you if you have not life together?
> There is no life that is not in community,
> And no community not lived in praise of God.[19]

Surely, in some measure, our universities must seek to embody a life together that anticipates that vision and sings God's praise.

16. Behind this sentence lies the brilliant diagnostic work in Alasdair MacIntyre, *After Virtue: A Study in Moral Theory*, 2nd ed. (Notre Dame: University of Notre Dame Press, 1984). See also George Steiner, *Real Presences* (Chicago: University of Chicago Press, 1989).

17. For a concise summary of Jean-François Lyotard's critique of metanarratives and an explanation of how the biblical narrative differs from modernist narratives, see Richard Bauckham, "Reading Scripture as a Coherent Story," in *Art of Reading Scripture*, 38–53.

18. See the discussion of interpretative "courtesy" (*cortesia*) in Steiner, *Real Presences*, 146–49; cf. Daniel Boyarin, *Carnal Israel: Reading Sex in Talmudic Culture* (Berkeley: University of California Press, 1993), 19–23.

19. T. S. Eliot, "Choruses from 'The Rock,'" in *The Complete Poems and Plays* (New York: Harcourt, Brace & World, 1952), 101.

2

||||||||||||||||||||||||||||||||||||||||

To Serve God Wittily, in the Tangle of One's Mind

||||||||||||||||||||||||||||||||||||||||

Jean Bethke Elshtain

SOMETIMES OTHERS ARE THE FIRST to notice. When my first book, *Public Man, Private Woman: Women in Social and Political Thought*, was published in 1981, I was criticized—indeed, in many instances it went beyond criticism to attack—by radical feminists, who at that point in time proclaimed that patriarchy (which seemed to mean any institution in which men were involved) should be "smashed," beginning with the family. Because I had found some compelling reasons for why families organized around configurations of men, women, and children could be found everywhere—and had, so far as we know, always existed—I was suspected of being soft on smashing. I had expected criticism, but I had underestimated the vehemence of the orchestrated campaign of criticism that followed publication of my book. In the years roughly between 1970 and 1988, receiving attacks was part of the deal if you were writing about feminism and not following the party line.

What I had not anticipated was that I would be suspected of being covertly religious, or perhaps even Christian. One reviewer of my book, writing in a leading journal of political science, went even further. Why was Elshtain even bothering to discuss the clearly benighted views of St.

Augustine, Martin Luther, and the like with such apparent interpretive charity? This reviewer suspected—although she hated to accuse anybody of this—that Jean Bethke Elshtain was a believer!

When I read these words, I was rather stunned. A believer? Really? I knew I was not a professional nonbeliever. I did not go around knocking religion. But I did not suspect that I wore my religious formation on my sleeve. To be sure, I spoke in the book of "bearing witness" and of "revealing" and of "when two or three are gathered together." I spoke of mutuality and community. I devoted the last chapter of that first book to a discussion of a vision of what I called "the ethical polity." But, a believer? Surely not any longer. Surely I had shed belief along the way like so many threadbare garments. Yes, there were moments when I backslid, took up St. Augustine's *Confessions* yet again, and found myself wandering into churches, even praying, although I had not planned to pray. I just "came to" and found that I was praying. But as a believer? The problem was, as I had learned in college, that one cannot prove belief, and that there is no compelling warrant for what believers claim to believe. I had become enlightened along the way! Thinking for oneself meant thinking *without* faith. And if faith precluded intelligent thinking, or if one could not think through or with faith, then I did not want any part of it.

But this was not working out the way it was supposed to. I said all the correct words. "Children should not be forced to be anything." They should "make up their own minds when they grow up." On and on. But the words rang increasingly hollow to my ears. What, I wondered, was to become of those of us who could not rid ourselves of faith, but who found equally troubling the naïveté of some believers as well as the arrogance of unbelievers who saw themselves as undoubtedly superior?

To Serve God Wittily . . .

As a graduate student, I had attended a lecture by one of the sprouts off the family tree Huxley—Sir Julian, I believe—and he assured those of us in attendance that by the year 2000, various phenomena would have disappeared from the face of the earth, eaten away by the corrosive acids of progress and spreading enlightenment. One of these phenomena was religion. A second was nationalism. I have forgotten the third. This is what is known as a failed prediction. Yet it affords some indication of the routine arrogance on display where religion is concerned.

Also during my student years, I had been drawn to Albert Camus's poignant project and his ongoing dialogue between the unbeliever and the Christian. His was such a powerful moral voice that I decided one could be a good, moral, decent person without being a believer. But maybe that was not where the heart of the matter lay. Maybe the heart of it all was not the "thou shalts" and "thou shalt nots" concerning conduct, so much as a fierce and terrible love: "For God so loved the world . . ." Perhaps this is what I had to learn to understand: God's love.

On some level I knew this already. But I needed to remember it, to pay attention, to unlearn so much of what I had learned during my college education so that I could be open to that love. I needed to understand that belief is not a matter of empirically testing the doctrine of the incarnation and finding it wanting and ticking it off the list, putting it into the "disconfirmed" column. I had tried to do this, knocking down my beliefs like so many bowling pins falling before the speeding ball of reason. But the beliefs kept popping back up. Perhaps I had it all wrong. I suspected that I did. I suspected that I needed to remember something, and I could not do that unless I unlearned the dogma that animates so much higher education—that faith and reason are incompatible, and that the life of the mind and the life of faith are mutually exclusive.

How, then, do we explain a St. Augustine? A St. Thomas? Such towering intellects. What did Augustine mean about "faith seeking understanding," the idea underlying his famous *credo ut intelligam*? Let's begin with my favorite lines from Robert Bolt's play about Sir Thomas More, *A Man for All Seasons*. Bolt puts some words in More's mouth. More tells his beloved daughter, Meg: "God made the *angels* to show him splendor—as he made animals for innocence and plants for their simplicity. But Man he made to serve him wittily, in the tangle of his mind!"[1]

To serve God wittily, in the tangle of one's mind! These are powerful and wonderful words. They draw us away from an excess of solemnity, which is death to witty scholarship. And they draw us into the tangle that is the human mind—that great and glorious instrument we either squander, use badly, or use well—*ad Dei gloriam*. To use well means, I believe, to recognize that our minds have not and cannot escape the noetic consequences of sin. Our minds cannot be perfect. Our knowledge is never complete. Humility is in order. Yet even allowing for all this, there really is, or can be, light shining in the darkness. Our epistemic urgency, our quest for knowledge, flows directly from creation itself. God would not have created us with intelligence to develop and use if this were not central to his pronouncement that creation is good. After all, we are asked to throw ourselves on God's love and mercy rather than into an abyss of ignorance. Critics of Christianity historically could point to such pronouncements as Tertullian's unfortunate "I believe because it is absurd" as proof positive that faith demands the resignation of intellect.

1. Robert Bolt, *A Man for All Seasons: A Play in Two Acts* (New York: Random House, 1962), 126.

Even Augustine's quite different and justly famous *credo ut intelligam*, "I believe in order to understand," came in for derision in many quarters, sometimes from those who failed to distinguish Augustine's position from Tertullian's, and sometimes from those confusing Augustine's position with a too-simple fideism or pietism that views the intellect with deep suspicion or even hostility.

The relationship between faith, reason, and learning that finally made sense to me was and is unafraid of intellectual engagement and is deeply committed to the life of the mind. It is embodied in a tradition that historically gave rise to such monumental tributes to the human mind's understanding through faith as St. Augustine's *City of God*, St. Thomas's *Summa theologiae*, Martin Luther's great works—this despite Luther's deep suspicions of overreliance on such pre-Christian philosophers as Aristotle—and Calvin's *Institutes*. Even the great mystics stressed certain attributes of mind—receptivity, a profound emptying of self in order that the mind and heart might be set afire by God's fierce love.

. . . In the Tangle of One's Mind

If you are a Christian in the early twenty-first century in a secular academy deeply suspicious of open faith, what will you find and how might you proceed? Most significantly, you find a routine omission of religious thinkers from the canon, an omission that undermines understanding and plays the intellect false. For example, it is a normal experience to look at a list of the canon in Western political thought and to find not a single "religious" text taken in its entirety. There will be excerpts, perhaps book 19 of Augustine's great *City of God*, or maybe a few pages from Aquinas's *Summa*, but usually nothing at all from the Reformers. Often enough, one simply leaps from Aristotle and perhaps a little Cicero, all the way to Machiavelli, as if the life of the mind ended in the third or fourth century and miraculously picked up again in the sixteenth century. Writers of more recent vintage such as Thomas Hobbes and John Locke—whose work is chock-full of religious dimensions, conflicts, and purposes—come in for similarly partial treatment. When I was in graduate school, there were versions of Locke's *Second Treatise* floating around that excised all the scriptural references, and editions of Hobbes's monumental *Leviathan* featuring only the first two books, omitting part 3, "Of a Christian Commonwealth," and part 4, "Of the Kingdom of Darkness."

In such a context, scholars prompted by Christian faith, serving God wittily in the tangle of their minds, can bring concepts and categories derived from faith and theology to bear upon their work. To do so has the effect, among other things, of showing the extraordinary illumination that can come from faith. There are so many powerful examples, but I will mention only three that I have addressed in my own work, in columns and op-editorials: just war, biogenetics, and economics.

The just-war tradition helps us to understand and to debate the justifiability of embarking on the use of coercive force and, further, whether the means being deployed, even in a just cause, are themselves licit or illicit.[2] The just-war tradition derives principally from St. Augustine's theological reflection upon the nature of justice and peace in a fallen world, so that one simply cannot understand many of the nuances of just-war positions in the absence of theological sensitivity. As I put it in another context:

> Viewing humanity through the lens of "original sin," just-war thinkers have historically expanded on understandings derived from theology: that human beings are broken and separated by sin and that this simply is the human condition between the fall and the end-time. At the same time, these torn and sinning creatures are haunted by the trace of their lost condition and yearn, therefore, for less alienated and fractured lives. Human motives and actions are always mixed: we both affirm and destroy solidaristic possibilities, often doing so simultaneously.[3]

In similar fashion, biogenetics is a field that cries out for the perspectives drawn from faith, as so-called "post" or "trans" humanists imagine a world in which the human being as creature no longer exists. Instead, a human-type entity will be something wholly of our own construction. Living in the United States, with its largely unregulated biogenetic industry, puts us especially at the mercy—unless government holds the line against this industry and its libertarian, rights-absolutist supporters—of these urgencies.

Economics is a particularly difficult subject because respected economists disagree on almost everything. But Christians of every political persuasion should ask themselves, "What is the nature of God's moral economy?" and by contrast reflect on their own economies and take stock accordingly. Minimally, I should think, we would all agree that God's economy of largesse and our economy of scarcity are bound to clash at particular points. Much of this is just in the nature of things in our fallen world. But there is also a good deal we can and should do, including challenging the notion of "abundance" that surrounds us.

---

2. See Jean Bethke Elshtain, *Just War against Terror: The Burden of American Power in a Violent World* (New York: Basic Books, 2003).

3. Jean Bethke Elshtain, "Just War and Humanitarian Intervention," *Ideas* 8, no. 2 (2001): 4–5.

When God promises that the faithful might live life "more abundantly," he wasn't thinking of SUVs and vacation homes. Perhaps we need to reflect long and hard on what constitutes "having enough" by contrast to "getting more."

These are but a few of the issues crying out for the power and insight that come from Christian understanding. Yet undoubtedly, serving God wittily in the tangle of one's mind—and doing so *publicly*—is bound to bring with it many frustrations. For example, I once participated in a discussion at the University of Chicago in which the question was God's economy and the market economy. My interlocutor was a faculty member from our economics department, one that has generated more Nobel laureates than any other department anywhere. I made a few points: God's economy does not begin with the presumption of scarcity and utilitarian cost-benefit analysis; God's economy demands that we morally evaluate and rank human activities. Along the way in this discussion, I was critical of the reductionistic anthropology—a fancy way of saying the wholly inadequate understanding of the human person—featured in economic theories wedded to a narrow, rational-choice approach. My criticism did not go over very well, to put it mildly. The good gentleman from economics threw his expertise down as a trump card. If you cannot do complex logarithms, you cannot talk about economics. I told him I would willingly give way if we were speaking of pricing mechanisms, or dozens of other economic phenomena. But he assumed that I was obliged to understand his perspective sympathetically—and that he was under no similar obligation in relation to my perspective. For in such matters, the unstated premise is that any perspective that begins with theological categories is intellectually bereft and cannot be defended rationally. That was basically the argument.

What does this add up to? Above all, do not be afraid. We are so easily embarrassed, or can be made to feel embarrassed, for sustaining the centuries-long effort of thoughtful Christians to bring together faith, scholarship, and the life of the mind. We worry that people will think we are wearing our faith on our sleeves, and that even the dynamic process of bringing concepts and categories to bear on a range of contemporary issues constitutes an example of such. We suppose others will imagine that we are not thinking at all, and that we want them to condone or to embrace our presumably uncritical perspective. If I have learned anything in my own pilgrimage, it is to put such fears, embarrassment, worries, and suppositions aside.

At the same time, however, public engagement of academic questions from the vantage of Christian faith may come in varied forms, some of which are more likely to prove useful and successful than others. In a law review piece of mine, I articulated some distinctions—some rules of engagement—about how believers should address the public square from the ground of faith.[4] I argued that there are three principal options:

- Full-bore "Christian" politics. The conviction that one must have a Christian position on everything. I rejected this position.
- Prophetic witness. This should be reserved for moments of great and fundamental crisis. An obvious example here is Martin Luther King Jr.
- Reasoned faith and respectful discourse. One need not bring the full panoply of reasons from faith to bear at each and every point. Some issues—like abortion—get to rock bottom very quickly. Others do not. One does not begin every discussion with "As a Christian . . . ," but rather lays out the reason-giving and tries to bring others on board. One's aim as a citizen is to persuade, not to forcibly convert. In opening oneself up to persuasion, one may open oneself up to conversion. But there are different mandates, offices, and vocations involved.

Put another way, there is a time and a season for everything. There is a line that separates one who, for example, sees the classroom as a forum for proselytizing—I have seen plenty of that over the years, and I have always opposed it. The examples I have in mind had to do with conversion to an ideology, like Marxism, rather than to anything religious. In a panel discussion one faculty member indicated that he graded students on whether they accepted the tenets of Marxist ideology, for if one understood those tenets, one obviously accepted them. It followed that students who raised criticisms had not understood "the theory" and could be graded down accordingly. Any Christian who did that would be given walking papers.

The classroom is an arena of understanding, of deepening complexity, in which one appreciates, as one teaches, the energy, illumination, hopefulness, and humility that flow from faith even as one is, well, rather ascetic in one's classroom practices. It took me many years to sort all of this out as I made my pilgrimage of the mind from childhood belief, to halfhearted yet dogged "unbelief," and through a complex detour back to belief—but a different, more complex, and more grateful belief than I had in my beginnings all those years ago. Reasoned faith and respectful discourse make it possible, whether in the classroom, the conference room, or the most public of forums, to traverse such a pilgrimage from naive belief to what Paul Ricoeur described aptly as a second naïveté, a

4. Jean Bethke Elshtain, "How Should We Talk?" *Case Western Reserve Law Review* 49, no. 4 (Summer 1999): 731–46.

disposition to be critically critical without falling over into the banality and paralysis of skepticism.[5] My own pilgrimage has been taking me in a southerly direction from Wittenberg to Rome. Yours may take you other places. In any case, however, we all need companions for life's significant journeys.

Tangling One's Mind in Christian Community

And here is where the notion of Christian intellectual community must come to the fore. My story is not of me alone, but of my interaction with and belonging to a community of interlocutors, some of whom have shared my faith, some of whom have not, but all of whom have challenged it. Thus, I am going to conclude by relating something about six of my book companions, my Christian and non-Christian guides. No story of the vocation of scholarship is ever complete without a testimony of this sort. The six for me are Albert Camus, Sigmund Freud, Dietrich Bonhoeffer, Hannah Arendt, Pope John Paul II, and St. Augustine of blessed memory. All are profiles in courage. All I discovered on my own rather than in or through any particular class. Because my story is inseparable from my ongoing dialogue with interlocutors whose thought I have made my own—and at one point you really do have to decide who you want rummaging around in your mind—my pilgrimage of the mind requires that I say something about each of these great figures.

Let me begin with Albert Camus. I discovered Camus when I was an undergraduate and read *The Stranger* in an honors literature course. Some of my classmates immediately became as absurd as possible. I, however, immediately grabbed *The Plague*, *The Rebel*, and *Resistance, Rebellion, and Death*. I saw that Camus lifted up the moral voice against the materialistic idols of the day. He was in ongoing dialogue with Christians. We dare not refuse that dialogue. In fact, with regard to many of the questions Camus takes up, I find myself on his side. Camus offers arguments

- against rational murder and "total"-itarianism.
- for ethical limits to political action.
- concerning the inseparability of moral and political questions.

His background included a thesis on St. Augustine and Neoplatonism. Read or reread the two sermons Camus puts into the mouth of the char-

5. See Paul Ricoeur, *The Symbolism of Evil*, trans. Emerson Buchanan (Boston: Beacon, 1967), 351–52.

acter Fr. Paneloux in *The Plague*, and you will emerge with a powerful sense of Camus's lifelong struggle with the theodicy question: If God is both all-powerful and all-good, whence evil?

Sigmund Freud, too, struggled to articulate the moral grounds for human decency in a world of practical atheism. Oh yes, there are many believers. But much if not most of the time, we proceed without what Bonhoeffer called "God as a working hypothesis."[6] Freud takes the moral measure of such a world. He called himself an atheist. Yet he offered his own version of loving the sinner and hating the sin. There is too much guilt, he insisted, and people were too hard on themselves, especially women who often lived lives involving unacceptable self-loss. He fought against the mechanistic and reductionistic mental scenarios of his time, with their often-cruel methods, in favor of more humane treatment of neuroses, consistent with human dignity. He argued that the first requirement of civilization is justice. The biggest challenge to civilization is the problem of cruelty and aggression. And in a Europe in which many educated, cosmopolitan European Jews denied their heritage and belief and hid it—especially if one came from a central Eastern European shtetl background—he never ran from his Jewish identity even though he did not practice the faith of his fathers and mothers. He argued to Christians that you could not be an anti-Semite without in some fundamental way being anti-Christian, even as he warned Jews against claiming a purity of identity.

Hannah Arendt found the courage to transform the victim identity of the refugee into the intellectual vocation of the adventurer of the mind. This great political theorist rejected "behavior" and instead celebrated both action and contemplation. She also challenged a teleology of violence even as she stressed "the political" as one way human beings reveal themselves one to the other. Her book *Eichmann in Jerusalem*, with its controversial phrase—"the banality of evil"—shows that she had studied her Augustine. She demonstrates that evil is not a grand, free-standing principle of its own but a dearth, a diminution, the work of horrifying men who are stuck in blind repetition of violence. Arendt also reminds us that the premier political faculty of the mind is "judgment"—that as citizens, we must discern, sift possibilities, and recognize that we live in a world of practical, not perfect, reason.

Dietrich Bonhoeffer, the great witness against Nazism, is a witness whom we, in turn, can witness through his writings, especially in his *Ethics* and *Letters and Papers from Prison*. A brilliant man unafraid of intellectual engagement, he took the measure of Nietzsche and Heidegger

6. Dietrich Bonhoeffer, *Letters and Papers from Prison*, ed. Eberhard Bethge (New York: Collier, 1972), 360.

and strengthened his theological thinking thereby. His life is all the more remarkable because, in so many ways, he is a faithful follower of Martin Luther, a figure not known for generating arguments for disobedience—to put it mildly! Yet Bonhoeffer insists that his views are entirely consistent with Luther's as he challenges totalitarianism with its impulse deeply embedded in "the triumph of reason," an aspiration of the French revolution. What the Nazis substituted was a triumph of the will.

Bonhoeffer sought to recapture some working notion of "nature" and the "natural" for Protestant ethics, finding in Nazism a violation of God's mandates and our status as created in the image of God. Disobedience, when it comes, comes reluctantly and tragically. One recognizes that one sins in calling upon oneself and one's coconspirators to assassinate Hitler. Yet what is to be done but to present oneself before God as a guilty person who acted in the name of concrete Christian responsibility, on behalf of "the bleeding brothers and sisters of Jesus Christ," the Jewish people?

Bonhoeffer also gives a powerful call for Christians to think and write with complexity. He hated mushy arguments and soft theology—and he feared that U.S. seminaries and divinity schools were already moving in that direction in the 1930s as various social and political agendas were substituted for intricate theological engagement and even for Scripture itself. His reference point was a course he was taking at Union Seminary in New York. During class, he found his fellow students giggling when Luther's doctrine of sin and free will was discussed: "How could anyone take such stuff seriously?" they seemed to be saying. For Bonhoeffer, anyone who believes it is funny to grapple with the basic stuff of abiding importance is obviously not a serious person. Given our contemporary crisis in Christian formation—much of it having to do with the life of the mind and with substituting simplistic politics and equally simplistic therapeutization for such a rigorous life—Bonhoeffer's tough-mindedness on these issues is more needed and more welcome than ever.

Pope John Paul II, one of the greatest historic figures of the twentieth century, is also a holy father of the intellect. He fashioned one significant encyclical after another, a surprising number focused centrally on the themes of the mind, such as *Veritatis splendor* (*Splendor of the Truth*) and *Fides et ratio* (*Faith and Reason*). As a philosopher, a teacher of Christian ethics at the University of Lublin, John Paul forged a dauntingly intricate encounter between the solid edifice of Thomism and the bracing currents of personalism and phenomenology. The full implications of this will be worked out during years to come. Throughout his papacy, he addressed himself to young people still in their years of formation. A typical passage demonstrates the powerful way in which he puts together human desires, thought, and faith: "In this creative restlessness beats and pulsates what is most deeply human—search for the truth, the insatiable need for the good, hunger for freedom, nostalgia for the beautiful, and the voice of conscience."[7]

Finally, consider St. Augustine. Here I hope you will grant me a small self-indulgence in resorting to a passage from one of my own books, *Augustine and the Limits of Politics*, where I interpret St. Augustine's understanding of knowledge:

> Although perfect self-knowledge is never possible, knowledge *is*. There is much we understand because we believe—not, however, from a stance of naïve credulity, or because belief somehow brings inquiry to a definitive halt. To the contrary: belief should spur understanding and sustain further inquiry.[8]

There is no finer way for me to conclude than by reference to a lyrical passage from St. Augustine expressing, or better yet, attempting to describe God's love. And remember, it is God's love and goodness that lie at the heart of the matter. We, his creatures, are the beings generated from that love, and in turn we love and serve by serving "wittily, in the tangle of our minds":

> My love of you, O Lord, is not some vague feeling; it is positive and certain. . . . But what do I love when I love my God? Not material beauty or beauty of a temporal order; not the brilliance of earthly light, so welcome to our eyes; not the sweet melody of harmony and song; not the fragrance of flowers, perfumes, and spices; not manna or honey; not limbs such as the body delights to embrace. It is not these that I love when I love my God. And yet, when I love him, it is true that I love a light of a certain kind, a voice, a perfume, a food, an embrace; but they are of the kind that I love in my inner self, when my soul is bathed in light that is not bound by space; when it listens to sound that never dies away; when it breathes fragrance that is not borne away on the wind; when it tastes food that is never consumed by the eating; when it clings to an embrace from which it is not severed by fulfillment of desire. This is what I love when I love my God.[9]

And moreover, *Dei gratia*, when we love our God, we do so with minds tangled—always inextricably, and hopefully wittily—in the fullness of Christian intellectual community.

---

7. Ioannes Paulus PP. II, *Redemptor hominis* (1979), §70.

8. Jean Bethke Elshtain, *Augustine and the Limits of Politics* (Notre Dame: University of Notre Dame Press, 1995), 32.

9. Augustine, *Confessions*, trans. R. S. Pine-Coffin (New York: Penguin, 1961), 10.6.

3

CHRISTIAN INTERDISCIPLINARITY

John C. Polkinghorne

ONE OF THE DEFINING CHARACTERISTICS of the modern research university is its emphasis on specialization. During my twenty years as a teacher and the leader of a research group in Cambridge University's department of applied mathematics and theoretical physics, I devoted my academic work to applying the principles of relativistic quantum theory in seeking to understand the behavior of the smallest particles of matter. I do not regret that narrow concentration—indeed, I regard it as having been part of my Christian vocation to use such talents as I had in this way. Engaging with a discipline in thorough detail teaches one something about the nature of knowledge—its subtlety, its interlocking complexity, the boldness required in intellectual venture, and the satisfaction that comes from attaining new understanding—insights that cannot be acquired through a more broad-brush approach to learning. Yet the insights gained in this way must also be set within a wider context.

I became aware of this wider context in a rather pragmatic way when for a while it became my responsibility, through my membership with the United Kingdom Science Research Council, to seek funding from the British taxpayer of some forty million pounds a year to support the work of our particle physics community. In discharging this task, I had to explain why an expenditure of this magnitude was needed so that we might be able to learn about the behavior of quarks and gluons, entities utterly remote from direct apprehension in everyday life. When all was explained about possible technological spin-offs from the activities of our community, the only final and appropriate response was that it is a human activity of intrinsic value to probe and understand the deep order and structure of the physical world in which we live. The ultimate motivation for particle physics was not to increase the gross national product, but rather to pursue knowledge for knowledge's sake. I did not then use as a public argument my private conviction that this latter belief had theological undergirding. Yet if pressed, I would have had to acknowledge that, for me, scientific exploration ultimately derives its justification from a desire, often unconsciously entertained, to learn something of the work of the Word "by whom all things were made, and without whom was not anything made that was made" (John 1:3 author's translation). Attempting to read the book of nature is an implicit act of homage to the Creator, and the sense of wonder that so often rewards the scientific inquirer after all the labor of doing scientific research is akin to an act of worship. These are themes to which I will return as my argument develops.

The Unity of Knowledge

I regard universities as being the institutionalized expressions of the value and validity of the human quest for knowledge. I believe that they are also called to be embodiments of the ultimate unity of that knowledge. This aspect of their academic witness is under threat today because of the relentless pressures that draw their faculty into becoming specialists who are no more than specialists, each "knowing more and more about less and less," as the saying goes. As the very name itself suggests, the true university is very much more than a loose federation of monodisciplinary research institutes, for logistical convenience located side by side on the same piece of land but without lively intellectual intercourse between them. A true university must seek the kind of unity within a common scholarly community that makes it capable of embracing and integrating the diversity of its specialties.

Those who adhere to a trinitarian theology will readily recognize that unity is not at all the same thing as homogeneity. The great mistake of the grand, but in the end unsuccessful, project of modernity was to suppose that there is a single universal rationality that applies across the board. The ghost of this misapprehension still lingers on, particularly in forms of scientistic reductionism that seek to cut down the rich variety of human experience into a truncated form that can then be forced to fit into the Procrustean bed of a crass kind of physicalism. The essence of rationality is to seek to conform our thinking modes to the actual nature of the objects of our thought. This means that we have to employ a variety of forms of rational expression to fulfill the task of gaining understanding, because the entities that we encounter are not all of one kind. We know sticks and stones in one way, other persons in another way, and the transpersonal reality of God in a third way.

From within physics itself we can easily illustrate this point about an open-ended epistemology and rationality, responsive in different ways to different dimensions of experience. There are two broad types of physical theory: classical mechanics, describing the kind of everyday behavior that Isaac Newton analyzed with such penetration in the *Principia*; and quantum mechanics, principally relating to the behavior of entities of the size of atoms or smaller. The former is based on a clear and determinate picture of the physical world, and the logic it employs is that of Aristotle, based on the law of the excluded middle: that there is no possible intermediate between A and not-A. The quantum form of physics is based on the unpicturable principle of superposition, which accommodates states that are mixtures of A and not-A. The existence of these middle terms, of a kind undreamed of by Aristotle, means that a different kind of logic has to be applied to the quantum world.[1] That world has to be encountered on its own terms, which include a Heisenbergian uncertainty clouding the picture of its processes. The thought patterns of commonsense expectation are not the measure of everything, even within science itself. So it is that the boundaries between different domains of rationality are subtle. They are not simple, linear frontiers, for they are mutually interpenetrating in fractal-like ways. Even in physics, such matters are by no means fully understood, and they give rise to perplexities.[2]

In the academic forum, pendulums of fashion swing as vigorously as they do anywhere else. The collapse of the modernist program has encouraged some to embrace the alternative of an extreme form of postmodernism. The result is that the discredited concept of a single kind of rationality has given way, in the minds of some, to the feeling that the choice of rationality is an à la carte matter, to be settled in accordance with personal inclination or social convention. It seems to me that leaping into the fire of postmodernism is no more satisfactory than staying in the frying pan of modernism. What we need is a temperate recognition that different forms of rational discussion are needed for different forms

1. See John C. Polkinghorne, *Quantum Theory: A Very Short Introduction* (Oxford: Oxford University Press, 2002), 37–38.
2. See John C. Polkinghorne, "Causal Nexus," forthcoming.

of encounter with reality, but the nature of these forms is controlled by the nature of the reality encountered.

This point of view makes sense only if we believe that experience really affords us contact with noumena (things-in-themselves) and that experience is not just the result of the appearances of phenomena in their play. As a scientist-theologian, I am an unapologetic believer in critical realism. The adjective "critical" is necessary because we certainly do not experience the naive objectivity of unproblematic encounter with reality (quarks are inferred and not directly observed). The noun "realism" is necessary because the world resists our prior expectations, and its stubborn actuality molds the shape of our thinking (it took about twenty years of intellectual struggle, largely experimentally led, before physicists reached the fully fledged realization of the quark structure of matter). I realize that critical realism is a contentious issue. Elsewhere I have tried to make my contribution to its defense,[3] and I do not intend to repeat those arguments now. Let me just say that the religious believer (and Judaism, Christianity, and Islam can all make common cause here) will see a realist position as being theologically underwritten by the conviction that the Creator will not be a deceiver. God enables us creatures, made in the divine image, to gain a true understanding of the works of creation.

In the search for unified knowledge and integrated understanding, we often have to be content with slow progress, and it would be a bad mistake to prematurely claim for a partial insight the status of a final solution. Yet there is a deep human conviction that, despite the difficulties encountered, unified theories and integrated insights are the legitimate, and indeed necessary, goals of intellectual endeavor. The unity of knowledge, on which the life of a true university is predicated, is indeed its proper aspiration. Ultimately, this is an article of faith that requires a theological foundation for its support. The world really is a cosmos and not a chaos, precisely because it really is a divine creation. Knowledge is one because God is one. A favorite epigram of mine is an observation by Bernard Lonergan, calling God "the unrestricted act of understanding, the eternal rapture glimpsed in every Archimedean cry of

3. John C. Polkinghorne, *One World: The Interaction of Science and Theology* (London: SPCK, 1986), chaps. 1–3; idem, *Reason and Reality: The Relationship between Science and Theology* (Philadelphia: Trinity Press International, 1991), chaps. 1–2; idem, *The Faith of a Physicist: Reflections of a Bottom-Up Thinker* (Princeton: Princeton University Press, 1994), chap. 2; idem, *Beyond Science: The Wider Human Context* (Cambridge: Cambridge University Press, 1996), chap. 2; idem, *Belief in God in an Age of Science* (New Haven: Yale University Press, 1998), chaps. 2, 5; and idem, *Faith, Science, and Understanding* (New Haven: Yale University Press, 2000), chaps. 2–3, 5.

Eureka."[4] The true university's quest for interdisciplinary truth may be properly called "Christian," not because of some imperialist attempt at takeover by the churches, but because those who seek the truth without reserve, whether they know it or not, are ultimately searching for the God and Father of our Lord Jesus Christ.

The centrifugal tendencies induced by specialization, which threaten the unity of the university community of searchers for truth, are thus counterbalanced by the centripetal effects of the intrinsic interconnectedness of knowledge. The new wine of increasing understanding bursts the old wineskins of disciplinary narrowness. This, too, can be illustrated from within the domain of science. We have every reason to believe that scientifically statable questions will eventually receive scientifically statable answers, however difficult at times it may actually be to find those answers. In this sense, the sciences do not need augmentation from outside of themselves. This judgment can only be reinforced by the observation that the detailed way in which scientists do their professional work does not appear to be shaped by broader considerations. Those who are Jews, Christians, Muslims, unbelievers, or whatever—all seem to function scientifically in the same sort of way.

Yet science has purchased its very great success in its own domain at the cost of the modesty of its ambitions. We have every reason to think that there are many questions both meaningful and necessary to ask that cannot be framed according to the narrow protocols of science. Their answering must lie outside of its self-chosen confines. If we are to pursue truth and understanding without reserve—a quest quite natural and congenial to the scientist—then we shall certainly have to move beyond science itself. The shape of this further stage in the quest for the widest possible intelligibility will be influenced by the broadness and depth of the view that one takes of the nature of reality. In other words, the search for understanding has to move on from physics to metaphysics. "Metaphysics" is not a popular word in many circles today, but it nevertheless represents an indispensable concept. Everyone, consciously or unconsciously, espouses a worldview. Whatever people may say, they can no more do without a metaphysics than they can speak a language without using prose. This is as true of the physical reductionists as it is true of anyone else. Such people certainly do not derive their scientistic principles from science itself. It is in forming this deeper view of reality, an essential setting for the exercise of an adequate interdisciplinarity, that religious insights and theological reflections have their role to play. That is why the notion of "Christian interdisciplinarity" is indispensable

---

4. Bernard J. F. Lonergan, *Insight: A Study of Human Understanding* (London: Longmans, 1958), 684.

in an exploration of faith as a foundation for intellectual community, for all of the academic disciplines, properly grasped, are ultimately self-transcending and oriented toward the unity of knowledge that holds together in God.

The Self-Transcendent Character of Academic Disciplines

Nowhere is the self-transcendent character of individual academic specialties more evident than within the sciences. Indeed, it is interesting and significant that some of the questions that take us beyond science actually arise out of the experience of doing science, even if they transcend its ability to furnish their answers. We may call them "limit questions," or "metaquestions," carrying us outside the borders of the simply scientific.

Why Is Science Possible?

One of these metaquestions is so simple that we seldom stop to think about it. It is just this: Why is science possible at all? Why can we understand the physical world so thoroughly? At first sight you might suppose that the necessities of evolutionary biology would provide a ready answer. If we did not understand the world in which we live, how could we survive in it? That is true, but only up to a point. We need to know that it is a bad idea to walk off the top of a high cliff, but it does not follow from this that Isaac Newton should be able—in an astonishing, creative leap of the human imagination—to see that the same force that makes the cliff dangerous is also the force that holds the Moon in its orbit around the Earth, and the Earth in its orbit around the Sun; or be able to discover the mathematically beautiful inverse square law of universal gravity, and hence to be able to explain the motions of all the planets in the solar system. There is something involved here far beyond mere matters of mundane utility. As Sherlock Holmes once said to a shocked Dr. Watson, "It does not matter to me in my work as a detective whether the Earth goes round the Sun or the Sun goes round the Earth." And about two hundred years after Newton, Albert Einstein comes along and, through another great creative imaginative leap that led him to general relativity, was able to start the formulation of a truly scientific cosmology, capable of giving us understanding of the whole physical universe.

These discoveries exhibit the amazing powers of the human mind. It does not seem at all plausible to suggest that they are just happy, accidental spin-offs from our ancestors having had to dodge saber-toothed tigers. One could make similar comments about our ability to understand the counterintuitive quantum world, as different in its character from the everyday world as its phenomena are distant from direct impact on our experience. Nevertheless, we can probe this subatomic realm and learn about its mysteries. And in fact, things are stranger than that, for it is mathematics that proves to be the key for unlocking the secrets of the universe. Time and again it has been our experience in fundamental physics that the theories persuading us of their verisimilitude by their long-term fruitfulness in explaining phenomena—these are also theories whose formulation is characterized by the abstract but unmistakable character of mathematical beauty. It was an eight-year search for a beautiful equation that led Einstein to the discovery of the fundamental formulae of general relativity. The great English theoretical physicist Paul Dirac once said that it was more important to have beauty in your equations than to have them fit experiment! By that he did not mean that empirical adequacy was irrelevant—no physicist could suppose that. However, initial difficulties in fitting experiment might have a number of venial explanations. Almost certainly the equations would have been solved using some approximation procedure, and perhaps the appropriate kind of approximation had not been made. Or maybe the experiments were wrong—we have known that to happen in physics a few times. So, if there seemed initially to be empirical problems, there might nevertheless be some hope of a way out. But if the equations were ugly . . . , well, then there was no hope at all. You did not have a chance.

This pursuit of mathematical beauty is no mere aestheticism on the part of theoretical physicists. This is made clear by its outstanding success as a strategy for gaining understanding. Dirac discovered his famous relativistic equation of the electron (inscribed on his memorial tablet in Westminster Abbey) precisely by seeking beauty in the mathematics. Once discovered, the equation gave an immediate sign of its convincing physical relevance by unexpectedly offering a natural explanation of an anomaly in the magnetic behavior of electrons that was already known but had been an unresolved problem to understand. Later, further thought about the properties of the equation led Dirac to the discovery of antimatter, a previously unknown and unsuspected phenomenon of fundamental importance. This kind of uncovenanted fruitfulness is very persuasive in showing that one is in touch with true aspects of physical reality.

When we use mathematical beauty in this way as a heuristic tool, something quite strange is happening. Mathematics is an abstract activity of the human mind, and its beautiful patterns do not have any obviously necessary relationship to the physical world around us. In other words, there is a mystery about this deep-seated connection between the mental world of mathematical entities and the physical world of objects, a quite astonishing example of interdisciplinary connection. Eugene Wigner, Dirac's brother-in-law and himself a Nobel Laureate for physics, once described this as "the unreasonable effectiveness of mathematics." He said that it was a gift that we neither deserved nor understood.

I do not know whether we deserve it, but I would certainly like to understand it. I would like to know why the internal reason of our minds and the external rational order of the world are so perfectly related to each other. Here is a metaquestion that arises from science, but goes beyond its power to answer, for science itself just takes advantage of this unreasonable effectiveness and, as Wigner acknowledged, it does not pretend to explain where it comes from. Looking beyond the horizon of science in a theistic direction opens up the possibility of saying more. Deep metaquestions of this kind will not have "knockdown," inevitable answers of a sort that it would be stupid not to accept immediately. This does not mean that answers cannot be given, but that they have to be defended by appeal to economy, elegance, and comprehensive adequacy, as is the case with all metaphysical claims.

Christian belief affords us a satisfying answer to why science is possible, why mathematics is so unreasonably effective. The reason of our minds and the rational order of the universe are integrated because they have a common origin in the Creator, whose mind and will is the ground of all that is. The deep intelligibility of the physical world is indeed a reflection of the mind of God. The mathematical physicist is privileged to catch a faint glimpse of the light of the Word, by whom all things were made. Within the wider horizon of theological understanding, the success of science is no longer an incredibly happy accident; instead, that success becomes intelligible to us.

Why Is the Universe So Special?

To be sure, the question of why science is possible is not the only metaquestion that compels physicists to look beyond their own disciplinary specialization for assistance. One might with equal interest ask: Why is the universe so special? The universe started extremely simple. Immediately following the big bang, the universe was an almost uniform expanding ball of energy, and we cannot have a physical system that is much simpler than that. Today, the universe is complex and diverse, with human beings the most complicated consequences known to us as the results of its fourteen-billion-year evolutionary development. Cosmic history is a history of immense fruitfulness, a thought in itself perhaps suggesting that there could be more going on than the strictly scientific story is able to tell.

As we have come to understand more and more of the details of this cosmic evolutionary history, we see that its fertility has depended critically upon the laws of nature taking quite specific forms, and the forces that these laws describe do have quite precisely the intrinsic strengths that they actually possess. Although, as far as we know, life only appeared when the universe was about ten billion years old, and self-conscious life when it was fourteen billion years old, there is a real sense in which the physical fabric of the world immediately post-big bang was already pregnant with the possibility of carbon-based life. Evolution was certainly an important component in the story of the emergence of life, but it was only part of that story. Only a world that was already "finely tuned" in its basic physical constitution could have been the setting for realizing that remarkable possibility.

I shall not go into the familiar detailed considerations that lie behind these conclusions of what has come to be called the Anthropic Principle.[5] In brief, a sensitive balance between gravity and electromagnetism is necessary if stars are to be able to burn steadily for billions of years, fueling the development of life on encircling planets. The character of the nuclear forces has to be just right to allow the chain of nuclear processes to take place, in stellar interiors and in supernovae explosions, and that alone can produce the heavier elements that are the chemical raw materials of life. Every atom of carbon in our bodies was once inside a star—we are literally creatures of stardust. The stellar production of this element that lies at the basis of all life was only a possibility because the precise form of the nuclear forces operating in our universe produces an enhancement effect (a resonance) at exactly the right energy to make the process feasible. When Fred Hoyle discovered this truly remarkable instance of "fine-tuning," he is said, despite a lifetime's inclination to atheism, to have concluded that the universe is "a put-up job." Fred could not believe that this delicate coincidence was just a happy accident. He felt that some Intelligence must lie behind the cosmic story. Even the immense size of the observable universe, with its 10^{22} stars, is necessary for it to have lasted the fourteen billion years that is the natural timescale for the development of conscious life. Moving to issues more parochially terrestrial, we may recall that the laws of matter must have among their consequences the remarkable and anomalous properties of water (such as becoming less dense near freezing point) that play so important a part in the processes of life.

5. See John D. Barrow and Frank J. Tipler, *The Anthropic Cosmological Principle* (Oxford: Oxford University Press, 1986); and John Leslie, *Universes* (New York: Routledge, 1989).

These anthropic insights have generated much discussion concerning what we are to make of their surprising specificity. The initial reaction of many scientists was hostile to the possibility that there might be a wider significance. The scientific community has an instinctive horror of the unique, and here was a suggestion, arising from within science itself, that there was something very particular indeed about our universe. We could no longer simply think of it as just an average cosmic specimen, of no especially interesting character.

Would it then be enough to treat anthropic fine-tuning as a mere brute fact, simply the way things happen to be? The universe must be compatible with our presence as observers within it, but the fact that this imposes such tight constraints upon its physical fabric is surely extremely surprising and potentially significant. It seems incredibly intellectually lazy just to say "We're here because we're here" and to leave it at that. There must be more to say and understand.

Two different strategies have been proposed by way of response. One suggests that there are actually many different universes, each with its own set of natural laws and circumstances, and that our observed universe is but one component in this vast and hypothetical multiverse. Our particular world then is special and suitable for life just by chance; it is simply the universe that happened to draw the winning ticket in the cosmic lottery of carbon-based life. The discerned particularity of our cosmos is thereby defused by making it just one among an almost infinite range of other universes. This is the response of a grossly extended naturalism, and although scientists have sometimes tried to trick out this proposal in speculative scientific dress, its character is clearly that of metaphysical conjecture. We have no adequate reason for an honest science to support so prodigal an array of many worlds with such a great variety of different laws of nature, all but one inaccessible to our investigation.

Any proposed answer to a metaquestion taking us beyond the narrow horizon of science will have to be metaphysical in its character. This is also true of the second strategy, which supposes that there is only one universe, but it is not just "any old world," for it is a creation that has been endowed by its Creator with just those finely tuned laws and circumstances that have enabled it to evolve conscious beings.

If both of these proposals have metaphysical status, how shall we choose between them? Considerations of economy and explanatory scope will be important. The supposition of many worlds only seems to do one piece of explanatory work: to assuage scientific embarrassment at the apparent specificity of our universe and to defuse the threat of theism. Belief in God, on the other hand, does a number of pieces of explanatory work in addition to giving an understanding of anthropic particularity. We have already seen how belief in God can cast light on the deep intelligibility of the physical world. Such belief also affords a basis for understanding the widespread claims of experiences of encountering the sacred, which in one form or another have featured in almost all cultures, with contemporary Western atheism being notably exceptional in this regard.

These two metaquestions being considered here have been the basis for an interdisciplinary engagement that amounts to a revival of natural theology in our time. It is, however, a revised natural theology when compared with its predecessors, such as represented in the writings of William Paley, for it is not concerned with rivaling science in trying to explain the happenings of the world, but rather with complementing science by making more intelligible what the latter has to take for granted: the form of the laws of nature. The new natural theology does not pretend to answer scientific questions; instead, it addresses the metaquestions that take us beyond science. I think this development represents real interdisciplinary progress in developing a positive relationship between science and theology. It is a limited exercise from the point of view of religious belief. It can be welcomed by all the Abrahamic faiths, because by itself it is as consistent with the God of Deism as it is with the Christian God, active providentially in history, whose steadfast faithfulness and care for human individuals is made known supremely through the life, death, and resurrection of Jesus Christ. I shall return to the issue of Christian specificity in due course.

What Moral Constraints Should Shape Scientific Inquiry and Application?

These limit questions are not the only interdisciplinary dimension within which the discourse of science needs to be located. It is also necessary to consider ethical issues. Science gives us knowledge, and then its lusty offspring, technology, takes that knowledge and turns it into the power to do things not previously possible. However, we should not do everything that can be done. From this fact arise the ethical questions that must properly be on the agenda of the true university. Academic scientists cannot absolve themselves from responsibility for the uses to which their discoveries may be put. After the end of World War II, many of the physicists who had been at Los Alamos were troubled by this realization. Yet the scientists cannot be left to themselves to be the sole judges in their own cause. Research is exciting, and the temptation is always to keep going. "We've done this, we've done that; come on, let's do the next thing." It is only too easy to become carried away by a kind of technological imperative. But the next thing may be something that should not be done. To scientific knowledge and technological power, therefore, we need to be able to add wisdom, the ability to discern and choose the good, and the ability to discern and refuse the bad.

Over many centuries religions have been reservoirs of wisdom, patiently accumulating experience of how ethically acceptable choices can be made. This is why Christian insight will certainly have significant contributions to make to the interdisciplinary discussion of the ethical uses of scientific discoveries. Yet religious people also have to recognize the novelty of many of the problems that face us today, which often do not have clear precedents in the moral thinking of the past. The Bible conveys important insights into moral principles and God's will for creation, but its pages do not offer, in any direct fashion, specific answers to many of the novel ethical problems of today.

Often perplexities arise, not from uncertainty about basic principles, but about how these principles actually relate to the case in question. For example, it is widely agreed to be a principle of medical ethics that interventions on a human being must be undertaken with fully informed consent and for the benefit of that person. But how does this apply to the very early embryo, say within the initial fourteen-day period, when there is no structure present other than that carried by the DNA in each undifferentiated cell? If the embryo is fully human from the moment of its formation, possessing the complete moral status of a person, then its destruction to yield a source of stem cells would be as morally unthinkable as would be the removal of the heart from a living person so that it could be transplanted into another. But perhaps human personhood is something that develops with increasing complexity of being, so that the very early embryo, though certainly entitled to a profound ethical respect on the basis of its potential humanity, has not yet attained the full moral status of a human being. If this is the case, then the possibility of using embryos before fourteen days for purposes that are medically serious, and for ends not likely to be attainable by a nonembryonic route, at least becomes an ethically conceivable possibility. The present state of legislation in the United Kingdom, in fact, corresponds to this latter judgment, so that embryo research of this kind can be licensed on a strictly assessed and case-by-case basis.

Which is the right conclusion? We shall not all be able to agree, despite the fact that we are all seeking to behave ethically in the matter of stem-cell research. Without going into the detail of the arguments, I point out that we cannot settle this matter simply by gaining more exact embryological information (although such knowledge is an important input into the discussion), nor by the deliberation of focus groups, nor by the clash of single-issue pressure groups, each seeing if it can shout louder than the others. Many factors have to be weighed and many insights taken into account. Temperate rational discussion must involve all kinds of participants, including both medical scientists and religious thinkers. In a word, it must be interdisciplinary. This kind of wide engagement in the search for truth and right conduct is something that universities are particularly well equipped to sponsor.

The Indispensability of Theology

Alas, the interdisciplinary community of scholars that enables universities to succeed often, in my estimation, fails to include an essential voice in the conversation: a department of theology.[6] Here I refer to "theology" and not just "religious studies." The latter, it seems to me, often tends to take a distanced and phenomenological view of what religion is about. "Muslims do it on Fridays, Jews on Saturdays, Christians on Sundays." I do not deny the value of this kind of investigation, but by itself it seems to me to be an inadequate approach to the issues raised by the widespread human encounter with the dimension of the sacred. Too often, religious studies brackets out the question of truth, an issue that is absolutely vital to religious believers. They are not simply concerned with a particular culturally formed way of life, but they also embrace that way of life because they believe it to conform to the character of ultimate reality—in the case of the Abrahamic faiths, to the nature and will of the God made known within their traditions.

One must admit that the question of theological truth is made extremely complex by the diversity of the world's faith traditions and the cognitive clashes between the claims that they make. These disagreements do not refer only to differences on rather specific matters (such as the status of the Torah, of Jesus, and of the Qur'an), but also to general worldviews: Is time a linear path to be trodden or a samsaric wheel from which to seek release? Is the human person an individual of unique and abiding significance in the sight of God, or recycled through a process of reincarnation, or ultimately an illusion from which to seek release? These are certainly not just culturally diverse ways of saying the same thing. The commitment to honest inquiry that should lie at the heart of university life has to take account of these perplexing disagreements.

Interdisciplinary discussion and interfaith encounter has to take place in a setting in which all participants seek to speak humbly but definitely from the integrity of their own positions. In the sphere of the faiths, in my opinion, nothing is gained by attempting to construct a kind of lowest-common-denominator religious point of view; this seems only

6. Cf. Polkinghorne, *Faith, Science, and Understanding*, chaps. 1–2.

to result in an account so diluted, or even banal, that it scarcely seems worth bothering about very much, or to be likely to excite the interest of many actual adherents of the faith traditions. For my part, I must hold fast to my conviction of the unique significance of Jesus Christ. This does not mean that I feel I have nothing to learn from the encounter with my brothers and sisters in other world religions, but our meeting must be on the basis of a candid affirmation of what each believes has been learned of the nature and purposes of God. In this firm but mutually respectful fashion, the ecumenical encounter of the world's faiths is a matter of great importance, but one that requires patience and persistence over a long time scale. It is a matter for the third millennium and not simply for the twenty-first century. Universities provide one of the settings in which this can take place.[7]

Let me therefore, by way of conclusion, try to summarize what I believe can be the Christian contribution to the soul of any true university. I can conveniently do so by indicating two roles that a department of theology can play and that make its presence indispensable to the character of a proper university.

Theological discourse operates at two levels. One of these is as a first-order discipline. In this role it is usually called "systematic theology." Its investigation is based on its own proper and basic resources—in the case of Christian theology, centering on the history of God's dealings with Israel; on the life, death, and resurrection of Jesus Christ; and on the continuing life, witness, and unfolding understanding of truth gained by the church under the guidance of the Holy Spirit. In this primary mode, theology develops its own style of thought and its own kind of rationality, in ways appropriate to actual encounter with the reality of God. In the case of Christianity, this requires the development of trinitarian modes of thought. Theology can no more be forbidden this use of its own rational

---

7. As a point of clarity, there is a worthwhile distinction to be drawn between the title of this volume, *Christianity and the Soul of the University*, and alternatives such as *The Soul of the Christian University*. I come from a country where there are no confessional universities, and for us, the concept of the Christian university is by no means unproblematic. A natural form of discourse in the British setting would be framed in terms of the Christian presence within the university. Our favored image is something like leaven in the lump rather than a gathered community, for there seems to be some danger if like talk only to like. I believe the critiques of unbelievers have a place within the providence of God, a thought reinforced by consideration of the fact that much orthodox Christian thinking has arisen as a response to the pressures of heterodoxy. I do realize that the overall situation in the United Kingdom is different, partly because we do not have a doctrine of the rigid separation of church and state overscrupulously enforced. I also know that many Christian colleges and universities in North America are places of integrity, academic excellence, and lively dialogue, and I am grateful for the privilege of having been able to visit such institutions. Nevertheless, I do not regret that my academic life and Christian vocation have been within an essentially secular but open system.

resources than science can be forbidden a similar freedom in relation to its observations of the history and nature of the physical universe. In the fulfillment of its proper task, systematic theology no more requires augmentation from science than science does from theology. First-order disciplines rightly defend the integrity that corresponds to their proper domains of inquiry. Without the presence of a department of theology, a university would lack due recognition of the dimension of encounter with the sacred and the transcendent, which is so significant a part of humanity's engagement with reality.

But theology has a further role to play, as a second-order discipline seeking to respect the insights of all the first-order disciplines and to integrate them into a religious worldview or theological metaphysics. This activity sometimes goes by the name of "philosophical theology." At this level Christianity can make a particularly vital—in my view, indispensable—contribution to the interdisciplinary life of a true university. That unity of knowledge, which is the foundational conviction on which the life of the university is built, is ultimately guaranteed by the unity of God. The possibility of truthful knowledge is guaranteed by the Creator's desire to make the divine will and nature known to creatures. Above all, belief in God is the single integrating idea that ties together in the most intellectually satisfying way the diverse richness of human experience.

I have already argued that the laws of nature, in their rational transparency and beauty, and in the fruitful potentialities that they contain, are not sufficiently self-explanatory to stand alone. Instead, their character, including our human access to it, is best understood as reflecting the status of the universe as a creation expressive of the mind and will of its Creator. As you would have expected from a scientist-theologian, the kind of natural theology that this gives rise to has been my principal example of the power of interdisciplinary thinking. Yet theological metaphysics has much more to offer.

For instance, human beings also have access to moral knowledge of a kind that seems to me to be as certain as any sort of knowledge that we might have. The conviction that torturing children is wrong is not some kind of curiously disguised strategy for successful genetic propagation, nor is it a tacitly chosen convention of society. Rather, it is a fact about the reality within which we live. What is the foundation of this fact? Where does moral knowledge come from? Or to take another example, what is the basis on which it is possible to argue, as we intuitively know we must, that we owe our respect to nature, and that it is not just there to be raped of its resources, with scant attention to its integrity or to the needs of future generations? While nonbelievers may follow these kinds of moral imperatives at least as responsibly as any Christian, they are hard put to explain why they should do so. In *The Selfish Gene*—in the course of which Richard Dawkins puts forth the bleak view that an evolutionary necessity to enhance gene propagation is the explanatory principle telling us what life is really all about—suddenly in the last lines of the last page, he says, "We, alone on earth, can rebel against the tyranny of the selfish replicators."[8] He clearly and sincerely believes that we should do so, but I do not see where this commitment could find an anchorage in the worldview that has been the subject of his book. For the Christian, our moral intuitions derive their validity from being intimations of the good and perfect will of our Creator.

Then there is human aesthetic experience.[9] I am sure that our encounters with beauty are not a kind of epiphenomenal froth; instead, they are engagements with a significant dimension of reality. What is the source of the authenticity of art? It is certainly not to be explained in terms of evolutionary argument. What is the survival value of the music of J. S. Bach? None, I think, but our lives would be greatly impoverished without it. The Christian can understand experiences of beauty as a sharing in the Creator's joy in creation.

Finally, there is human encounter with the reality of the sacred. For me, no metaphysical view could begin to be adequate that did not take into full account the life, death, and—I certainly wish to say—resurrection of Jesus Christ. God is the ground of all reality, the integrating factor that ties together the multidimensional richness of human experience. A true theory of Everything is not superstring theory, but Christian theology. Bearing witness to that is the indispensable contribution that Christian interdisciplinarity can make to the soul of the university.

8. Richard Dawkins, *The Selfish Gene* (Oxford: Oxford University Press, 1976), 215.

9. See Anthony Monti, *A Natural Theology of the Arts: Imprint of the Spirit* (Burlington, VT: Ashgate, 2003).

4

THE CHRISTIAN SCHOLAR
IN AN AGE OF WORLD CHRISTIANITY

Joel A. Carpenter

IN RECENT YEARS, NATIONAL CONFERENCES on Christian faith and the life of the mind have become an annual moveable feast, traveling from Notre Dame to Calvin to Pepperdine and to Baylor, among other places. A common desire for integrity in academic and intellectual life is drawing Christians together from a variety of traditions. The broad and bold mandate for the Baylor meeting asserts that Christianity offers a "comprehensive, unsurpassable, and central account of human life and the world" that aims at an "all-encompassing" vision. Yet the topics and perspectives on the docket seemed rather limited, given the universal rhetoric. Those of us who are committed to this mandate need to become even more evangelical and catholic in vision. By way of illustration, consider two recent visitors to my office.

One was the Rev. Dr. Musiande Kasali, a Congolese theologian who is a seminary president in Nairobi, Kenya. President Kasali had some news for me: "The Lord is calling me to found a Christian university," he told me, saying that it would most likely be in Beni, in the eastern Congo. I was astonished. Beni was the epicenter of the brutal civil war in the Congo that has claimed some 3.3 million lives since 1998. Dr. Kasali explained:

"We must rebuild our nation. We need Christian leaders who will serve God's reign. Surely we have seen enough of Satan's hand in our land." One can hardly imagine a more impossible place to build a Christian university, but Kasali and his countrymen have heard God's call.

The other visitor was Dr. Young-sup Kim, the academic dean of Handong Global University in South Korea. Handong was founded in 1995 by a Korean nuclear engineer who dreams of its becoming an evangelical MIT. This university is assembling a strong Korean faculty on a gleaming new campus, with about three thousand high-achieving students. Handong is not content to stop there; it is busy replicating itself in two other Asian sites: Uzbekistan and Manchuria. At Calvin College, we worry about spreading ourselves too thin, so we have shelved some of our more ambitious dreams. Yet we look at our Korean counterparts and marvel at their vision and energy.

Few of the topics or speakers for the recent conferences on Christianity and higher education relate directly to Kasali and Kim.[1] Christianity and the life of the mind are profoundly contextual, and we are living in a time of some seismic shifts in context for Christianity and its role in the world. For the past millennium, Christianity and Christian consciousness have been tied to Europe, and our conversation here about Christianity and the life of the mind bears the deep stamp of European culture. Today, however, Christianity is in deep decline in Europe and yet is rising elsewhere. Christian scholars must reorient their course accordingly. If we journey much deeper into this new century with our eyes on the North Atlantic shores, we may hinder Christian scholarship's ability to help the church navigate the new global reality.

Christianity Moves South and East

Becoming a World Religion

There is a great demographic shift underway in world Christianity. In 1900, some 80 percent of the world's Christians lived in Europe and North America. A century later, 60 percent of the world's Christians are living in Africa, Asia, and Latin America.[2] Christian adherence is waning in the North but rising in the South and East. In Great Britain, for example, only about one million of the 26 million members of the Church of England attend

1. One exception was Tite Tiénou's excellent plenary address, "Christian Scholarship and the Changing Center of World Christianity," in *Christian Scholarship . . . for What?*, ed. Susan M. Felch (Grand Rapids: Calvin College, 2003), 87–97.

2. David B. Barrett and Todd M. Johnson, "Annual Statistical Table on Global Mission: 2004," *International Bulletin of Missionary Research* 28, no. 1 (January 2004): 25.

on Sundays. In Nigeria are 17.5 million Anglicans, and their churches are packed on Sunday. Half of the world's Anglicans now live in Africa.[3]

The rise of non-Western Christianity has come as a huge surprise to the secular West. Historian Dana Robert points out that, thirty years ago, Christianity outside the West was thought to be a product of European imperialism, and it was expected to wither and die in the postcolonial era. As Robert wryly observes, one of the great ironies of our times is that "the process of decolonization . . . freed Christianity to be more at home in local situations."[4] Christianity grew much more rapidly after the end of the colonial empires than during them. In 1900, there were only about 9 million Christians in all of Africa. A half century later, this number had tripled, to about 30 million. By 1970, however, this number nearly quadrupled, to over 117 million. Today, the number has more than tripled again, to an estimated 382 million Christians in Africa.[5]

Even so, the notion that Christianity in Africa, Asia, and Latin America is a Western import remains strong. One recent theory is that it is part of some vast right-wing conspiracy: an exported American fundamentalism of either the Pat Robertson or the Opus Dei variety.[6] These views ignore the copious research that shows the new Christianity to be homegrown.[7] Western religious agents, ideas, and products surely are flowing freely around the globe, but so is the new Christianity. The United States still leads the world in mission sending, but it also receives the largest number of foreign missionaries.[8]

3. Bill Bowder, "Worship Numbers Fall Again," *Church Times*, http://www.churchtimes .co.uk/churchtimes/website/pages.nsf/httppublicpages/5D2740B09B60101080256FA2001 F459D (accessed November 14, 2005). Ruth Gledhill, "Archbishop Thanks Africa for Lessons on Faith," *Times* (London), July 26, 2003; Charlotte Allen, "Episcopal Church Plays Russian Roulette on the Gay Issue," *Los Angeles Times*, August 10, 2003; and Diane Knippers, "The Anglican Mainstream: It's Not Where Americans Might Think," *Weekly Standard* 8, no. 47 (August 25, 2003): http://www.weeklystandard.com/Content/Protected/ Articles/000/000/003/008jiufd.asp (accessed November 14, 2005).

4. Dana Robert, "Shifting Southward: Global Christianity since 1945," *International Bulletin of Missionary Research* 24 (April 2000): 53.

5. Barrett and Johnson, "Annual Statistical Table on Global Mission," 25.

6. See, for example, Steve Brouwer, Paul Gifford, and Susan D. Rose, *Exporting the American Gospel: Global Christian Fundamentalism* (New York: Routledge, 1996).

7. For a sense of the scope and thrust of this work, see (and follow the citations of) three recent overviews: David Martin, *Pentecostalism: The World Their Parish* (Oxford: Blackwell, 2002); Paul Freston, *Evangelicals and Politics in Asia, Africa, and Latin America* (Cambridge: Cambridge University Press, 2001); and Philip Jenkins, *The Next Christendom: The Coming of Global Christianity* (New York: Oxford University Press, 2002). Jenkins gives important coverage to Roman Catholicism and the Anglican communion, while Martin and Freston look at the more Protestant, mostly Pentecostal, side.

8. Michael Jaffarian, "What the WCE2 Numbers Show," *International Bulletin of Missionary Research* 26 (July 2002): 130. He refers to David B. Barrett et al., eds., *World Christian Encyclopedia*, 2nd ed. (Oxford: Oxford University Press, 2001).

As Christianity takes root in the South and the East, it is being transformed. Never before has the world seen the faith of the cross expressed in so many languages and cultural forms. Increasingly, these facts contradict the assumption that it is a European faith. African Christian scholars, for example, see Christianity as an African religion, not an import. That is the main point of Kwame Bediako's stirring and provocative *Christianity in Africa: The Renewal of a Non-Western Religion*.[9] Lamin Sanneh's eloquent new self-interview, *Whose Religion Is Christianity? The Gospel beyond the West*,[10] takes on the assumptions and questions he has most frequently encountered from Western intellectuals to portray a stunning portrait of a post-Christian West and a post-Western Christianity. If Christianity is becoming predominantly non-Western, then what happens in Africa, Asia, and Latin America will have a growing influence on what Christianity will be like worldwide. Conversely, what happens in Europe and in North America will matter less. Says Tite Tiénou, the West African theologian who now heads Trinity Evangelical Divinity School, "The future of Christianity no longer depends on developments in the North."[11] Missions historian Andrew Walls concludes that "it is Africans and Asians and Latin Americans who will be the representative Christians, those who represent the Christian norm, the Christian mainstream, of the twenty-first and twenty-second centuries."[12]

Only a few years ago, such assertions would have seemed vastly overblown, but the tragic events of September 11, 2001, and the subsequent wars have begun to awaken us to the "globality" of contemporary life. One of the surprises is its religiosity. Says Peter Berger, formerly a high priest of secularization theory, "The assumption that we live in a secularized world is false." The assumption that "modernization necessarily leads to a decline of religion" has proved to be mistaken. Globally interactive modernity has proved to be a powerful vehicle for religious interaction and competitive expansion, as traditional religious and communal boundaries have broken down.[13] The rising Christianity of the South and East is no longer distant or exotic. It is changing the whole church.

9. Kwame Bediako, *Christianity in Africa: The Renewal of a Non-Western Religion* (Edinburgh: Edinburgh University Press, 1995).

10. Lamin Sanneh, *Whose Religion Is Christianity?* (Grand Rapids: Eerdmans, 2003).

11. Tite Tiénou, "Christian Scholarship and the Changing Center of World Christianity," 91.

12. Andrew F. Walls, "Christian Scholarship in Africa in the Twenty-first Century," *Journal of African Christian Thought* 4, no. 6 (December 2001): 47.

13. Peter L. Berger, "The Desecularization of the World: A Global Overview," in *The Desecularization of the World: Resurgent Religion and World Politics*, ed. Peter L. Berger (Grand Rapids: Eerdmans, 1999), 2.

Contributing New Leaders

One important indication of the change underway is that Southern and Eastern Christianity is providing the global church with new leaders. The twentieth century was an ecumenical age, but European and American leaders dominated. The balance of power and authority is changing. In the Catholic Church nearly 40 percent of the cardinals eligible to vote for John Paul II's successor were from the third world. At the 1998 Lambeth Conference of Anglican bishops, Africans and Asians were in the majority, and they reshaped the theological and pastoral agenda. They set aside overtures for ordaining practicing homosexuals and instead emphasized the church's calling to evangelize, combat poverty, and overcome political oppression. In 1999, the World Alliance of Reformed Churches (WARC) named Setri Nyomi, an Evangelical Presbyterian theologian from Ghana, as its executive head. A keynote speaker at the WARC gathering, a theologian from Singapore, warned that the ecumenical leaders from Europe were out of touch with the deep spiritual yearnings of the world's people. In August of 2003, the World Council of Churches named Samuel Kobia, a Methodist from Kenya, as its new executive secretary. Kobia leads an organization whose income has been cut in half in recent years. He remarked that one thing he would bring to the World Council in a time of fiscal crisis was an African Christian "capacity to be hopeful" even in critical situations.[14]

Offering New Lines of Thought

Hope amid suffering is indeed one of the salient lines of thought emerging from Southern Christianity, whether in Latin American liberation theology or in the amazing theological cauldron of South Africa.[15] Likewise, forgiveness and reconciliation have emerged as main themes. Desmond Tutu's *No Future without Forgiveness*, a meditation on the work of the South African Truth and Reconciliation Commission, comes immediately to mind.[16] Questions about Christian identity in plural settings and queries about the presence of God in the pre-Christian past also pervade Southern and Eastern Christian thought—witness

14. "Kenyan Takes Lead of World Church Council," *Grand Rapids Press*, September 6, 2003.

15. For example, see Desmond Mpilo Tutu, *Hope and Suffering: Sermons and Speeches* (Johannesburg: Skotaville Publishers, 1983). The bibliography in John W. de Gruchy, *The Church Struggle in South Africa*, 2nd ed. (Grand Rapids: Eerdmans, 1986), 280–89, suggests the breadth and volume of theological creativity and inquiry arising from the crisis over apartheid.

16. Desmond Mpilo Tutu, *No Future without Forgiveness* (New York: Doubleday, 1999).

the work of Kwame Bediako.[17] Some of the most creative theology in North America arises from its communities of color, whose experiences of oppression and marginality have brought profound reflection on the meaning of the gospel. Black theology's contributions are well known, and we should recognize those of American Latino theologians, notably Virgilio Elizondo's meditations on the "Galilean" experience of Mexican American *mestizos* and Justo González's perspectives on U.S. Latino *evangelicos*.[18]

Christian theology eventually reflects the most compelling issues from the front lines of mission, so we can expect that this theology will be dominated by the issues rising from the global South. I find it striking, however, to see the extent to which North American academic theology still focuses on European thinkers and post-Enlightenment intellectual issues. Western theologians, liberal and conservative, have been addressing the faith to an age of doubt and secularity, and to the competing salvific claims of secular ideologies. The new Christianity will push theologians to address the faith to the most pressing issues in its new heartlands: poverty and social injustice; political violence, corruption, and the meltdown of law and order; and Christianity's witness amid religious plurality. They will be dealing with the need for Christian communities to make sense of God's self-revelation to their pre-Christian ancestors. Theologians everywhere will be pondering Christianity's answer to the spiritual hunger and searching in global mass culture.

Engaging New Lines of Action

New patterns of popular religious action add evidence that non-Western Christianity is rising. The new Christianity partakes of a global flow of religious ideas, expressions, and products. These global flows now go in all directions. The great missionary movement is not over; it has become omnidirectional. There are four hundred thousand missionaries in the world, but most are not from Europe and North America. I visited Nigeria in 1990 and met with some American and Canadian missionaries. They lamented that instead of the five hundred comrades

17. John S. Mbiti, *African Religions and Philosophy* (London: Heinemann, 1969); Harry Sawyerr, *God: Ancestor or Creator? Aspects of Traditional Religious Belief in Ghana, Nigeria, and Sierra Leone* (London: Longman, 1970); C. G. Baëta, ed., *Christianity in Tropical Africa* (London: Oxford University Press, 1968); Kwame Bediako, *Theology and Identity: The Impact of Culture upon Christian Thought in the Second Century and Modern Africa* (Oxford: Regnum Books, 1992); and idem, *Christianity in Africa: The Renewal of a Non-Western Religion* (Maryknoll, NY: Orbis, 1995).

18. Virgil Elizondo, *Galilean Journey: The Mexican-American Promise* (Maryknoll, NY: Orbis, 1983); and Justo L. González, *Mañana: Christian Theology from a Hispanic Perspective* (Nashville: Abingdon, 1990).

they had in 1960, now there were only one hundred. Many of the enterprises they had started were fading. The next day the missions director of the Nigerian sister church of this mission, now two million strong, told me about its nine hundred missionaries, serving sacrificially in rural northern Nigeria, and in Niger, Cameroon, Chad, Burkina Faso, and darkest London. Welcome to the new world of foreign missions. Brazilians head to Portugal, Angola, and Boston. Indian Pentecostals are founding rapidly growing churches in Nepal. South Koreans are everywhere. New churches are springing up in diaspora communities. The largest church in London is Pentecostal, led by a Nigerian. The same is true in Kiev. Some researchers doubt that the new Southern Christianity will break out from these communities into resolutely secular Europe, but it is too soon to tell.[19]

In the United States, a much more assimilative culture, "mainstream" American Christianity is absorbing aspects of the new world Christianity, which has been arriving in force with recent immigrants. More than 60 percent of them come from the global South and East. Demographers predict that in another quarter century, the United States population will look like that of California, with no ethnic or racial group comprising a majority. Kenneth Prewitt, former director of the U.S. Census, states, "We're on our way to becoming the first country in history that is literally made up of every part of the world."[20] The vast majority of the new Americans are Christians. This fact may seem self-evident when considering the Latinos, but the majority of the African immigrants also are Christian, one half of all Arabs in the United States are Christian, and a disproportionately large minority of the Asians are Christian.[21] New congregations, with varieties of Christianity rarely seen here before, are growing across the American urban landscapes. West African Pentecostal churches are thriving in Houston, where eighty thousand Nigerians reside. Around my former home in suburban Philadelphia, every Protestant church in the township had a Korean congregation

19. See Gerrie ter Haar, *Halfway to Paradise: African Christians in Europe* (Cardiff, UK: Cardiff Academic Press, 1998).

20. Joel L. Swerdlow, "Changing America," *National Geographic* 200, no. 3 (September 2001): 46.

21. R. Stephen Warner, "Coming to America: Immigrants and the Faith They Bring," *Christian Century* 121, no. 3 (February 10, 2004): 20–23. On Christianity's disproportionately large representation among America's Asian immigrants, Koreans are a prime case in point. While 25 to 30 percent of South Koreans are Christians, about half of the South Koreans entering the United States are Christian. Due to the church's vigorous outreach and service to the ethnic community, Christian adherence among Koreans living here reaches 80 percent. See Pyong Gap Min, "The Structure and Social Functions of Korean Immigrant Churches in the United States," *International Migration Review* 26, no. 4 (1992): 1370–94.

sharing the building, and at nearby Westminster Theological Seminary, a quarter of the students were Korean.

The Catholic Church has been the historic haven of immigrant communities in America, and it is being transformed by Latino immigration. Some three thousand Catholic parishes now offer Spanish services. Catholics also provide communities of faith for other growing groups, such as Filipinos and Vietnamese. In each of these traditionally Catholic immigrant communities, new varieties of evangelicalism—mostly Pentecostal—are developing. About one-fifth of American Latinos are now *evangelicos*, many led by missionary bishops and apostles. One is my neighbor down the block, Pastor Antonio Rosario, from the Dominican Republic. He oversees the ministry of three Latino Adventist congregations in Grand Rapids, meanwhile teaching in the Hispanic ministry program at an Adventist university nearby. In sum, the United States is not becoming secular like Europe. It is not being overrun by non-Christian faiths either. But the nature of its Christianity is changing. As the sociologist Stephen Warner put it recently, "Immigration is creating not so much new diversity in American religion as new diversity within American Christianity."[22]

Building New Centers of Learning

Circling back now to Dr. Kasali and Dr. Kim, we see that they represent yet another trend: non-Western Christianity's growing investment in higher education. Three years ago, in a hastily conducted study, I found more than three dozen new evangelical universities in the global South and East.[23] When I presented my findings at an international conference, other participants told me of many more universities I had missed. Regularly now I converse with Christian leaders, ranging from Haiti to Irian Papua to Ethiopia, who like Dr. Kasali have heard God's call to found a Christian university. So what is going on?

This movement marks an important stage in the development of non-Western Christianity. There are many places now where conversionist Christianity is no longer new on the ground, nor still in a nascent, awakening phase. A second generation is coming to the fore, and the outlook and agendas are changing. Like the Methodist and Pentecostal movements of the past, the new Christian groups arising in many places are evolving from peace-disturbing, establishment-upsetting religious

22. Warner, "Coming to America," 20. Insightful on these points as well is Jenkins, *Next Christendom*, 105–13.

23. This paper, "New Evangelical Universities: Cogs in a World System of Players in a New Game?" was published in two installments in the *International Journal of Frontier Missions* 20, no. 2 (Summer 2003): 55–65; and 20, no. 3 (Fall 2003): 95–102.

upstarts into settled denominations and fellowships. With revival fires no longer flaring and in some need of tending, institutions or "fireplaces" are being built. There is a rising generation to equip, and a surrounding society in which to minister for the longer term.[24]

The new Christianity is growing most rapidly among the world's poor, who according to sociologist David Martin often become an "aspiring poor." They believe that God wants to deliver them from hopelessness, spiritual emptiness, and material poverty. A university education and a good job become worthy Christian aspirations, as does a rising desire to save and serve troubled societies. From their situation, frequently on society's margins, evangelicals have tended to be preoccupied with evangelization and basic discipling, with little thought to playing some influential social role. As these movements have grown and prospered, however, they have gained salience, and with greater visibility and institutional heft has come a greater sense of social responsibility.[25] Early evangelical forays into politics, as sociologist Paul Freston has shown, frequently focus on support for parties and governments that will act most favorably toward the faithful.[26] In time, however, these groups may recognize a responsibility for nation building or rebuilding. Hear the mission statement of a new Pentecostal institution, Central University College in Accra, Ghana. It aims to advance "the great commission of our Lord Jesus Christ in its multifaceted dimensions, . . . to exhibit His Kingdom ethics and to spread its justice and righteousness in the world."[27]

These new Christian universities give off echoes of our own past. Nineteenth-century Baptist and Catholic missionaries in the American West founded new universities in such wild places as the South Bend of the St. Joseph River in Indiana and on the banks of the Brazos in the Republic of Texas. These "uncommon schools," according to historian Timothy Smith, "were the anvil upon which the relationships between the people's religious traditions and the emerging political and social

24. For example, see R. Stephen Warner, *New Wine in Old Wineskins: Evangelicals and Liberals in a Small-Town Church* (Berkeley: University of California Press, 1987), 284–95, regarding the important difference between "nascent" and "institutional" religious orientations.

25. David Martin, *Tongues of Fire: The Explosion of Protestantism in Latin America* (Oxford: Blackwell, 1990), especially chap. 11, "Protestantism and Economic Culture: Evidence Reviewed," 205–32; see also idem, *Pentecostalism.* Concerning the aspiring poor, see idem, "Evangelical Expansion in Global Society," Position Paper 115, Currents in World Christianity Project (1999): 27–29.

26. Freston, *Evangelicals and Politics in Asia, Africa, and Latin America.*

27. Central University College, undergraduate catalog, 2000–2002 (Accra: Central University College, 2000), 6.

structures were hammered into shape."[28] The new world Christianity is repeating this process. It is relying on higher education to address the summons of Jesus to "teach the nations." So what do all of these developments have to do with us as Christian scholars?

New Mandates for Christian Scholarship

A brief glimpse at the new Christian universities, and indeed at the origins of our own institutions, reminds us of their essential nature. Christian higher education is missionary work, and it long has been so. The universities of the Middle Ages emerged out of monastic missionaries' attempts to bring literacy and basic Christian knowledge to pagan Northern Europe, and then to give more advanced equipage to the leaders of society. The basic academic work was a Christian engagement with the ancient pagan culture.[29] From the ante-Nicene theologians forward, Christian intellectuals have worked, in the light of the gospel, to appropriate and improve upon pagan wisdom. Throughout the history of Christianity, argues Andrew Walls, a "lively concern for Christian living and Christian witness has repeatedly called scholarly activity into existence."[30]

Walls shows that wherever Christian missionaries went, their encounter with new cultures "caused them to translate books and to write new ones." Whole new fields of inquiry rose from their efforts: the study of languages and literatures outside Europe, comparative linguistics, anthropology, comparative religion, and tropical medicine. The modern, secularized universities have forgotten the origins of these fields, but they arose, Walls insists, out of "the desire that Christ should be known in other cultures."[31]

Reorienting Current Strategies

The scope and thrust of Christian scholarship has therefore long reflected the scope and thrust of Christian mission. What we now tend to view as the universal outlook of the secular academy is in fact, Walls argues, "a heavily indigenized, highly contextual," and historically forget-

---

28. Timothy L. Smith, *Uncommon Schools: Christian Colleges and Social Idealism in Midwestern America, 1820–1950* (Bloomington: Indiana Historical Society, 1978), 5–6.

29. On this point, see John Van Engen, "Christianity and the University: The Medieval and Reformation Legacies," in *Making Higher Education Christian: The History and Mission of Evangelical Colleges in America*, ed. Joel A. Carpenter and Kenneth W. Shipps (Grand Rapids: Eerdmans, 1987), 19–37.

30. Walls, "Christian Scholarship in Africa," 44.

31. Ibid., 45–46.

ful view of reality. The resulting intellectual edifice is a great fortress of post-Enlightenment, post-Christian rationalism and empiricism, shaped by a Euro-American context. It has been laid siege by the postmodernist philosophers, but they too operate with naturalistic assumptions that are much too confining for thoughtful Africans and Asians. Despite the burgeoning industry of studying non-Western cultures, Walls insists that the Western academy's approach does not represent a "world standard" but in fact betrays "pre-Columbian maps of the intellectual universe."[32] Western Christian scholars struggling to work faithfully within this realm have focused on the challenges of post-Enlightenment secularity, with strategies that are highly contextualized to the North Atlantic situation. That has been our context, but the one we now face is changing. Therefore, our strategies need to change. Before suggesting how they should be transformed, please allow a short review of the main strategies that Western Christian scholars have used:

1. Fostering Christian humanism: Recover and reapply the cultural wisdom of the Christian past, mostly with European Christendom in mind. Example: The Erasmus Institute at Notre Dame.
2. Highlighting the religion factor: Question the secular assumptions of the academy by uncovering the religious dimensions and dynamics of culture, past and present. Example: The Paul Henry Institute for the Study of Christianity and Politics at Calvin College.
3. Promoting theism: Argue for the rationality and coherence of theistic belief, outlook, and action. Example: The Center for Philosophy of Religion at Notre Dame.
4. Serving the present age: Put Christian beliefs, perspectives, and values to work as critical tools for reforming work in society. Example: The Center for Law and Religion at Emory University.
5. Building strong movements: In order to advance all of these strategies, find ways to stimulate and support Christian scholarly activity and productivity by creating sustainable networks, programs, and institutions to foster such work. Example: The Pew Evangelical Scholars Initiative.

These are all good strategies, and I do not counsel abandoning any of them, but in this new era of global Christianity, each of these strategies needs some "reorienting."

32. Andrew F. Walls, "Of Ivory Towers and Ashrams: Some Reflections on Theological Scholarship in Africa," *Journal of African Christian Thought* 3, no. 1 (June 2000): 1–2.

Decentering Christian Humanism

The first strategy, the Christian humanist strategy, is perhaps the most tied to Europe and the West. For a millennium, secular and religious scholars alike have assumed that European civilization and Christianity are fundamentally linked. In the face of multiplied attacks, Christian humanists have fought to preserve and uphold the insights of the Western Christian past. I applaud those efforts, but this strategy needs reforming. Christianity has become a predominantly non-Western faith, and the Western Christian heritage now looks much less central, standard, and normative. Western Christian humanists will be tempted to resist this decentering because it resembles one of the most influential lines of secular assault. For three centuries, scholars have used knowledge of the world's great non-Western civilizations to attack Christianity's claims to "a comprehensive, unsurpassable, and central account of human life and the world."[33] Would not a de-Westernizing of the Christian humanist approach actually concede the game to the relativists?

No. Just the opposite is true. Among the problems of Western Christian humanism is that the West is not very Christian anymore. Christianity thus can be treated as a fading tribal religion. Identifying religions with regional civilizations, à la Samuel Huntington, reduces religion to a function of its regional culture.[34] But a more global view of Christianity allows it to break out of this cultural-religious essentialism. The world's regions are religiously plural, more so than ever, since Christianity now thrives in each of them. Christian humanism is now free to do its discerning and converting cultural work all over the world.

Does this mean we should neglect the study of Christianity in the West? Not at all, but we will pursue those studies with new questions, ones raised by Christianity's new situation in the world. Last summer while visiting in Tuscany, I was struck by how relevant the story of medieval and renaissance Italy is for non-Western Christians today. The Italians were trying to build a more just and merciful society in a chaotic postimperial,

---

33. Edwin J. Van Kley, "Europe's 'Discovery' of China and the Writing of World History," *American Historical Review* 76 (April 1971): 358–85, illustrates how knowledge of Chinese civilization began to challenge the centrality of the biblical narrative and European church history in the writing of world history during the eighteenth century. Grant Wacker, "A Plural World: The Protestant Awakening to World Religions," in *Between the Times: The Travail of the Protestant Establishment in America, 1900–1960*, ed. William R. Hutchison (New York: Cambridge University Press, 1989), 253–77, shows a similar crisis in nineteenth-century Protestant theology.

34. Samuel Huntington first laid out his theory of civilizational competition and conflict in "The Clash of Civilizations?" *Foreign Affairs* 72 (Summer 1993): 22–49; then in fuller fashion in idem, *The Clash of Civilizations and the Remaking of World Order* (New York: Simon & Schuster, 1996).

postpagan situation. Out of that experience arose the likes of St. Francis of Assisi, Dante Alighieri, and St. Catherine of Siena. The Italians also encountered the daunting virtuosity of Greco-Roman visual arts, and over successive generations, from Giotto to Michelangelo, they developed a powerful new Christian synthesis. Who knows what wonders of grace may await us as we move from pondering this legacy to transposing its method and example in places like post-Confucian Korea?

Understanding the Desecularization of the World

One of the more favored and fruitful contemporary strategies among Christian scholars is highlighting the "R Factor." A cadre of evangelicals and Catholics in American political science used it to build an influential religion and politics study sector within the American Political Science Association. Because of this group's influence, the election coverage in 2004 simply assumed that religious commitment matters in political opinion and behavior. There still are vast reaches of the academy, however, where scholars merely assume that religious dimensions of society and culture are determined by other, more elemental forces. Why does such reductionism persist? The social sciences still work in the shadow of the Peace of Westphalia, the bargain struck to keep religion out of European public affairs. Yet the more we focus on the global South and East, the less sustainable this paradigm seems. The grand expectation that modernization and globalization would lead to secularization is being proved false. Rising Christianity in the global South, argues my sociologist colleague Paul Freston, is globalization from below, part of the "desecularization of the world" that Peter Berger and others see happening today.[35]

There is a huge agenda arising from these discoveries. All of the big ideas in modern social science—modernization, secularization, globalization, democracy, pluralism, human rights, and capitalism—are ripe for revision. The European pattern now appears to be an anomaly, not the paradigm shaper we have made it to be. Christianity's entry as a new social, political, and economic factor in many places needs careful attention. It is one of the greatest worldwide developments of our

35. Paul Freston, "Globalization, Religion, and Evangelical Christianity: A Sociological Meditation from the Third World," in *Interpreting Contemporary Christianity: Global Process and Local Identities*, ed. Ogbu Kalu (Grand Rapids: Eerdmans, forthcoming); see also Berger, *Desecularization of the World*. Other suggestive reviews of the prospects for globalization and religious resurgence to revise social-scientific paradigms are in an issue dedicated to "Religion and Globalization" in *Hedgehog Review: Critical Reflections on Contemporary Culture* 4, no. 2 (Summer 2002).

time. Christian scholars should take the lead in examining its impact and implications.

Changing Debates: From Unbelief to Rival Spiritualities

The third strategy for Christian scholarship, promoting theism, also has been a deeply contextualized Western approach. It assumes the need to respond to the post-Enlightenment naturalism and skepticism of the "cultured despisers of religion," as Schleiermacher put it. The need continues because such views still prevail among Western intellectuals and elites. Going forward, however, Christian philosophers and theologians will need to argue for Christianity among competing religious claims. There is plenty of theism and spirituality around, and the privilege once granted to naturalism is no longer automatic. The more insistent questions now arise from rival revelations. So Christian philosophers and theologians should give more attention to testing the coherence of Christianity over against other religious and ethical systems. To focus so intently on secularity, European style, increasingly will mean putting one's main forces into a rearguard action.

The various fields of Christian theology are in for a major reorientation if they are going to address the worldwide church's most pressing questions. The church history syllabus, for example, needs a complete redrafting. It has become untenable to teach the subject as a continual westward migration and to treat Christianity in the global South and East as a recent footnote.[36] In biblical studies, a fresh set of questions and opportunities arise. As Christian people with worldviews and cultures much closer to the biblical writers interpret the Scriptures, the privileged place of historicism in biblical studies seems increasingly problematic. As Andrew Walls recently quipped, "Paul uses exegetical methods that would be ruled out of court in a seminary exercise."[37] The Scripture Project, a four-year inquiry at Princeton's Center for Theological Inquiry, is coming to similar conclusions, in part because of its appreciation of questions raised by non-Western interpreters.[38] Systematic theology in the Western tradition notoriously underestimates its cultural embeddedness, even among the apostles of process and flux. Yet Kwame Bediako speculates that European theology became overly abstract and disembodied because, unlike Africans, pre-Christian Europeans had no great Creator God to identify with the God of the Bible. The "god" of European

36. A valuable beginning is Wilbert R. Shenk, ed., *Enlarging the Story: Perspectives on Writing World Christian History* (Maryknoll, NY: Orbis, 2002).

37. Walls, "Of Ivory Towers and Ashrams," 2.

38. Ellen F. Davis and Richard B. Hays, "Beyond Criticism: Learning to Read the Bible Again," *Christian Century* 121, no. 8 (April 20, 2004): 23–27.

usage is an abstraction, the singular of "gods," not the name of a personal deity already known to the Northern peoples.[39] Western, post-Enlightenment theology, says Andrew Walls, is "pared down theology, cut and shaved to fit a small-scale universe," but in contrast, most Africans live "in a larger universe," with open frontiers.[40] Their kind of Christianity is now at the center of worldwide faith and practice, and theology will need to respond accordingly. Systematic and historical theologians of the North Atlantic world have assumed that they need to tutor African, Asian, and Latin American graduate students in the "great tradition" of the European theological canon. The day is coming, however, when instead of encouraging their African doctoral students to dissertate on Friedrich Schleiermacher or Karl Barth, Euro-American theologians will be running to African theological centers to gain a fresh understanding of how to apply the wisdom of the Scriptures and the premodern theologians.[41]

Renewing and Reforming the Academy

The main mandate and strategy for Christian scholarship is to do intellectual work for the divine project of straightening the world's crookedness, making its rough places plain, and making all of life fruitful in fulfilling its created purpose. Through their research and teaching, Christian scholars are called to propagate perspectives, skills, and understanding that, as theologian Neal Plantinga, puts it, "can be thrown into the struggle for shalom, the battle for universal wholeness and delight."[42] Contemporary universities proclaim their mission in similar and actually derivative terms, minus the transcendent norms and aims. They have made great contributions toward curing diseases, improving agriculture, cultivating the arts, advancing technology, and addressing a variety of human needs and issues. Christian scholars can and should participate in these efforts to serve the present age; but do we have any-

39. Bediako, *Theology and Identity*, 269–71. See also Andrew F. Walls, *The Missionary Movement in Christian History* (Maryknoll, NY: Orbis, 1996), 35, 70–71.

40. Walls, "Christian Scholarship in Africa," 49.

41. A pioneering work of this sort is Bediako, *Theology and Identity*. A yearning for theology that is less abstract and more concrete and pastoral is pushing a number of Western theologians back to premodern theology. See, for example, Ellen T. Charry, *By the Renewing of Your Minds: The Pastoral Function of Christian Doctrine* (New York: Oxford University Press, 1997). In part because of the new salience of religious devotion emanating from the global South and East, Oxford theologian Alister McGrath joins those who see atheism waning; see his book *The Twilight of Atheism: The Rise and Fall of Disbelief in the Modern World* (New York: Doubleday Anchor, 2004).

42. Cornelius Plantinga Jr., "Educating for Shalom: Our Calling as a Christian College," http://www.calvin.edu/about/shalom.htm (accessed August 27, 2005).

thing singular to offer to this great enterprise? Rather than pausing to ponder this question, Christian scholars need to be agents for renewal and reform within the university at a time when these noble aims are endangered. An excellent strategy for reform would be to give priority to the human needs most pressing for non-Western Christians.

For guidance, I turn again to Andrew Walls, the best Northern interpreter of this strategic moment. He sees growing corruption within the house of learning. The earlier excitement over major discoveries and new fields of inquiry seems to be giving way, Walls says, "to recycling age-old materials, to trivial novelty-seeking and hair-splitting."[43] Professors are choosing research topics based on their market value. Doctoral students chat cynically about how to pad their *vitas* with more publications. Government funders channel their reduced appropriations toward immediate payoffs for the national economy, and researchers increasingly depend on corporate funding. Medical researchers, Walls observes, obtain their funding "from drug companies, whose priorities are best served from the afflictions of the affluent world, and foundations, whose consciousness of suffering is also concentrated there. Yet the big killer diseases wreak their havoc . . . across Africa and Asia." Walls tells of university colleagues seeking funding from biscuit manufacturers for "research in dunking cookies," and from tobacco companies for "an academic school of business ethics." He calls Christian scholars to cleanse scholarship of these polluting forces and reorient it according to a Christian vision to serve the present age.[44]

What would such a reorientation look like? Assuming even good and proper current uses of their intellectual gifts, Christian scholars might think about applying their talents and energies in directions that better correspond with the outlook and concerns of world Christianity. Biomedical scientists working in immunology might refocus their research from replacing joints to conquering AIDS or malaria. In addition to investigating teenage alcoholism in the Upper Midwest, social scientists might point their students toward child nutrition in the Upper Volta region. Rather than addressing vibration noise in SUVs, engineers could develop more durable small-plot tractors. A Fulbright fellowship in Ireland might be fun, but why not try for one in Eritrea instead? Faculty exchanges coming North can be equally fruitful. Fund some out of your own campus resources. I know of one small group of professors who have created a self-funded resource pool that enables one of them to serve in Africa every couple of years, rather than waiting for their sabbaticals.

43. Walls, "Christian Scholarship in Africa," 45.
44. Ibid., 47–48.

Relocating Christian Scholarship

We Christian scholars are quite naturally absorbed in our own work, our own immediate situation. To this point I have been trying to persuade you to reorient *your* scholarship, focusing on what new interests *we* might develop, what new strategies *we* might pursue. But if worldwide Christianity is going to mature and grow strong in all of these new places, then Christian scholarship needs to grow in them too. Some non-Western Christian scholars are confident that their academic movements will catch up with the church growth and provide some strategic leadership.[45] Yet others look at the current state of the knowledge industry and acknowledge that, as Walls puts it, "the rule of the palefaces over the academic world is untroubled."[46] Tite Tiénou says that a "Western hegemonic postulate" is at work in the intellectual world today. The ideas and research of Asians and Africans are still treated mainly as the exotic raw materials with which the Northern intellectual aristocrats can furnish their ivory towers. Northerners continue to assume the right to intellectual rule, and Southern intellectual development remains stunted. Unless Northern Christian scholars can develop just and reconciling relationships with their Southern colleagues, the reorientation for which I have been pleading will become yet another occasion for intellectual imperialism.[47]

The heart of the matter is to serve the faith and its intellectual mission, not to serve ourselves. What North American Christian scholars need most, Tiénou insists, is to become good listeners. True Christian scholarship requires humility and mutual dependency, letting agendas arise from the insights of the whole group. Christian scholarship is profoundly communal, and the makeup of our community has changed dramatically. So must the content, accent, and direction of its thinking.

With those aims in mind, here are some thoughts for a North-South dialogue about strengthening Christian scholarship. These ideas will certainly need to be tested, tempered, translated, and probably transformed; they are open to reproof and correction.

First, while there is great promise in the movement to found Christian universities, I see potential for disappointment. The new Christian universities, like other new private universities worldwide, focus on technical, commercial, or professional programs, with few courses that offer a broader knowledge of the world. They tend to reflect the secular

45. Bediako, for one instance, is quite sanguine; see idem, *Christianity in Africa*, 253.

46. Andrew F. Walls, "Structural Problems in Mission Studies," *International Bulletin of Missionary Research* 15, no. 4 (October 1991): 152.

47. Tiénou, "Christian Scholarship and the Changing Center of World Christianity," 92–96. This paragraph follows Tiénou in referring to Bediako and Walls, as cited above.

and instrumental values that drive Western intellectual hegemony, and they do not acquaint students with the depth and breadth of the Bible's *shalomic* vision. These new universities urgently need to develop an education that partakes of Christ's lordship over all of creation. With this task, Christian scholars from North America have experience that their counterparts might adapt for their own approaches.

Second, there is a promising non-Western movement to study the faith's cultural mission, and it should grow and broaden. Among evangelicals, whose work I know better than Catholics', I think of the Kairos Center in Buenos Aires; the Akrofi-Christaller Centre in Akropong, Ghana; and the Institute for Studies in Asian Church and Culture in Manila. These agencies tend to operate mainly in theology and range out from there into some "cognate" cultural studies. I long to see this movement grow more institutional nodes and networks, multiply by mentoring a new generation, and regenerate the arts and sciences. North Americans have been working on this broader project, and we have something to share if we can do that humbly, expecting to receive more wisdom than we give.

In broader programmatic and institutional terms, we need to leverage the accomplishments of the movement's pioneers. This growth can happen by mounting concerted projects, strengthening intergroup networks, building the capacity of their institutions, and raising up new leaders with a broadening range of scholarly interests. The heart of such work would come out of local genius, initiative, and materials. We will not see well-endowed institutions like the Kroc Institute at Notre Dame, but there are other models for Christian communal thought and action. One with roots in India, Andrew Walls reminds us, is the ashram, a community of scholars living a simple life of devotion and study, not unlike the medieval monasteries.[48] From such modest but focused initiatives can come much that is fruitful.

In particular, I consider the Akrofi-Christaller Memorial Centre for Mission Research and Applied Theology in Akropong. This institute was founded in the late 1980s by Kwame Bediako and a circle of evangelical leaders in Ghana to foster African Christian thought and apply it to creative ministry. The Centre occupies the buildings of a mid-nineteenth-century theological seminary. I remember visiting the Bediakos there in 1990. Kwame spoke, with a prophetic gleam in his eye, of the day when this Centre would attract Christian scholars from across Africa and the North to learn more about Christianity's taking root in African culture. I marveled at his faith and vision. Today the Centre's buildings, lovingly restored and expanded, bustle with activity. The Bediakos convene research conferences and hold seminars with African graduate students, working

48. Walls, "Of Ivory Towers and Ashrams," 4.

in a degree program with the University of Natal at Pietermaritzburg, South Africa. The Centre's journal publishes these programs' results. Here is a powerful model for strengthening Christian scholarship.

What role is there for Northern Christian intellectuals and resources in such development? One of mutuality. The Akrofi-Christaller Centre has benefited from the Northern Christian scholarly enterprise in several ways, and has given back many benefits as well. First, Bediako acknowledges an intellectual debt to Andrew Walls, who sponsored his dissertation twenty years ago and is a frequent visiting lecturer and program adviser. Walls insists that his own thought has been converted by his African partners. Second, Bediako had his first opportunities to network internationally because of some programs organized and funded by the International Fellowship of Evangelical Students, the Lausanne Committee for World Evangelization, and the World Evangelical Fellowship. Through these agencies, third-world theologians raised their sights more broadly, and North Atlantic theologians gained critical perspectives in return. Third, the Centre has received project grants from Northern funders, who in turn had their outlook and priorities transformed. Fourth, Bediako built partnerships with academic centers, such as Walls's Centre for the Study of Christianity in the Non-Western World at the University of Edinburgh, the faculty of theology at the University of Natal at Pietermaritzburg, and with Calvin College. Yet all of this work grew from a locally owned institution. Northern partners are invited guests, funding and institutional ties are diverse, and there is minimal danger of dependency.

In sum, Northern scholars can serve the new Christianity in several ways. First, by reorienting our own work. Second, by opening new programmatic approaches. Third, by allowing non-Western Christian intellectuals to share in our projects here and shape our agendas. Fourth, by accepting their invitations to share in mutual projects and learning elsewhere. Fifth, by prodding Christian philanthropists and funding agencies to invest in new ways, new directions, and new places.

This reorientation business is not easy. I recall pushing the scholars at the Institute for the Study of American Evangelicals to do some reorienting. They resisted, because they were happily conducting studies deeply situated amid white American evangelicals; but Mark Noll and Edith Blumhofer now testify that their work has been transformed. The sacrifice, they insist, is worth it.

The Fullness of Christ

Why should we be doing this reorientation? First, the health and integrity of our calling depends on it having vital ties to God's mission in the world, and that mission has taken some dramatic turns. Second, so long as the history of redemption continues to unfold, we have much more to learn about the fullness of Christ, about the gospel's full range and power. Every time the gospel is translated into a different culture, Andrew Walls and Lamin Sanneh remind us, we learn new things about the gospel. From the Jews came the truth of Jesus the Messiah; from the Greeks, Christ the cosmic Lord. To the Romans and Northern Europeans, Jesus came as the justifier of the guilty; to the African Americans, Jesus is the liberator of the captives. Who knows what new rich depths of the wisdom of God await us in the gospel's encounter with the cultures of the South and East?[49] There may be sacrifices ahead if we reorient our work, but the joy of discovery and the delight of new fellowship will more than repay us. There are whole new horizons opening up. The range and scope of the Christian intellectual calling have never been greater.

49. Andrew F. Walls explains this idea in his recent book, *The Cross-Cultural Process in Christian History* (Maryknoll, NY: Orbis, 2002), 74–81. See also Lamin Sanneh, *Translating the Message: The Missionary Impact on Culture* (Maryknoll, NY: Orbis, 1989), especially chap. 2, "Mission and the Cultural Assimilation of Christianity: The Hellenistic Factor," 50–87.

5

FAITH, FORTITUDE, AND THE FUTURE OF CHRISTIAN INTELLECTUAL COMMUNITY

David Lyle Jeffrey

GEORGE BERNARD SHAW ONCE DELIVERED his opinion that "a Catholic university is a contradiction in terms." I cannot presume to know what this particular dictum of his conjures up for others; in my case, it makes me wonder if Shaw found the conjunction "Catholic" and "university" oxymoronic, how would he have reacted to "Baptist university" or even "Christian university" for that matter?

The historic facts are, nevertheless, that even the secular university, both as Shaw knew it and as we have inherited it, has a Catholic foundation. A secondary tributary for us in America is an educational tradition most surely to be aligned with evangelical or Reformed Protestants. There would have been no Oxford or Cambridge without the first stream, and no Harvard or Princeton without the second stream (nor, if we consider Baptists, the University of Chicago, Brown, or Rochester either).

But Shaw's quip is no mere laughing matter. It goes right to the heart of the question, as we all now have to deal with it, and perhaps most

precisely in its explicit attack on association with the term "Catholic."
What Shaw was thinking about was *authority—Magister*. His particular
target was the church's *magisterium*, especially the teaching authority of the church as a constraint upon inquiry, and more generally the
question of authority in relation to higher learning. In my view, Shaw's
opposition to Catholic higher education identifies an issue with which
we all have to wrestle. We (especially Protestant Christians) have not
dealt with this issue very well, and if we want to talk coherently about
the possibility of a *university*—which really is that—and which is also,
in any meaningful sense *Christian*, we will have to find ways of addressing Shaw's representative objection straight-on instead of ducking
away from it. Shaw spoke—and still speaks—for secularist resistance
to the very existence of higher learning that dares to presuppose God.
His barb—aimed at John Henry Cardinal Newman, among others—was
that Christians could not really make the case for God stick, intellectually, and that all they really wished to do was to establish a subcultural
enclave in which they could evade their accountability to the pressing
needs of a wider society. As so often happens in the Christian life, our
adversaries may have seen more clearly than we ourselves where both
our duty—and our temptation—lies.

Shaw's aphoristic critique is, after all, a précis of many principled
voices of resistance to us, at least since the early eighteenth century. In
response to these pressures, whether from those candidly outside orthodox Christian filiation, or those extremely uncomfortable and only
nominally within it, two dominant Christian educational strategies have
been developed.

The first of these was in fact a strategy of separation—religious retreat and a construal of higher education as a dictate of the needs of the
church. It is still one pole of Christian educational practice. It lies behind
many Christian colleges, both Catholic and Protestant. It is invoked in
almost all critiques of Christian higher education, even by those who
would actually like it better if this allegation of separatism were entirely
true and we Christians did just hole up with our coreligionists and stay
there—self-marginalized.

A second strategy has been that of selective participation—an openness to secular learning and its fashions, to dialogue on generous terms.
This involves an implicit acceptance of post-Enlightenment liberalism
except for an additional emphasis on faith as a qualitative enrichment,
a dividend in good citizenship. More than the first option, this strategy
lies behind universities of a Protestant heritage in particular. Yet increasingly, these qualities have become identified with Catholic universities
too. When thoughtful secularists observe this model, especially in our
own time, they sometimes begin to wonder if, from such an accommo-

dating stance, we are really making any distinctive contribution that grows out of our religious worldview. Are we perhaps just secularists with an archaic hint of, say, Methodist DNA, or with filial obligations to rich founding families who were Baptists?

This is to paint with too broad a brush. Nonetheless, the broad brush sets up our question again: What is—or rather, what would be—a Christian university, and how could such a university form a worthwhile or even distinctive intellectual community?

Perspective

We should preface this question, as many good scholars have, by first asking, What *was* the Christian university? By now we have at least some sense of our history.[1] We need no rehearsal of the impressive intellectual and spiritual foundation we share: the commitment of Christians to truths for the sake of Truth, and the redemptive view of all the treasures of wisdom that Ambrose and Augustine found hidden in Christ. We recognize the enormous productivity of the intellectual energies of later medieval academics such as Anselm, Albert, Aquinas, Bonaventure, and Wycliffe, who in their intellectual inquiries knew no trepidation because they were confident, as Wycliffe succinctly put it, that "God cannot contradict himself."[2] To this lineage we could add the probing educational philosophies of John Comenius, Isaac Watts, and John Locke.

But that was then, and this is now. These mighty voices of our tradition have faded out of currency among us. The soul of the American university, some argue, has been sucked dry, and only a few scattered evangelical scholars, a handful of colleges, and a few hard-headed and breast-beating Catholics are left alive to tell each other how once it was, or ought to have been.

And maybe it is almost that apocalyptic—though in my view, for which I press, our situation is much more positive. There are, after all, many excellent Christian institutions of higher learning. Most, it is true, are colleges, but they are hardly negligible. And still in the world are what

---

1. For example, consider Charles Homer Haskins, *The Rise of Universities* (Ithaca, NY: Cornell University Press, 1966); E. Harris Harbison, *The Christian Scholar in the Age of the Reformation* (New York: Charles Scribner's Sons, 1956); George M. Marsden, *The Outrageous Idea of Christian Scholarship* (New York: Oxford University Press, 1997); and idem, *The Soul of the American University: From Protestant Establishment to Established Nonbelief* (New York: Oxford University Press, 1994).

2. John Wycliffe, *De veritate sacrae scripturae*, ed. R. Buddenseig, vol. 1 (London: Trübner for the Wyclif Society, 1905), 202.

may without hyperbole be called Christian universities—Notre Dame, Pepperdine, and Baylor perhaps among them.

But our question remains, still imperfectly answered. For while we know something of what we mean by "university," we know less—or at least we are disinclined quite specifically to declare ourselves—about what we mean by "Christian."

What Is a University?

Because, for the guilds to which we belong, it is much easier to say what a university is than to say what a Christian is, let us dispense with the apparently easier item first. Again, I resort to the broad brush. I simply list, without elaboration or defense, six characteristics that secular reflection on the university more or less concurs are sine qua non for use of the term. All are continuous with their medieval prototype, and all have been present whenever the university has itself attained excellence:

- Independence. Freedom from micromanagement by its supporting institutions or the civil order.
- Judicious impartiality. What the eighteenth century called "disinterestedness"—not a lack of interest but a resistance to raw advocacies so that the faculty of discernment might apply itself to understanding and the truth of things, an effort that has in the end practical civic value outweighing the swings of party spirit. It is what makes synthesis and reconciliation possible.
- Bookishness. Scholarly pursuit that makes reflective intellectual activity the essence of the university's work-to-do, rather than, for example, the making of machines or money.
- Commitment to the advancement of knowledge. Not simply archival or antiquarian in its commitment to tradition, the university builds upon its reflective and mnemonic resources by questioning and in principled fashion pursuing answers to questions that may not have been asked before.
- Commitment to pass on the deposit of learning, much as the church has traditionally been committed to pass on the deposit of faith. In order for intellectual richness to be maximized, the corporate body should lose as little as possible of value.
- Centering culture. Since the Middle Ages, when culture was fundamentally religious, to the twentieth century, when it has been fundamentally secular, the university has, by both design and effect, been at the center of culture—articulating, shaping, and debating

options and prerogatives. Here is the sphere in which intellectual freedom, essential to academic work, interacts with moral obligation and social responsibility. It is the sphere in which the humanities and the arts disciplines have traditionally staged the key debates and offered leadership, but from which they have, for a complex of reasons, recently pulled back, to the detriment of all concerned.

If you accept, at least as a crude outline, this notion of what a university is, we can go forward to our qualifier, "Christian."

What Is a "Christian" _____?

Strictly speaking, as many have observed, the word "Christian" suffers diminishment when it is not used as a noun. To be a Christian, strictly speaking, is to be a person under obedience to Christ. To be under obedience to Christ is to have heard the Great Commandment (Matt. 22:34–40//Mark 12:28–31), the Great Commission (Matt. 28:18–20), the Sermon on the Mount (Matt. 5–7), and even the prayers of Jesus for his followers (as in John 17), and to be taking them seriously enough that a certain clarity about first-order obligations is more or less reflexive. When we say of someone—even a fellow academic—"That person is a Christian," what we are saying, or should mean, is that she (or he) is one for whom the claims of Christ have a greater hold upon her reflective intelligence than any other claims, including those of her academic guild. For after all, "no one can serve two masters" (Matt. 6:24).

I suspect, however, that in the academic setting few of us often use the term "Christian" in this clear-minded way, as a primary and denoting noun. As in the context of our discussion here, we use it as a modifier, an adjective, ostensibly to qualify some other noun. When we do that, the term "Christian" itself inevitably is qualified, for in the conjunction of terms, it is the noun that takes precedence, and we all know it. There are many parallels: "Italian-American" or "Polish-American" come to mind. But to the degree that there is real and vibrant life in the first term, there is a subtle but real sense in which the weight of emphasis shifts away from the second, so that it also is being "modified," as with "Mexican-American" or "African-American." These terms still have the force of meaningfully referring back to the realities denominated by the first noun in the pair. Others exhibit little or no fruitful tension: If I should say to you that I, too, am a hyphenated citizen, a Canadian-American, you might laugh. There are some institutions in America whose name includes the term "Christian" with as little or less modifying force.

If my examples invoke the concept of dual citizenship, it is because I sense here an instructive analogy. "Christian/university," "Christian/philosopher," "Christian/intellectual"—are these not evocations of two realms now, two citizenships? For Albert, Aquinas, and Bonaventure, it was not so; for us, it is so. And thence comes our topic and thus our task: If there is to be real meaning in the conjunction "Christian university," there must remain such authority in the first term—cultural, intellectual, and moral authority—that it is not altogether modified out of relevance by the second.

"In . . . [Christ] are hidden all the treasures of wisdom and knowledge" (Col. 2:3). Do we really believe that? If so, our sense of what a university is will arise from that confidence, that first order of intellectual affection.

Citizenship in the Guilds

Apprenticeship in our era, apprenticeship in our respective guilds, is overwhelmingly an induction into a narrower and technical, not merely secularized, understanding of the university's multifold tasks. Hypertrophy in the disciplines, the fragmentary and even atomizing character of their development, accentuates a general modern movement away from integration of any kind. The result, as now countless academic jeremiads have made more or less public, is a crisis of moment for the secular university itself.[3] Our own version of it—only the deeper for its necessarily more direct resistance to separating intellectual freedom from community responsibility, and separating the pursuit of private enterprise from the claims of public vision—actually has a bearing upon, and should be of direct value to, resolution of this wider intellectual crisis in the Western university.

Why do I claim that Christian academics "necessarily" must more directly confront the increasingly general separation of intellectual or academic freedom from the mutual obligations of intellectual community? Because all of us are members of the body of Christ. Yes, we are also members of some academic guild, perhaps one that more or less self-consciously offers us (unlike St. Paul, I speak only metaphorically) the inducements of a harlot. And we find it rather too easy to rationalize a preoccupation with these inducements; like our Master, we have no aversion to ministry to harlots. We engage them, as he by a certain will did, in deep and reflective conversation. And we will gladly bear the brunt

3. See, for example, David Lyle Jeffrey and Dominic Manganiello, eds., *Rethinking the Future of the University* (Ottawa: University of Ottawa Press, 1998); Marsden, *Outrageous Idea of Christian Scholarship*; and idem, *Soul of the American University*.

of our pharisaical coreligionists' scorn as we tipple and convivially dine with these folk, and even more scurrilous publicans, for we do it all on impeccable authority. But there is a limiting line there somewhere.

Early on, few of us find that our doctoral programs engage the "Christian," even in fields where "Christian" is central to the discipline, in any very nuanced, discerning, or mature fashion.[4] Typically, the opposite occurs: we are expected to see the rectitude of Shaw's oxymoron (above) and quickly to shed our interest in these matters. Moreover, motives for matriculation regularly become mixed with mammon. Quickly enough we learn that for survival's sake we should fashion our professional self-image so as to make it appear to our superiors and peers that loyalty to our guild outweighs loyalty to our university, as also to the gospel. We are inclined to suspect that we will have "academic freedom" to the degree that we keep in mind what, as Richard Rorty says, our peers will let us get away with saying.[5] We learn to rankle no Romans; we confront few Pharisees. But in such a case, academic freedom has been sadly corrupted, and that on several counts. For the Christian, in whose mind academic freedom should seek its roots in the second clause of the Great Commandment as much as the first, the "perfect law of liberty" (James 1:28; 2:8) is an outwardly directed freedom. As the text makes plain, it is a freedom to love the neighbor as one's self. In a Christian context there can be no virtuous practice of academic freedom that does not seek the common good—the "commune profit," as John Gower put it—of the whole body of Christ.[6] But this view, like most other communitarian convictions, has fallen on hard individualistic times, in which academic neighbors may regard as truest charity a firm commitment to leave each other alone.

For Christians in the university, what Michael Beaty, Todd Buras, Larry Lyon, and others have called the "two-spheres" approach is thus for many just a sensible survival strategy.[7] For others, even in nominally Christian universities, it seems that the only way to make progress, either

4. See Bob R. Agee, "The Outrageous Idea of a Christian University—The University and the Church: Understanding the Paradigms," *Carson-Newman Studies* 9, no. 2 (1999): 130.

5. See Alvin Plantinga, "On Christian Scholarship," in *The Challenge and Promise of a Catholic University*, ed. Theodore M. Hesburgh (Notre Dame: University of Notre Dame Press, 1994), 280.

6. See Russell A. Peck, *Kingship and Common Profit in Gower's* Confessio Amantis (Carbondale: Southern Illinois University Press, 1978), xxi; 18–19.

7. See Larry Lyon and Michael Beaty, "Integration, Secularization, and the Two-Spheres View at Religious Colleges: Comparing Baylor University with the University of Notre Dame and Georgetown College," *Christian Scholar's Review* 29, no. 1 (1999): 73–112. Also see Michael Beaty, Todd Buras, and Larry Lyon, "Christian Higher Education: An Historical and Philosophical Perspective," *Perspectives in Religious Studies* 24 (1997): 145–65.

with personal intellectual life or with corporate academic development, is by a diplomatic management of divided loyalties. Rationalizations, often with the best of intentions, abound.

And this two-spheres approach, pragmatically speaking, has served many purposes, including the would-be tolerant purposes of our non-Christian colleagues. Many of these colleagues would be willing for the spheres of faith and reason to coexist almost indefinitely, as long as we more or less continuously and therapeutically assure them that it will be on terms dictated by what counts as reason—that it will be the norms of the secular university that determine what shall be the acceptable intellectual and social implications of the term "Christian."

That is why I agree with those who think that for the purposes of granting "Christian" its necessarily authoritative stature in the Christian university, the two-spheres approach, whatever its transitional value, will no longer do. The "add-on" defense for religion, as Beaty, Buras, and Lyon have shown, is in fact often a version of me-tooism, a hyperreflex of fashion-conscious American Christianity in the twentieth century; yet it can involve such an extreme rejection of separateness from the mainstream culture as in effect to deny the Christian obligation to be countercultural. On the other hand, the faith/knowledge separation, so easy for antiauthoritarian Protestants, can be at the very core of that disobedience to Christ that the church must address. In the two-spheres model, the second term almost always eventually overcomes the first. David Solomon's prediction that institutions like Notre Dame and Baylor must inevitably also succumb to it is not, on the evidence of past examples, unwarranted.[8]

Indifference to the drift, as though these were matters merely of taste or the market, is in fact already a de facto choice. As Rowan Williams, archbishop of Canterbury, recently put it, "If you think you are being neutral about the moral and spiritual ethos of a school, you are in fact generating an ethos of individualism, functionalism, and ultimately fragmentation."[9] In other words, intellectual neutrality kills; in particular, it is fatal to Christian academic community.

Where we Christians might have suggested alternative models for development, we have, too often I fear, been content simply to show that we too, despite our somewhat awkward subcultural peculiarities, can move in solidarity with the general herd. The neutral or broad way, we

8. W. David Solomon, "What Baylor and Notre Dame Can Learn from Each Other," *New Oxford Review* 62, no. 10 (1995): 19.

9. Rowan Williams, in his first major address on education given to the Association of Anglican Secondary School Heads, annual conference, September 11, 2003, at Exeter. See http://www.archbishopofcanterbury.org/sermons_speeches/2003/030911.html (accessed August 27, 2005).

imply, is our way too. We have often failed, as Charles Habib Malik has suggested, even to provide a useful Christian critique of the general fate of the university.[10] Even now, when our minds as a community (thanks to Marsden, Plantinga, Pelikan, Schwehn, Wolterstorff, Carpenter, Noll, Holmes, et al.) are working better on this than two decades ago, are we ready yet to say what a truly Christian university would be like? What would be *distinctive* about it *intellectually*?

I am not sure. What I am sure about is that others are now listening to see what, if anything, we might have to say.

Constructive Criticism from Outside

We may even say, in a sense, that neighbors not of our community have joined our conversation, at least temporarily. This is something to be welcomed. Insofar as their attention does not move us either to defensiveness or to what is more to be pitied, a fawning insipidity that leads us to play up to their camera rather than really put our minds to the issue—we should be grateful. Whatever is distinctive and whatever we may hope to be worthy in our identity cannot but profit from intelligent questions. Our identity—not simply as academics or as citizens, but rather our identity as credible adherents, followers, and students of the teaching of Jesus—demands our careful attention to those who have tried to understand us in something at least akin to our own terms.

Most will remember, a few years ago, an issue of *Atlantic Monthly* that focused on the topic at hand. In the lead article, Alan Wolfe makes three apparent criticisms of evangelical higher education. (In effect, they boil down substantially to one criticism.) And though he is talking mostly about evangelical colleges, what he says certainly applies to the possibility of a credible Christian university such as what Baylor, among others, aspires to be.

First, Wolfe finds that evangelicals in particular "have created institutions as sensitive and caring as any in America," but often at the cost of moral and intellectual discernment, to the degree that they have "no adequate way of distinguishing between ideas that are path-breaking and those that are gibberish."[11] For example, in some quarters if M. Scott Peck is talk-show popular, he becomes an authority more compelling than Moses; no matter how new-agey and incoherent he remains even

10. Charles Habib Malik, *A Christian Critique of the University* (Downers Grove, IL: InterVarsity, 1982).
11. Alan Wolfe, "The Opening of the Evangelical Mind," *Atlantic Monthly* 286, no. 4 (October 2000): 65.

to his interpreters, he "works" for some because above all they want to be "with it."

Second, Wolfe finds that therapeutic culture comes too easily to evangelicals, precisely because, if I follow him, therapeutic culture is a safely secularized version of the good news and therefore entails little scandal or social stigma. But this me-tooism, he claims, creates an oddly unevangelical political correctness and leads to intellectual flaccidity:

> A therapeutic sensibility and a culture of nonjudgmentalism are inappropriate for hiring new faculty members, evaluating them for tenure, developing a syllabus, grading undergraduates, mentoring graduate students, writing books, or conducting experiments. All these tasks involve making judgments about who or what does or does not achieve a certain threshold of validity or excellence.[12]

To the degree that our incapacity for discerning excellence applies, it cripples ambitions for the development of any kind of serious university.

Finally, Wolfe reflects a very old view—one that Catholics and Jews as well as eighteenth-century dissenters firmly agreed on: "When it comes to the life of the mind, democratic sensibilities aren't always a help. Once sentenced to intellectual mediocrity because they kept too many ideas out, conservative Christian institutions face the prospect of returning to mediocrity because they let too many in."[13] The odd attraction of postmodernism for many evangelicals, he claims, owes more than anything to their legacy of antiauthoritarianism, their resistance to authority of any kind. Wolfe's imperious rhetoric aside, I have come to recognize a little truth in this; as in so many other matters, we may sometimes have shown ourselves more interested in relevance than in coherence.

Now we see how it is that all of Wolfe's points resolve into one. Our problem, much like that of Adam and Eve as Milton so shrewdly presents them in the primal garden, is that we will go to pretty much any option that leads us away from thinking clearly about authority above the self—about, for example, the biblical imperative to make connections between love and obedience. Wolfe does not say it, but the widely shared Western suspicion of any and all authority—recall the 1960s mantra "Question authority"—is the secularized legacy of an intellectually shopworn Protestantism; it is also, as Wolfe does not perhaps fully understand, why evangelicals tend to reject (or at the least steer away from) Catholics, even transparently saintly Catholics, as full partners in the intellectual work to be done. They do not trust Catholics, who have had more of value to say—forever, really—than anyone on the integration

12. Ibid., 69.
13. Ibid.

of faith and learning, whose vision of *fides quaerens intellectum* originated the university in the Middle Ages and still undergirds most of the most compelling products of such integration that evangelicals study today. To some fundamental degree, this is not because of this or that doctrinal difference, but rather, I think, because Catholics have insisted upon the necessity of transpersonal authority, both in matters of faith and in matters of reason. It may also be because they are viewed as having too strong a sense of community: they are not dependable enough as populists, or to invert the point, are insufficiently individualistic in matters of mind and heart. Evangelical Protestants want to say "I believe" or "I think that"—Catholics tend to want to say "The church teaches," and evangelicals find that disturbing. Evangelicals tend to prefer and even trust a more radical individualism. Yet all the while, many of us who call ourselves Baptists or evangelicals—and Wolfe is right about this, isn't he?—are obliged to put enormous amounts of energy into educating boards of regents and wider communities of church-based support away from the anti-intellectualism that is, after all, quite precisely a function of *their* radical individualism.

The Issue

Another way to describe our quandary—and I do so because, for both consistency's sake and the sake of our unity, it follows here—is to say that to some degree we Protestants have naturalized our resistance to Christ. We say we are accountable to the Scriptures, but we insist that only our own personal, anarchic, and subjective interpretations of the Bible, malleable and protean according to our current prejudices, will do. Currently, for example, we are happy to quote the Great Commission, but we are less happy to remember the Great Commandment; much of the Sermon on the Mount is cliché for us, and some of it, like the bit about not serving two masters, goes unremarked. As for the great high-priestly prayer of Jesus in John 17, that we all be made one, even as he and the Father are one—we do not much like to think about that prayer, let alone pray with Jesus.

In the Middle Ages, the very word "Uni-versity" implied, as often recognized, the many turning toward the One: with the diversity of human labors and vocations, we return—for reference, communion, corporate self-understanding, community, and a common sense of purpose—to that One in whom all our wisdoms are hidden, and whose members, like spokes of a wheel, we are to be as the world turns.

What is needed, for the church as for any cultural extension of it that would be meaningfully Christian, is a reestablishment, in reflective tranquility and deep study, of the teaching authority of Jesus at the hub. If we can somehow find a way to deal appropriately with this issue, we then (and probably only then) can coherently address the key question: Can there be such a thing as a Christian university that functions as an intellectual community?

The Experiment

Since there is, by my reckoning at least, still no fully satisfactory exemplar of the Christian university in America today, we must imagine the task of helping to build one in purely experimental terms. Here are some hypotheses on which I would like to see experiments:

- That theology—a truly rigorous philosophical theology, be built up over a generation or two to the point where it could once again and more credibly become "queen of the arts."[14] For this to happen, theology would need to acquire our brightest and best, apprenticeship in theology would need to require countercultural and truly radically higher standards than now prevail, and a commensurate prestige would need to be granted the discipline. (I love to think that some visionary Christian philanthropist may help to fund a program in which brilliant practitioners of one of the major intellectual disciplines, say at about the age of forty-five to fifty, could be identified and supported at full academic salary for about five years of top-level theological training, then turned loose to practice a theology informed by and grounded in the intellectual disciplines for the benefit of the wider church.)
- In the interim, philosophy—including philosophy of education, philosophy of history, history of philosophy, philosophy of science, epistemology, and philosophy of religion—would need both to become crackerjack good and capable of much more than technical preoccupations, and thus capable of giving leadership to intellectual and spiritual self-definition in the Christian university. This will require faculty members who have the stature and independence of mind to be able to critique the norms and prejudices of their academic guilds as well as the conventional secular pieties of our wider academic culture.

14. See Donald A. Carson, "Can There Be a Christian University?" *Southern Baptist Journal of Theology* 1 (1997): 20–38; and Douglas Harink, "Taking the University to Church: The Role of Theology in the Christian University Curriculum," *Christian Scholar's Review* 28, no. 3 (1999): 389–410.

- All other disciplines must be built up in a similar fashion, cultured, with faculty who possess and continue to acquire the highest possible levels of (1) commitment to Christ and (2) disciplinary excellence. Without intellectual integrity, piety in the university soon becomes odious—and on these grounds perhaps has become odious to many.

- Further, a communing community must be formed, a faculty that commits to common worship and prays with a common purpose. Any idea that this may be accomplished simply by having all faculty members from a single denomination or general category of Christians is delusory, in my view. There is more divergence among Baptists, for example, on everything I have talked about today, or among Catholics or Methodists or Lutherans, than between Christ-directed intellectuals and laypeople across and beyond these traditions. Part of the countercultural courage we need is to experiment obediently toward fulfilling the will of Christ so clearly expressed in John 17.

It may be that our tacit question ought not to be "Can there be a Christian university?" but rather, "Can there be a Christian university that lacks the conviction to put its theology at the core?" I do not think so—at least not for long. Protestant evangelical educators need to find their own versions of a mission statement for the Christian university, a statement that allows for it to be a place where

> aided by the specific contribution of philosophy and theology, university scholars will be engaged in a constant effort to determine the relative place and meaning of each of the various disciplines within the context of a vision of the human person and the world that is enlightened by the Gospel, and therefore by a faith in Christ, the *Logos*, as the center of creation and of human history.[15]

These are the words of John Paul II, from his *Ex Corde Ecclesiae* (*Apostolic Constitution on Catholic Universities*), but they surely have a contribution to make to all our conversations.

A Christian Faculty

One cannot build a Christian university without a Christian faculty, and such a faculty's real and ongoing needs must then be met. In a measure not now that widely evident:

15. Ioannes Paulus PP. II, *Ex Corde Ecclesiae* (1990), part 1, §16.

- We need understanding of a scriptural worldview and loyalty to it. We need to know and love the Christian metanarrative.
- We need theological leadership—intellectually and spiritually authoritative because it is continually earning that authority. There needs to be a level of theological inquiry that is capable of reminding us fruitfully of the ultimate unity of truth, and of teaching us again and again how it is a requisite of the search for truth that the enterprise be a corporate, communal endeavor.
- We therefore need a community of faith. As Mark Schwehn and Doug Harink say, we cannot be Christian without it.[16] We need to be the gathered church, even as we research, teach, and think. We need to share spiritual focus much more than we do. We need worship as this focus, and not just fellowship.
- As members of such a community, we need obedience in Nietzsche's sense—"a long obedience in the same direction"—to our intellectual vocation as an outworking of our spiritual vocation, our share in responding to the authority of Christ and the church.[17]
- We need freedom in the biblical and not the Nietzschean sense, freedom that is self-effacing and generous, a "free spirit," freely therefore to obey and freely to give. May it be said of us, as Chaucer said of his fourteenth-century Oxford academic, "Gladly would we learn and gladly teach!"
- We need to be able to pursue research that is pure; also, we need to do research that is targeted, focused, as Harold Attridge has said, toward answering the big (and often therefore theologically laden) questions.[18]
- We need, to a degree that almost all universities in the twentieth century have neglected to their peril, "translators"—accomplished polymathic scholars whose mature share in the community task is to bridge the disciplines and to help set them in conversation with each other and with the philosophers and theologians.

Much of this *is* countercultural. But if the experiment, or even parts of it, should work, it may contribute, as no mere conformity to the imperatives of the multiversity ever could, to the collective good of human intellec-

---

16. See Mark R. Schwehn, *Exiles from Eden: Religion and the Academic Vocation in America* (New York: Oxford University Press, 1993), 22–43; and Harink, "Taking the University to Church," 389–410.

17. See Schwehn, *Exiles from Eden*, 45.

18. Harold W. Attridge, "Reflections on the Mission of a Catholic University," in *Challenge and Promise of a Catholic University*, 20.

tuality and culture—including the minds and culture of many who will not ever be "Christian," even in the most nominal sense of the word.

So then, at last, to the implicit question in my title: Is there a future for Christian intellectual community among the colleges and universities of America? My answer is strongly yes, but with these provisions: As long as there are communities of scholars who make it their business to privilege faith that seeks understanding over professional self-interest looking to find some vestigial reason to believe, then there will be a future. As long as there are institutions in which the practice of academic freedom is not merely a protection for narrow agendas and advocacies, but is richly grounded in that larger Christian principle of love of the neighbor—then what the apostle calls "the perfect law of liberty" may grace our learning with sufficient self-effacement and charity toward the common good of the wider church we serve. As long as we do not permit ourselves to become double-minded and hence unstable in all our ways (cf. James 1:8), and as long as our faith is unwavering, accompanied by fortitude and perseverance, then there will be a future worthy of our charitably patient endeavors. Under these conditions, we may yet fulfill our calling and actually be the Christian intellectual communities our denominational sponsors and forebears have, however unwittingly, prayed we would become.

PART 2

VITAL
PRACTICES

6

||||||||||||||||||||||||||||||||||||||||||

DOUBT AND THE HERMENEUTICS
OF DELIGHT

||||||||||||||||||||||||||||||||||||||||||

Susan M. Felch

DOUBT MAY NOT BE THE quintessential virtue of the modern university, but it is a quality of mind highly valued in the academy. To doubt what has been taught, what has been believed, even what has been experienced—such doubt has long marked the passage from childish belief to mature reflection. Higher education, particularly education in the humanities, has often equated such maturity with the development of a certain type of critical thinking, with doubt that is not just neutral *un*belief, but doubt that is a deliberately cultivated critical distance, a *dis*belief that the *Oxford English Dictionary* defines as "positive unbelief." The modern academy has seen such doubt, such positive unbelief, as a valued commodity because it pares away extraneous theories, experiences, emotions, and narratives to arrive—if not at the truth—then at least at a better or more useful or perhaps more provocative explanation for observed data.

In the postmodern academy—or at least among our current students—doubt often loses this cutting edge and instead spreads out into an ironic or cynical miasma, an unwholesome, menacing atmosphere of uncertainty, characterized not by the paring down of unhealthy or outgrown choices but by the production of a paralyzing plethora of alternatives, none of which carries enough weight to interest students for very long. They look out over a flattened moral landscape that does little to excite their imagination.

In what follows, I argue that doubt and the critical distance it engenders should not be allowed to shape the geography of our classrooms. Indeed, giving doubt this kind of priority allows a part to substitute for the whole. Rather than helping our students grow up, such privileging of doubt hampers our students' progress from adolescence to mature adulthood. As an alternative, I suggest that we try the hermeneutics of delight.

On Doubt, Faith, and Delight

There is no doubt that doubt has its proper place in scholarly and pedagogical agendas, and not just as the way to begin a paragraph. The doubt that lurks behind such statements as "I have questions about . . . ," or "I wonder about . . . ," or even "Is it possible that . . . ?" is an essential part of learning about the world. This doubt is plural; it is "doubts about"—a common noun followed by a preposition and its object. As such, it has a proper part to play in the classroom and in scholarly projects.

A problem arises, however, when doubt becomes a singular proper noun—Doubt with a capital D, reified doubt, calcified doubt, the doubt that by a false etymology we have confused with "doughty," as in brave, formidable, and capable, and have too often claimed as education's patron saint. This is the doubt that claims a privileged status, that demands a critical, distanced methodology for intellectual work. Such doubt often shapes our classroom lectures and discussions, as well as our own scholarly projects; it constitutes the landscape in which we pursue our intellectual quests. And this doubt is often directed against religious faith: it is not by chance that the first definition of doubt in the *Oxford English Dictionary* points to religion, reporting that the noun frequently means "uncertainty as to the truth of Christianity or some other religious belief or doctrine." Even in the Christian university, putting everything in doubt—including Christian faith, belief, and doctrine—is often seen as the first methodological step to genuine inquiry.

We might think that the antidote to such reified, calcified doubt is faith, and in a certain sense, that is true. Faith, the writer of the book of Hebrews tells us, "is the assurance of things hoped for, the conviction of things not seen" (Heb. 11:1), and those two words, "assurance" and "conviction," provide an alternative methodology to the uncertainty of doubt. We can seek out understanding with the confidence that there is a goal to be obtained and truth to be learned. But "things hoped for" and "things not seen" remind us that such confidence is in an ultimate outcome, indeed, an ultimate person. Along the way, we see in a glass, darkly—and that sounds like a synonym for doubt, or at least for "doubts about." Furthermore, doubt and faith are not precisely parallel terms. Faith is not simply a methodology—a way of thinking or a quality of mind. It is also a body of content—the *confession* of faith summarized in the Christian creeds—and the fidelity, or faithfulness, we *profess* in words and deeds as Christians. While the plural common noun, "doubts about," can play a role in the faith we profess, faith, in its many dimensions, is more comprehensive than both "doubts about" and reified doubt.

So I propose that we consider delight as an alternative to doubt, that we turn to delight to shape the geography of our classrooms and our own scholarly projects. Faith may wend its way across the landscape of doubt or the landscape of delight, but delight provides us with the richer aesthetic and moral topography through which to chart our course as scholars and teachers as we confess and profess our Christian faith.

Is "delight," however, the best term to use? Certainly, we can think of others: "love," "wonder," "joy." Perhaps "gladness" works, recalling Chaucer's Oxford student who would "gladly learn and gladly teach." Or we might choose "beauty," "the marvelous," or "the sublime." All of these terms form a constellation that evokes a sense of receptivity and expansion, qualities fundamental to a landscape of delight, and each is worth further exploration. But I have chosen "delight" as the central word for three reasons.

First, it echoes the language of Horace in the *Ars poetica* (line 333), which says that the goal of literature is *aut prodesse . . . aut delectare*, "to teach or to delight, but preferably both at once." This conjunction of teaching and delighting is taken up by Sir Philip Sidney in the sixteenth century, who completes the triad by adding the Augustinian notion of "moving to action." Sidney argues that literature excels the other arts and sciences because it teaches, delights, and moves us to take action.[1] Indeed, literature instructs and moves us to action precisely because it delights. To hear a story, children come in from play, says Sidney, and old people will abandon a warm fire. What makes literature particularly powerful is its ability to bind ideas and pleasure and stimulus to action all together in a single, exciting package. And because ideas, delight,

---

1. Philip Sidney, *The Defence of Poesy* in *Sir Philip Sidney: The Oxford Authors*, ed. Katherine Duncan Jones (Oxford: Oxford University Press, 1989). Augustine writes that the good educator will always speak "so as to teach, to delight, to sway," for "teaching your audience is a matter of necessity, delighting them a matter of being agreeable, swaying them a matter of victory" (Augustine, *Teaching Christianity [De doctrina christiana]*, trans. Edmund Hill [Hyde Park, NY: New City Press, 1996], 4.12).

and action come all bound up together in real life as well, to experience literature is to come close to experiencing life in all its complexities. Literature, in fact, comes closer to replicating life than do other disciplines (for Sidney, history and philosophy are the textual foils against which literature proves its value) because it provides an opportunity to test one's mettle in a secondary world. And by journeying through that world, through the landscape of delightful devices, we are best able to learn. But as Sidney also reminds us, a hermeneutics of delight does not seal us inside an enclosed aesthetic domain; instead, it propels us back into the primary physical world, wiser and better prepared to act. What we practice in the secondary world of literature we perform, knowingly or not, in the "real" world. To some extent, we are, or we become, what we read.

Second, delight retains a sense of that "aha" moment of surprise and discovery that is essential to good education, and Sidney deepens its meaning by contrasting it with laughter. We laugh, he says, at incongruity, at things that are disproportionate to one another. Recall your favorite *Far Side* cartoon, and you will understand what Sidney means. What makes humor funny is the juxtaposition of elements that normally would not stand side by side: cows opening a freezer and discovering packs of hamburger inside; giant insects holding a jar that contains a small boy. Delight, on the other hand, comes from things that fit together; it elicits a sigh of satisfaction, a sense of rightness. To be sure, we can experience delight and laughter at the same time, as when lovers express their joy at being together with extravagantly foolish language, but the two responses are essentially different. "Delight hath a joy in it," says Sidney, "either permanent or present. Laughter hath only a scornful tickling."[2] And it is precisely delight's emphasis on joy rather than scorn that makes it appropriate for the classroom.

Third, delight reaches out to embrace both the concept of light and the notion of formative reading. In the sixteenth century, "delite" began to be spelled "delight," enhancing the connection between joy and light, while its Latin root, *delecto*, calls to mind the *lectio*, or reading aloud, that forged a link between medieval devotional and pedagogical practices.

The very expansiveness of the word "delight" suggests that the hermeneutics of delight offers not a constricted pathway of precept and rule, or a blinkered reduction to critical doubt, but rather a rich aesthetic landscape that encourages the learner—and the scholar—to look up and around rather than merely down or forward. And although I would not be adverse to arguing that literature in general and stories in particular provide the best means for moral education, what I want to claim *here*

---

2. Sidney, *Defence of Poesy*, 245.

is that all our academic disciplines depend upon narrative structures both large and small, and therefore are amenable to a hermeneutics of delight. In other words, I would not agree with Sidney that *only* the discipline of literature teaches, delights, and moves to action, but rather that all of our disciplines have the potential to do so.

Questing through the Landscape of Delight

The image of the Christian scholar-teacher riding through the landscape of delight comes to me, I must confess, from the genre of romance. Not the romance of boy meets girl, but the great medieval-quest romances of Arthur, Gawain, Lancelot, and the whole Round-Table crew, and in particular, from the revision of those romances by Edmund Spenser in his late-sixteenth-century tale, *The Faerie Queene*. In the prefatory letter to *The Faerie Queene*, addressed to Sir Walter Raleigh, Spenser states his intention to meld the genre of romance—with its questing knights and dragon-filled adventures—with the most serious of educational goals, the formation of mature persons. He intends *The Faerie Queene* "to fashion a . . . noble person in virtuous and gentle discipline," in other words, to draw out, to educate, mind and heart toward maturity.[3] And he deliberately chooses the romance landscape for this educational mission precisely because it offers a hermeneutics of delight. To those who object to his "method" of education, arguing that good discipline should be "delivered plainly in way of precepts, or sermoned at large" rather than "cloudily enwrapped in Allegorical devises," he replies that good teaching is much more "profitable and gracious" when it uses example rather than rule.[4] Here Spenser is following his own immediate exemplar and fellow countryman, Philip Sidney. Thus, I follow Spenser and illustrate my claims about the landscape of delight from *The Faerie Queene*.

In the first few stanzas of *The Faerie Queene*, Spenser introduces us to two main characters: the Redcrosse Knight, a young and untried adolescent decked out with the armor of God and ready to plunge into his first set of adventures, and Una, a quiet but confident young woman whose parents are under siege by a fearsome dragon. Redcrosse Knight has been charged by the Faerie Queene to fight the dragon, but in true romance style we do not actually reach Una's home country and the dragon until near the end of book 1. This delay is not merely a narrative strategy; in Spenser's hand it is also a necessary aspect of education. Moral, mental, and spiritual formation cannot be rushed, and as we first meet him, the

---

3. Edmund Spenser, *Poetical Works*, ed. J. C. Smith and E. de Selincourt (Oxford: Oxford University Press, 1970), 407, spelling modernized by the author.
    4. Ibid.

Redcrosse Knight is in no way ready to meet the challenge the dragon poses. So Spenser dumps the Redcrosse Knight and Una into a textured, three-dimensional landscape, where they spend delightful hours riding through a forest, but also where they listen to a catalog of the names of the trees, lose their way, encounter and conquer the Monster Error with her ugly and swarming brood of baby books, chat, and generally begin to grow up. The landscape through which they travel is dense with experiences: they see, hear, touch, taste, and feel the world, and yet not every experience is immediately transmuted into an assessable educational objective. The catalog of trees, for instance, is simply a constitutive feature of all tall tales and offers an opportunity for Spenser to add an English touch to his romance while playing around with the sound of words: "The sailing Pine, the Cedar proud and tall, / The vine-prop Elm, the Poplar never dry."[5] This landscape of delight is richly aesthetic, sensual, in love with the stuff out of which the world is made: trees, clear streams, lowering rain, well-made shields, and stout horses.

It is also a landscape in which lurk dangers, and Redcrosse Knight's judgment is tested particularly when he rushes foolhardily into Error's den, ignoring Una's warning to wait:

> Be well aware, quoth then that Ladie mild,
> Least sudden mischief ye too rash provoke:
> The danger hid, the place unknown and wild.[6]

And later he extracts himself from Error's clutches only when he hears Una shout:

> Add faith unto your force, and be not faint:
> Strangle her, else she sure will strangle thee.[7]

He acts on her advice. Here, as we can see, the Redcrosse Knight would have benefited from a little doubt, as in *"doubt about* the wisdom of rushing into Error's den." "Doubt about" is certainly *part* of the landscape of delight, and "doubt about," properly used, restrains impetuousness with a quiet attentiveness.

John Donne, a man who knew something about doubt himself, put it this way at the conclusion of his third satire:

> . . . doubt wisely; in strange way
> To stand inquiring right, is not to stray;

5. Ibid., 4 (I, viii).
6. Ibid., 4 (I, xii).
7. Ibid., 5 (I, xix).

To sleep, or run wrong, is. On a huge hill,
Cragged and steep, Truth stands, and he that will
Reach her, about must, and about must go,
And what the hill's suddenness resists, win so.[8]

Like Una, Donne recommends a wise doubt; or rather, he doesn't recommend a wise doubt, for Donne, as does Spenser, refuses to harden doubt into a noun. Instead, he retains doubt as a verb: to doubt wisely is to actively engage in serious inquiry; to doubt wisely is to ask questions about; to doubt wisely requires a disciplined and quiet attentiveness, in contrast to the careless sleep that will later overwhelm the Redcrosse Knight, or the wrongheaded rush that propels him into Error's den. But within the landscape of delight, wise doubting is only one action, and a limited action at that. For as Donne recognizes, within that landscape, indeed dominating it, is Truth, a "huge hill, / Cragged and steep," and to reach that Truth, Donne, the Redcrosse Knight, and we alike must move through our doubting to continue the task of ascending her steep and difficult heights. We "about must, and about must go, / And what the hill's suddenness resists, win so."

Donne's equation of doubt with stillness might seem counterintuitive to us at first. On further reflection, however, we notice the importance of the restraining adverb. To doubt "wisely" is to ask questions while we stand still, looking around as we sort out the next best step to take. But to reify doubt is to let questions pool out from our own standpoint and flatten the landscape of delight; it is to mistake a part for the whole, and to substitute a rich diversity of aesthetic experiences for only the mode of critical questioning; it is to reduce the plenitude of the landscape of delight—with its catalog of trees, wandering paths, and multilayered adventures—into the poverty of single, reductive methodology: that of critical distance, suspicious questioning.

We may be guilty of teaching such reductive methodology in the very way we design our assignments. We often ask students, for instance, to argue against a particular statement or idea. Indeed, an essential component of the classical oration, a rhetorical structure still useful for developing argumentative essays, is the refutation, a statement that stands in opposition to the main thesis.[9] The easiest way to write a refutation

8. John Donne, *The Complete English Poems of John Donne*, ed. C. A. Patrides (London: J. M. Dent & Sons, 1985), 228, spelling modernized by the author.
9. The traditional parts of a classical oration are the exordium, which introduces the topic and grabs the audience's attention, often with an anecdote; the narration, which explains the significance of the topic and states the thesis; the partition, which outlines the various parts of the argument to follow; the digression, which amplifies the argument by means of stories or other "tangential" elements; the confirmation, which develops each

is to construct an objection that can be demolished in the subsequent paragraphs; doubt, critical distance, is used here as a reductive tool to strengthen one's own position. The better way to write a refutation is to consider a substantive objection that may nuance the original thesis, perhaps either by restricting or broadening its scope.

So, for instance, a student paper may argue that Shylock, in Shakespeare's *The Merchant of Venice*, is a villain because he claims a pound of flesh from his business rival. The thesis might find itself chastened not so much by the more obvious "Hath not a Jew eyes?" speech,[10] which after all does argue for universal human vindictiveness, but more by the conclusion of that scene, in which Shylock learns that his daughter has carelessly traded her mother's ring for a monkey. The doubt enacted by this refutation (the loss of his wife's ring constitutes Shylock, at least temporarily, as a sympathetic victim, who grieves his family's loss) presses a student to a more carefully nuanced consideration of Shylock's villainy. In this case, "doubts about" Shylock's villainy cause a student to look up and around in the play, to wander about in a broader landscape of aesthetic delight rather than moving too quickly to judgment and critique.

More broadly, however, asking students to write only argumentative papers increases the likelihood that they will mistake the part for the whole; that they will see the educational enterprise as consisting mainly, if not entirely, of analysis and critique; that the geography of their minds will be reduced to the landscape of doubt. The classical oration itself hints at a better way. Not only does it call for partition—a description of the *various* ways in which a writer will defend and, indeed, explore his or her thesis—but also for that wonderful component, the digression. A digression is exactly what it sounds like—a rhetorical byway that lets a writer play around with a suggestive tangent. Digressions may merely

---

part of the argument in turn; the refutation, which states an objection to the thesis and answers that objection; and the peroration, which restates the thesis and wraps up the argument. Cf. *Silva Rhetoricae*, http://humanities.byu.edu/rhetoric/silva.htm (accessed August 29, 2005).

10. Shylock says to Salerio, another Venetian merchant, "Hath not a Jew eyes? Hath not a Jew hands, organs, dimensions, senses, affections, passions? Fed with the same food, hurt with the same weapons, subject to the same diseases, healed by the same means, warmed and cooled by the same winter and summer, as a Christian is? If you prick us, do we not bleed? If you tickle us, do we not laugh? If you poison us, do we not die? And if you wrong us, shall we not revenge? If we are like you in the rest, we will resemble you in that. If a Jew wrong a Christian, what is his humility? Revenge [the Christian responds with revenge rather than with humility]. If a Christian wrong a Jew, what should his sufferance be by Christian example? Why, revenge. The villainy you teach me I will execute, and it shall go hard but I will better the instruction" (Shakespeare, *The Merchant of Venice*, 3.1.55–69).

provide opportunity for rhetorical showmanship; but at their best they enrich an essay not through direct argument or critique, but by way of similitude, in developing analogies that suggest and deepen and augment the original thesis. Digressions in a classical argumentative essay, or more creative genres that use adduction rather than simple induction or deduction, help students to see and embrace the plenitude of the world in which they live; digressions give them ways of talking about the world that do not always reduce it to argument/counterargument, thesis and defense, critique and judgment. The thesis-driven, five-paragraph, argumentative essay—a stripped-down version of the classical oration that is rooted in doubt—is a useful tool, but it is only a single tool in what should be a well-stocked rhetorical toolbox. The world is rarely so simply understood or opponents so easily demolished as five paragraphs may lead a student to believe.

But if reified doubt flattens the aesthetic landscape and reduces diverse experiences to the single mode of questioning, it also flattens the moral landscape and reduces the number of moral responses, for doubt insists upon distance and distrust. Spenser illustrates this descent into distance and distrust at the beginning of the second canto. Following their initial shared adventures, Redcrosse Knight and Una come to the house of Archimago, the hypocritical villain and archenemy of the Faerie Queene. In a complex and comic scene, Archimago sets out to sidetrack the Redcrosse Knight from his appointed quest by deceiving him as to Una's true nature. Archimago arranges for Redcrosse Knight to be rudely awakened in the middle of the night and hustled into Una's bedroom. There he sees Una, his true love, in bed with another knight. Redcrosse Knight immediately abandons everything he knows about Una—her virtue, her faithful companionship on their adventures thus far, her willingness to stand by him when he foolishly rushed into Error's den—and doubts her integrity. And this doubt leads him to a single moral response—distrust tinged with disgust. Una's roles as daughter, companion, and friend; her steady and trustworthy character; the moral weight she bears in the romance as witness to the unified truth—all of these collapse into a single description: she now becomes simply "the woman who betrayed me."

Unfortunately for Redcrosse Knight, doubt has not here clarified his vision but obscured it: the Una the Redcrosse Knight sees in bed with another knight is not Una at all but a simulacrum, a false Una, created by Archimago himself. With a mind clouded by doubt, however, Redcrosse Knight is unable to understand this more complicated, nuanced, and sculpted moral landscape. He does not, for instance, stop to talk with the false Una, to ask what she might be doing with another knight, or to consider alternative interpretive scenarios other than the one posed by doubt. He succumbs to reified doubt, a skeptical methodology that systematically excludes alternatives and leads him to an either/or conclusion: either Una is true, or she is not. And relying on his own judgment and critique, Redcrosse Knight brands Una as false, leaves the house of Archimago under cover of darkness, and begins a downward spiral of misadventures through an increasingly flattened aesthetic and moral landscape that ends in the dungeon of pride and the cave of despair. Not until he is reunited with Una and led by her to the House of Holiness does he once again encounter genuine aesthetic richness and regain flexible moral responsiveness.

The problem with critical distance, as the incident with Redcrosse Knight highlights, is that it often distances us from the wrong thing. Rather than engendering humility with regard to our own perceptions, reified doubt is skeptical about others, about the world itself, and especially about God. It distances us from the very realities that could broaden and enrich our perspectives, redirect our anxieties, and correct our fears. It impoverishes our experiences, makes us draw back too quickly from complex situations, and at the same time hustles us forward toward judgment, forestalling the quiet space in which we might "doubt wisely." All too often, such reified doubt, such critical distance, is a burden we as professors impose on our students, which they then mistake as their own dawning awareness, much as Redcrosse Knight mistook Archimago's deception for his own critical thinking. It is ironic that the very openness and maturity that proponents of critical thinking wish to inculcate in late adolescents can disappear into the rigidity of a secondhand critical distance, or reified doubt, which imprisons their minds and souls.

The Plenitude of God's Landscape of Delight

The aesthetic and moral poverty of reified doubt contrasts with the plenitude that is the very heart and soul of Christian witness about the world, ourselves, and God. And this plenitude marks out the landscape of delight that, in contrast to the flattened landscape of doubt, is three-dimensional, full of valleys and mountains and rivers and trees that invite exploration rather than hedging that landscape of delight about.

The opening account of creation in Genesis 1 is nothing if not a narrative that overflows with plenitude and welcomes us into an ever-expanding landscape of delight. God not only speaks the world into existence; he also lovingly crafts its particulars on six successive days. God not only speaks all things into existence; he also divides them: light from darkness, waters above the firmament from those below, seas from dry land. God not only makes and divides the great spaces, but he also names them: day, night, heaven, earth, sea. God not only speaks, divides, and names his creation; he also fills it up with greater and lesser lights, fish and fowl, vegetation, and all the creeping things—each multiplying furiously after its own kind. Nor does plenitude end in Genesis 1. Genesis 2 (v. 18) reminds us that it is not good for 'ādām to be alone: a community of two is the irreducible minimum not only for companionship but also for fulfilling *our* task of working in the world, whether that task be physical or intellectual.

After the fall, Psalms, Job, and the Prophets witness that a single lament is insufficient to give voice to our griefs. The historical books of the Old Testament and the Gospels of the New Testament speak to our need for multiple perspectives of the same event, for accounts that will bear witness to the rich experiences of lived reality. The book of Proverbs reminds us that we need moral flexibility: when do I *not* answer a fool according to his folly (26:4), and when *do* I answer a fool according to his folly (26:5)? Here the wisdom writer does not set up a dilemma of doubt as I have done, by phrasing these two alternatives as questions and demanding a choice between them. Rather than opposing them in a logical dyad (either A or B), the writer simply states two propositions, or perhaps better yet, lays out two scenarios: "Do not answer fools according to their folly" and "Answer fools according to their folly." These proverbs invite us to pause when we are confronted by foolishness, to consider each situation as a unique event, to think carefully about the response that will best move the fool (who all too often is ourselves) toward wisdom. Rather than relativism (holding that it does not matter which alternative we choose) or reified doubt (holding that we cannot know the right choice), the proverbs urge us toward moral plenitude—toward active, responsible, ongoing engagement in the messy, complicated details of real life.

Our theological doctrines, as well, force us to say more rather than less. To take just one example, the body of Christ is one holy catholic and apostolic church, but it is composed of many members, each of whom is gifted in unique ways. It is surely no accident that the eschatological vision of this body depicts a city, full of living creatures, and angels "numbering myriads of myriads and thousands of thousands," and "a great multitude which no one could number, from every nation, from all tribes and peoples and tongues, standing before the throne and before the Lamb, clothed in white robes, with palm branches in their hands, and crying out with a loud voice, 'Salvation belongs to our God who sits upon the throne, and to the Lamb!'" (Rev. 5:11; 7:9–10 RSV). Indeed, in this account from the book of Revelation, the many tongues praising God are the eschatological realization of the many tongues unloosed at Pentecost, and both narratives witness against the reductive, proud, singular language of the Tower of Babel. The many tongues also remind us that a Christian understanding of complexity is centered in persons—from creation to the Trinity to the incarnation to the church. The foundation of faith is, indeed, community.

This is the consistent witness of our primary narrative, the Bible, and our secondary narratives, the creeds. We "believe in one God, the Father Almighty, Maker of heaven and earth," says the Nicene Creed, and also "in one Lord Jesus Christ, . . . God of God, Light of Light, very God of very God, begotten, not made, being of one substance with the Father." And we "believe in the Holy Spirit, the Lord and Giver of life, who proceeds from the Father and the Son, and who with . . . [them] together is worshipped and glorified." God is one, but God is three. Christ is both divine and human, without confusion or division. The Father is the maker of heaven and earth, but all things were made by Christ, and it is the Holy Spirit who is the giver of life. To recite the Nicene Creed is to confess that in our religious account of the world, at the heart of our Christian faith, is plenitude, a rich aesthetic and moral landscape, where to know anything truly is always to know more than one thing alone.

Equally important, in this aesthetic and moral landscape, is this fact: to know anything truly is to know it not alone. Indeed, God himself says, "It is *not* good for '*ādām* to be alone," and God makes this pronouncement "not good" in Eden, before the fall (Gen. 2:18). The delight Adam feels as he sees Eve, "Bone of my bone / flesh of my flesh," is an acknowledgment of increased plenitude (2:23). Even Eden can be better, more full, more complete, more complex. In Eve, Adam meets not a mirror image of himself but a true companion who with him can pursue the joint calling to work in the world and worship God.

Reified doubt, on the other hand, as we saw with the Redcrosse Knight and Una, not only flattens the aesthetic and moral landscape but also tends to collapse the boundaries of the self and others, thus fostering an unhealthy subjectivity. Again, to revert to the *Oxford English Dictionary*, the first definition of doubt says it is the "(subjective) state of uncertainty with regard to the truth or reality of anything."

The Redcrosse Knight, consumed by doubt, merges the complex, personal, three-dimensional Una into a single extension of himself: she becomes merely "the woman who betrayed me." And once the Redcrosse Knight merges Una into his own subjectivity, he feels free to discard her. By violating the boundaries of her personhood, he deprives himself of her necessary and external point of view and opens himself up to be absorbed into the false world of the counterfeit Duessa.

As a number of theorists have explained, radical doubt is not a methodology that a person can consistently maintain if one wishes to live in the world rather than in an insane asylum. Without beginning with a modicum of trust—for instance, with the assumption that another person is talking sense, not gibberish—a person is reduced to a solipsistic existence. Indeed, it was just this realization of the basic moral necessity of trust that moved Augustine along from skepticism to faith. In the *Confessions*, he testifies that

> little by little, Lord, with a most gentle and merciful hand you touched and calmed my heart. I considered the innumerable things I believed which I had not seen, events which occurred when I was not present, such as many incidents in the history of the nations, many facts concerning places and cities which I had never seen, many things accepted on the word of friends, many from physicians, many from other people. Unless we believed what we were told, we would do nothing at all in this life. Finally, I realized how unmoveably sure I was about the identity of my parents from whom I came, which I could not know unless I believed what I had heard.[11]

Because trust is necessary for life, reified doubt can be pernicious, for it sneaks something into belief under the guise of questioning everything. Satan's interrogative in Genesis 3, "Did God say, 'You shall not eat from any tree of the garden?'" is all the more dangerous because it is manipulative and dishonest under the guise of asking a question. Eve's answer—and more important, her own attitude toward God—is shaped not only by the false information embedded in the question, but also by a methodology of doubt that pares away the rich possibilities of the garden. Doubt, in other words, draws Eve away from looking around at the plenitude of the garden—with its implications of the generous Creator—and redirects her attention to a set of binary alternatives: "If God has refused you the fruit of this tree, God must not be good; and if God is not good, you need not obey God." And doubt likewise collapses necessary boundaries—"You will be like God," Satan murmurs—while insinuating a new set of beliefs.

Plenitude within Boundaries and the Bonds of Community

True plenitude needs boundaries, and the biblical and theological witness to plenitude insists on delineated borders: the proper division of light from darkness, waters from dry land; the creation of humanity in God's image but not identical to him. Hence, the desire to erase that boundary, to be like God, constitutes the primal sin. The Chalcedonian

---

11. Augustine, *Confessions*, trans. Henry Chadwick (New York: Oxford University Press, 1991), 6.5.

Creed thus insists on Christ's divinity and humanity, without confusion or division.

These deeply Christian conjunctions of plenitude, boundaries, persons, and communities are echoed by the Russian thinker Mikhail Bakhtin. He observes that "aesthetic culture is a culture of boundaries and hence presupposes that life is enveloped by a warm atmosphere of deepest trust."[12] But when this trust is shattered, and the I-for-myself becomes the most important category—as in the immanentization of God or the psychologization of God and religion—the lived life "tends to recoil and hide deep inside itself, tends to withdraw into its own inner infinitude, *is afraid of boundaries*, strives to dissolve them, for it has no faith in the essentialness and kindness of the power that gives form from outside; any viewpoint from outside is refused."[13] But when the view from the outside is refused (as when Redcrosse Knight discards Una), it is difficult to develop judgment, the ability to arrive at a sound or correct notion or to apprehend mentally the relation of two objects. Without a true intellectual community, it is difficult if not impossible to pursue intellectual tasks with integrity, because a single point of view is insufficient to embrace the plenitude of the world.

Spenser's own narrative technique is as scrupulous about boundaries as it is about plenitude. His allegorical devices are not mere husks to be discarded for the real "moral" of the story. The Redcrosse Knight is a Christian everyman: outfitted with the armor of God, sent into the world, and faced with temptations—to most of which he succumbs. But he is also a typical eighteen-year-old, brash and self-confident on the surface, seething with worries on the inside, and wracked with sexual desires and insecurities. It is just that enriched realism, as we are caught up in the Redcrosse Knight's misadventures, that allows us to be educated within a rich aesthetic and moral landscape. For Spenser, choosing the genre of romance with its "allegorical devices" is not merely imitating Sidney by combining teaching and moving with delighting. He is also laying out an educational landscape that deeply reflects his reformed sacramentalism.

In Calvin's (and Spenser's and Augustine's) understanding of the sacraments, the outward physical element—bread, wine, or water—is "a visible sign of a sacred thing, . . . a visible form of an invisible grace."[14] Physical reality and spiritual reality are not merely symbolically joined—as in

12. Susan M. Felch and Paul Contino, eds., *Bakhtin and Religion: A Feeling for Faith* (Evanston, IL: Northwestern University Press, 2001), 203.

13. Ibid.

14. John Calvin, *The Institutes of the Christian Religion*, trans. Henry Beveridge, from the author's last (1559) edition (Grand Rapids: Christian Classics Ethereal Library), 4.14.1; http://www.ccel.org/ccel/calvin/institutes.html (accessed August 29, 2005).

Zwingli. Nor are they merged in a transubstantial union. Rather, they are intimately related—they look at one another face to face, we might say—without being merged into one. There is a true representation and "sacramental union" between outward signs and the things they signify (Westminster Confession, chap. 27), a union neither "empty and hollow" (Belgic Confession, art. 33) nor claiming identity between sign and signified. Bread remains bread, its physical boundaries intact; and the spirit is renewed spiritually, by the Spirit of the Triune God, "who has not a body like us."

This intimate and yet unmerged relationship can also be seen in the "general" sacraments. In the *Institutes*, Calvin holds that the term "sacrament" includes "all the signs which God ever commanded men to use, that he might make them sure and confident of the truth of his promises."[15] Two natural objects that God deepens into sacraments by the word of his promise are the tree of life in the Garden of Eden as a pledge of immortality, and the rainbow as a pledge that the earth will not be destroyed by a flood. Calvin concludes:

> These were to Adam and Noah as sacraments: not that the tree could give Adam and Eve the immortality which it could not give to itself; or the bow (which is only a reflection of the solar rays on the opposite clouds) could have the effect of confining the waters; but they had a mark engraven on them by the word of God, to be proofs and seals of his covenant. The tree was previously a tree, and the bow a bow; but when they were inscribed with the word of God, a new form was given to them: they began to be what they previously were not. . . . For why is the shapeless and the coined silver not of the same value, seeing they are the same metal? Just because the former has nothing but its own nature, whereas the latter, impressed with the public stamp, becomes money, and receives a new value. And shall the Lord not be able to stamp his creatures with his word, that things which were formerly bare elements may become sacraments?[16]

We need physical representations because we ourselves are bodies. But we also need physical representations to be deepened into significance. Calvin quotes John Chrysostom's sixtieth homily: "Were we incorporeal, he would give us these things in a naked and incorporeal form. Now because our souls are implanted in bodies, he delivers spiritual things under things visible. Not that the qualities which are set before us in the sacraments are inherent in the nature of the things, but God gives them this signification."[17] Similarly, Calvin claims of general sacra-

15. Ibid., 4.14.18.
16. Ibid.
17. Ibid., 4.14.3.

ments that the tree of life was a real tree and the rainbow was a real bow. Indeed, says Calvin, if anyone looks at a rainbow and contends "that the variety of colours arises naturally from the rays reflected by the opposite cloud, let us admit the fact."[18] But while the distinctness of physical things remains unchallenged—things remain things—their meaning is deepened by the language that interprets them: deepened into grace by the promises of God's word; deepened into aesthetic and moral education by the allegorical devices of Spenser's *Faerie Queene*. If by virtue of God's word, a tree becomes more than a tree, it nevertheless does not cease to be less than a tree. If by virtue of Spenser's genius, the Redcrosse Knight becomes an emblem of the Christian life and therefore more than a questing knight, he does not become less than a questing knight. And it is a hermeneutics of delight that allows us to experience the world with this deepened and enriched sense of realism.

In moving from a special hermeneutics of the sacraments to a general hermeneutics of the imagination, Spenser retains Calvin's understanding of the relation of physical things—creation, the world, literary genres, the romance, heroes and dragons and monsters, real things with their own integrity and boundaries—with spiritual realities. His allegorical devices do not collapse character into meaning, thing into spirit. But rather, as with the sacraments, one is related to the other by means of words, by the naming (or preaching) that "makes us understand what the visible sign means." For "a sacrament consists of the word and the external sign." Allegories, like sacraments, "lead [us] by the hand to that to which the sign tends and directs us" without collapsing distinctions, and like sacraments, they move us toward action.[19]

This deepening of things via the word, deepening of persons in community, of unmerged boundaries, is what ultimately fashions the noble person in virtuous and gentle discipline, what educates the mind and heart toward maturity. And for those of us who confess the faith and profess the faith, this progress toward maturity best unfolds in the company of others who also take up their journey within the landscape of delight.

---

18. Ibid., 4.14.18.
19. Ibid., 4.14.4.

7

CHRISTIAN HOSPITALITY IN THE INTELLECTUAL COMMUNITY

Aurelie A. Hagstrom

SADLY, IT IS NO EXAGGERATION to say that many church-related schools in the last century have downplayed or even forsaken their Christian heritage and identity.[1] The Christian character of American colleges and universities, often taken for granted in bygone years, more recently has prompted debate, contention, and embarrassment. Where dissension is absent, confusion too often abounds. No longer can we say that "everyone knows" what it means to be Catholic, Baptist, or Lutheran; hence, what it means to be a Catholic, Baptist, or Lutheran university is equally opaque. Nor in a post-Christian culture can church-related colleges and universities simply rely on such things as mandatory chapel attendance, compulsory theology classes, or strict student-life policies to sustain an institution's Christian character.

---

1. Recent studies that trace the loss of Christian identity in church-related colleges and universities are George M. Marsden, *The Soul of the American University: From Protestant Establishment to Established Unbelief* (New York: Oxford University Press, 1994); and James Burtchaell, *The Dying of the Light: The Disengagement of Colleges and Universities from Their Christian Churches* (Grand Rapids: Eerdmans, 1998).

In such times as these, we must think anew about how to ensure that our Christian colleges and universities remain vibrant institutions capable of flourishing in the future. And among the requisite strategies for such renewal, we need not only excellent Christian scholarship, but also a revival of concrete, integrative practices to sustain the life of the Christian community.

One relevant strategy for renewal, and the one to which I want to turn attention, is constituted by the Christian virtue of hospitality. Its importance as a key virtue for Christian higher education is conveyed well by Elizabeth Newman: "The practice of hospitality—by reflecting a larger tradition and thus the formation of specific virtues—creates a place (a space) for Christian identity to appear as a whole way of life. The practice forms our understanding of the intellectual life and even more our understanding of the final goal of higher education: love and faithfulness to God."[2] My argument, in short, is that Christian higher education must recover and appropriate hospitality as a theologically significant moral category, one that benefits both the cultivation of community within colleges and universities as well as the pursuit of scholarly inquiry in the classroom. As a historic Christian practice, hospitality is distinctly communal and self-giving, embodying a way of being and thinking about the "other" or the "stranger." It rests on the basic conviction that in welcoming others we are also welcoming God, and by welcoming God we are participating in God's reconciling love for the world, manifest in God's Triune nature.[3]

The practice of hospitality represents fruitful terrain for colleges and universities that want to cultivate stronger and more faithfully Christian ways of regarding such diverse aspects of university life as academic freedom, faculty hiring, and student-life policies. As a signal virtue of Christian thought and life, hospitality is especially helpful for those struggling with the Christian character of their institutions precisely because it applies both inside and outside the classroom; it integrates both ideas and practices. It is grounded not only in the conceptual theological framework of being Christian, but also in the concrete embodiments of Christian practices. Hospitality is fundamentally an expression of and witness to God's grace, since all of us are guests of God's hospitality and are called to embody that hospitality to others through word and deed alike. As such, it may help to bridge the conversation between those concerned about whether a university is sufficiently "Christian" in its daily

---

2. Elizabeth Newman, "Hospitality and Christian Higher Education," *Christian Scholar's Review* 33, no. 1 (2003): 87.

3. See Reinhard Hütter, "Hospitality and Truth," in *Bound to Be Free: Evangelical Catholic Engagements in Ecclesiology, Ethics, and Ecumenism* (Grand Rapids: Eerdmans, 2004), 62–68.

campus life, and those who are concerned to protect academic freedom and promote rigorous scholarly inquiry in the classroom.

One qualification demands attention from the outset: hospitality reflects a radically different and compelling alternative to tolerance. Hospitality, I maintain, is preferable to tolerance principally because tolerance—unlike Christian hospitality—is unable to sustain either communities or conversations in moments of intellectual, moral, or religious crisis. Tolerance is ill suited to address matters of deep controversy because of its tendency to trivialize what is most important to us. It is, in fact, a false sort of engagement. Rather than demanding a true acknowledgment and embrace of the other, tolerance instead involves a type of "entertainment" of the other. Rather than the costly, risky engagement of hospitality, tolerance superficially entertains another's worldview, beliefs, and values. This "entertainment mode" of tolerance—what Stanley Fish has described as boutique multiculturalism—has no built-in telos or end that would arrive at an objective moral truth.[4] Tolerance is more an exercise in abstraction—a distancing from distinct moral settings; it is a mode that fits aptly with a postmodern, pluralistic world in which truth is always elusive and, in fact, infinitely deferred.[5]

By contrast, hospitality is incarnational, morally attuned, and prompted by commitments to truthfulness in word and deed. It does not exist as a disembodied attitude toward others, but instead brings concrete strangers together in rituals of peaceful engagement. Christian hospitality grows out of the morally rigorous demands of Jesus Christ's unsurpassable example. And while skirting false dichotomies between legalism and latitudinarianism, hospitable Christians remain steadfastly committed to "whatever is true, whatever is noble, whatever is right, whatever is pure, whatever is lovely, whatever is admirable" (Phil. 4:8 NIV). They remember that Christian hospitality must follow the pattern of God's hospitality to us, extended supremely through Christ's death for us "while we were still sinners" (Rom. 5:8 NIV). In all these ways, hospitality surpasses tolerance by demanding a personal, authentic encounter that is self-emptying and open even to those with whom we have deep philosophical, theological, and political disagreements. Hospitality thus involves far greater commitments and costs than mere tolerance, which aspires to little more than "entertaining" those who, while different from us, are nice to us, so that we in turn may be nice to them.

4. See Stanley Fish, "Boutique Multiculturalism: Or, Why Liberals Are Incapable of Thinking about Hate Speech," *Critical Inquiry* 23 (Winter 1997): 378–95.
5. Hütter, "Hospitality and Truth," 66–67.

Hospitality: Definitions and Descriptions

Hospitality above all is a biblical phenomenon that is developed as a moral category in both the Old and New Testaments, one that Scripture exegetes, theologians, and ethicists have rediscovered as a sustaining virtue for Christian community of all kinds. Biblically, for example, one finds the practice of hospitality in evidence when Abraham welcomes the three heavenly visitors at Mamre in Genesis 18 and thereby opens himself to the surprising revelation of God's promise and plan. The New Testament notion of hospitality is evidenced in experiences like the countercultural table fellowship of Jesus of Nazareth in Luke's Gospel.[6] Eating with the outcast tax collectors and sinners, Jesus welcomes all and invites them into the kingdom of God through his healing words of forgiveness.[7]

Regarded more theologically, hospitality can serve as a coherent theological framework that connects thoughtful faith with daily life and the concerns of social justice.[8] Indeed, properly understood, hospitality becomes a means by which we, in earnest commitment to God's redemptive work in the world, share in the labors that bring nearer the realization of the kingdom of God among us. God thus is the host who offers a radical hospitality to the human race, which is in need of redemption from sin and death. The death and resurrection of Jesus is God's hospitality to the world, offering an invitation to us for forgiveness, healing, and the fullness of redemption. We participate in the extension of this hospitality to the world when we bear witness to his kingdom in word and deed. Theologically, we can speak of a "hospitality of truth," which is our responsibility always to bear witness to his truth and to give a reason for the hope that is within us.

Put into explicitly ethical terms, hospitality to the stranger can operate as a metaphor definitive of the Christian moral life in general. Hospitality

6. See D. E. Smith, "Table Fellowship as a Literary Motif in the Gospel of Luke," *Journal of Biblical Literature* 106 (1987): 613–38. Also helpful is idem, *From Symposium to Eucharist: The Banquet in the Early Christian World* (Minneapolis: Fortress, 2003).

7. Cf. Gillian Feeley-Harnack, *The Lord's Table: The Meaning of Food in Early Judaism and Christianity* (Washington, DC: Smithsonian Press, 1994); Joachim Jeremias, *The Eucharistic Words of Jesus*, trans. Norman Perrin (New York: Scribner, 1966); and Arthur Just, *The Ongoing Feast: Table Fellowship and Eschatology at Emmaus* (Collegeville, MN: Liturgical Press, 1993).

8. Christine Pohl, *Making Room: Recovering Hospitality as a Christian Tradition* (Grand Rapids: Eerdmans, 1999), 8. In addition, see Gary Macy, *The Banquet's Wisdom: A Short History of the Theologies of the Lord's Supper* (Mahwah, NJ: Paulist Press, 1992); and Abraham Malherbe, *Social Aspects of Early Christianity*, 2nd ed. (Philadelphia: Fortress, 1983).

in this vein has stimulated the work of a number of scholars in recent years.[9] Thomas Ogletree explains:

> For moral understanding, the central thrust of the metaphor of hospitality is to break the preoccupation of ethical theory with perceptions and reasonings stemming from a given actor's own vantage point in the world . . . [and thus underwrite] a de-centering of perspective. To offer hospitality is to welcome something new, unfamiliar, and unknown into our life-world. . . . Hospitality designates occasions of potential discovery which can open up our narrow, provincial worlds.[10]

Ogletree points to the ways in which hospitality goes beyond simply referring to literal interactions with strangers. On a deeper level, it suggests an attention to "otherness" in a variety of forms. This attention to the other includes receptivity, openness, regard for characteristic differences in the experience of others, and efforts to transcend artificial barriers. "For theological ethics, the religious sense of otherness is foundational," he writes.[11] In similar fashion, Lucien Richard's *Living the Hospitality of God* expresses concern for the "other" or stranger and offers a paradigm for the Christian's orientation in and perspective on the world:

> Reflection on the Scripture's teaching on hospitality to the stranger offers a particular lens or key by which Christians interpret circumstances and realities in their attempt to envision the whole of life in relation to God and to the other. . . . Such a command provides the possibility of a critical stance towards present forms of existence and order in the social world. It can lead us to an acceptable model of humanhood and calls us to social action on behalf of a new earth.[12]

At their best, theologians like Ogletree and Richard develop the moral imperatives of the practice of hospitality in terms of its broader biblical context: the kingdom of God. The kingdom of God was the main theme of the preaching of Jesus (Matt. 4:17; Mark 1:15; Luke 11:20). The kingdom is not a place or a thing, but an activity, the reign of God over his creation. This sovereign rule of God breaks into human history

---

9. Thomas Ogletree, *Hospitality to the Stranger* (Philadelphia: Fortress, 1985); John Koenig, *New Testament Hospitality* (Philadelphia: Fortress, 1985); Pohl, *Making Room*; Monika Hellwig, *Guests of God: Stewards of Divine Creation* (New York: Paulist Press, 1999); Brendan Byrne, *The Hospitality of God* (Collegeville, MN: Liturgical Press, 2000); Lucien Richard, *Living the Hospitality of God* (New York: Paulist Press, 2000); and Darrell Fasching and Dell deChant, *Comparative Religious Ethics: A Narrative Approach* (Oxford: Blackwell, 2001).

10. Ogletree, *Hospitality to the Stranger*, 2.

11. Ibid., 3.

12. Richard, *Living the Hospitality of God*, 1–2.

through the words and deeds of Jesus and is established in a definitive way through his cross and resurrection.[13] The full realization of God's kingdom will come with Christ's glorious return at the end of time. It is within the already/not yet dynamic of the kingdom of God that Christians are called to exercise the mission of mediating the kingdom to the world. In the interim between the ascension and the parousia, the Holy Spirit empowers the church for mission in promoting and mediating the kingdom of God through word and deed.

The moral imperative of hospitality to the stranger is to be understood within this context. The kingdom, while eschatological, is not simply otherworldly. It breaks into the here and now and brings about a social transformation. God's reign reverses social order and turns the values of the world upside down.[14] The kingdom reintegrates the poor and marginal into society and emphasizes radical inclusiveness. All are invited and welcome, but especially the poor, the outcast, the sinner, and the stranger. The kingdom generates invitation, welcome, and challenge. It overturns discrimination, exclusion, and marginalization in all their forms.[15] As Sallie McFague writes, "The central symbol of the new vision of life, the Kingdom of God, is a community joined together in a festive meal where the bread that sustains life and the joy that sustains the spirit are shared with all."[16] The kingdom of God is a realm of hospitality.

Hospitality in the Christian University

How can the Christian practice of hospitality serve as a moral category for the enrichment of life within the Christian academy? In the first instance, it can help us to frame questions of diversity on our campuses. For example, students from different religious traditions who are welcomed to our campuses are guests of our hospitality. They are the "others" who challenge us to make room, be receptive, and remain attentive to their worldviews. The sponsoring religious community of the university is the "host," whether Catholic, Lutheran, Baptist, or Methodist. And those students, faculty, administrators, or staff from diverse religious traditions, who are part of the campus community, are the "guests." Understanding the character of both roles is important, because clarity on these points allows the host and the guest to be true to their own

13. See John Bright, *The Kingdom of God* (New York: Abingdon, 1953).

14. See Frank Matera, *New Testament Ethics* (Louisville: Westminster John Knox, 1996).

15. Richard, *Living the Hospitality of God*, 40–41.

16. Sallie McFague, *Models of God: Theology for an Ecological Nuclear Age* (Philadelphia: Fortress, 1987), 173.

identities in an atmosphere of mutual acceptance and welcome, and to do so without compromising into a bland relativism that diminishes the uniqueness and gifts of these identities.

Pushing the metaphor of hospitable host and welcomed guest one step further makes the point. In one sense a host is the one who sets the banquet table. Within the context of a church-related institution, the "table is set" in a certain way according to the sponsoring religious community. Guests are welcomed to the table, but the hosts are not expected to change the table setting simply because the guests are not used to the hosts' habits and customs. The religious identity, praxis, and worship of the host are not abandoned in the interchange of hospitality. Indeed, it is only the clear identity of the host that makes the guest feel secure and welcome. If the customs or habits of the table manners of the host are unclear or ambiguous, the guest feels awkward and unsure of how to behave or react. The Catholic, Lutheran, Baptist, or Methodist identity of the university has to be clear to others who are welcomed as guests.

Some might object that a host should accommodate the guest and even change any practices, customs, or rituals necessary to make sure one's guests are comfortable. However, Newman points out, "From this perspective, hospitality then simply underwrites the ideology of pluralism and diversity, . . . where we simply allow or tolerate different points of view."[17] While a thoughtful practice of hospitality may require a certain flexibility of the host, the identity, traditions, and praxis of the host (and the guest) must be clearly maintained. The alternative is to let hospitality give way to the relativistic banalities of mere tolerance, denying host and guest alike the honest opportunity to judge, instruct, or learn from the other.

Hospitality, therefore, does not prohibit the judging, analyzing, and classification of the other. Nor does Christian hospitality imply a type of unconditionality and openness without any distinctions whatsoever. In fact, such free-floating unconditionality impinges on the integrity of both host and guest. Newman makes the helpful suggestion that the rubric of "making distinctions but not drawing boundaries" can be instructive here. Indeed, authentic engagement can happen only when real differences between host and guest are acknowledged, not ignored.

> Practitioners of hospitality are justified or are displaying faithfulness to this practice (and thus to God and the world) when they judge or make distinctions about those ideologies or practices that contradict or even negate hospitality. . . . Such drawing of distinctions . . . rests in the realization that truth cannot be coerced, but remains vibrant by the power of persuasion or attraction. Inasmuch as hospitality genuinely

17. Newman, "Hospitality and Christian Higher Education," 85.

acknowledges the other as both similar (a child of God) and other, . . .
then it is a practice that allows for genuine difference to appear and true
engagement to take place.[18]

Christian colleges and universities must honor the truth about differences and distinctions in any practice of hospitality on their campuses.
Reinhard Hütter claims that although this truth about differences can
be painful, we cannot trade truth for hospitality: "Heaven's hospitality
turns out to be painful because it does not trade truth for hospitality.
. . . Hospitality can only be truthful and thus true hospitality if it does
not betray the nature of the host and so does not undercut the truth that
presupposes a personal relationship."[19]

Beyond informing general issues of campus diversity, hospitality may
also provide a helpful context for conversations about academic freedom,
which can be an "intellectual hospitality" on our campuses. One thing
that happens as a result of Christian hospitality, concretely expressed for
example in table fellowship, is conversation as host and guest tell their
stories. This interchange is encouraged by the experience of hospitality. Indeed, the atmosphere of invitation, welcome, and *communio* of
persons is precisely what gives rise to sharing and storytelling. It also
provides a context within which healthy debate and disputation may take
place. When there is a level of trust between the host and guest, both
are empowered to tell their story of how they understand the world and
reveal their views on the "Good." For this reason, table fellowship offers
a setting where hostility can be transformed into hospitality, where the
stranger may be welcomed as guest and eventually as friend. But even
this transformation from stranger to guest to friend does not imply
conformity or sameness between host and guest. Neither party loses
the particularity of identity, traditions, and praxis. To erase differences
would be a concession to the false sort of politically correct engagement
known as tolerance, explained above as entertainment rather than authentic encounter.

As host, a church-related university's sponsoring religious community
tells its story in a variety of ways across campus life. Mission statements,
curriculum, student-life policies, and faculty-hiring procedures are but
a few examples of how this story is told. This is the "narrative" of the
host, if you will. And when the guests hear this story, they cannot then
expect the host to change it. Likewise, the guests have a right to their
own stories, without the host forcing them to change their perceptions,
convictions, and values. In this context academic freedom can flourish,

18. Ibid., 87, 89.
19. Hütter, "Hospitality and Truth," 59–60.

as long as the host's narrative is understood and respected, and as long as it is likewise understood that the whole life of the campus is fundamentally oriented to this story, without apology.

Here we raise a perhaps controversial question, whether or not a robust intellectual hospitality allows for the possibility of conversion. Does academic freedom in Christian higher education curtail or even prohibit Christian proclamation of the gospel? Within a hospitable dialogue between the Christian host community and its non-Christian guests, is there space for proclaiming the need for gospel conversion? Or would such a challenge be "inhospitable" to the guests? In my judgment, dialogue and proclamation must be linked. To dialogue with others presumes that we have something to share. In the case of the Christian host, this "something" is Jesus Christ. Thus, dialogue is not separate from the proclamation of Christ. It is precisely in the hospitable proclamation of the gospel that the Christian host community honors truth and maintains integrity. Ralph Wood puts the point keenly and explicitly, though in a spirit of "fear and trembling":

> Our welcome to Hindu and Sikh and secular students alike must be so generous that we do not merely tolerate them and thus trivialize their differences with us. Our commonality does not lie in some storyless and deracinated humanity that we supposedly share. Christians believe that we have something far deeper and more concrete in common with them— namely our shared creation and redemption in the God of the Gospel. Faith in this Lord requires that we extend non-Christians the hospitality that takes them seriously. Such seriousness requires us not only to honor their own narratives by studying the texts and traditions that undergird them, but also to contest these narratives with our own. This contestation must never be harsh or coercive but always generous and persuasive. Even so, our non-Christian students and faculty must be made aware that their own conversion remains a very real possibility. When this happens it is a matter of neither conquest nor defeat, for our one true and only common ground is Golgotha. For there lies, we believe, the one victory in which no human being is defeated.[20]

True Dialogue in the Kenotic Model of Jesus Christ

The radical character of Christian hospitality as a practice conducive to the true dialogue of intellectual community stands in stark contrast to mere tolerance. Hospitality is much more engaging, risky, and costly than is the meager tolerance of diversity for its own sake. Hospitality

20. Ralph Wood, *Contending for the Faith: The Church's Engagement with Culture* (Waco: Baylor University Press, 2003), 122.

takes the identity, story, and tradition of the guest seriously as a foundation for table fellowship and meaningful dialogue, and it does so without pretending to be less than one is as a Christian, vacating one's own theological identity or story, or taking recourse in small talk or superficial celebration of "difference" for its own sake. Hospitality rightly regarded thus moves beyond reticent and sheer tolerance to embrace genuine dialogue, a basic form of "engagement of the other." Dialogue has its "own integrity" and above all else is "a manner of acting, an attitude and a spirit . . . which implies concern, respect, and hospitality towards the other."[21] Hospitable attitudes such as attention, receptivity, and openness are typically expressed in dialogue and conversation. The hospitable "creation of a free space" most often begins in the experience of dialogue, as Richard explains:

> Hospitality involves a way of thinking without the presumption of knowing beforehand what is in the mind of the other; dialogue with the other is essential. I must let the other tell me who he or she is. Hospitality decenters our perspective; my story counts but so does the story of the other. . . . To welcome the other means to let the other tell his or her story. So listening becomes a basic attitude of hospitality. Being hospitable means being genuinely open to the other, interested in sharing, learning, and receptive to the learning the other might possess.[22]

Such welcome and reciprocity for the sake of wisdom, while central to hospitality, is absent from the spirit of politically correct tolerance.

At the other end of the spectrum, the hallmark of hospitality is not conflict. The spiritual activity of conversation or dialogue is not about argument, contention, or controversy. It is not about winning a debate or "coming out on top" in a contest—though the interlocutors may leave their exchange transformed by the encounter. The spirituality of dialogue is characterized by the same virtues as hospitality: gratuitousness, welcome, receptivity, and a recognition of interdependency with others. A spirituality of hospitality opens up the capacity for dialogue. The free space opened up in a spirituality of hospitality invites the engagement of conversation and transforming interaction with others, even those with whom there are deep differences and disagreements.

The Christian theological underpinning for intellectual community so regarded derives from the kenotic model of Jesus Christ. Indeed,

21. Pontifical Council for Interreligious Dialogue, *Dialogue and Proclamation*, no. 29 (1991); http://www.vatican.va/roman_curia/pontifical_councils/interelg/documents/rc_pc_interelg_doc_19051991_dialogue-and-proclamatio_en.html (accessed August 29, 2005). Cf. Michael Barnes, *Theology and the Dialogue of Religions* (Cambridge: Cambridge University Press, 2002).

22. Richard, *Living the Hospitality of God*, 12.

the very spirituality of conversation I am presupposing demands an attitude of *kenosis*. If one is full of oneself and seeking only one's own interests, there is no room for the free space of true encounter and dialogue. A spirit of self-sufficiency can lead to the conviction that nothing can be gained by dialogue and conversation. Self-emptying servitude, on the other hand, implies a continuous movement of conversion, dying to self in order to live for God. This dynamic is necessary for the openness required for dialogue. Dying to self does not mean, however, setting aside elements of personal identity or beliefs out of fear that they might hinder true dialogue with others of different races, cultures, ethnicities, and religions. *Kenosis* actually requires an affirmation of one's own identity. Paradoxically, the more one is rooted in one's own identity and traditions, the more open one can be to others.

For this reason, some of the obstacles to genuine dialogue include selfishness, self-absorption, and arrogance. True dialogue does not leave room for smug self-reliance or a demand to have one's own way. Impatience can also prevent true encounter since dialogue is always a process that takes time. Usually there are no quick results or easy answers when dealing with highly complex issues and concerns with others. Lack of respect often hinders dialogue because the identity, views, and convictions of the other are not taken seriously or welcomed. A shortage of humility also constitutes an obvious obstacle to hospitable dialogue since it prevents the possibility of receiving and learning from the other. Suspicions about the other's motivations for engaging in dialogue can also inhibit an authentic encounter.

True dialogue in the context of Christian hospitality is certainly not an easy task. It is hard to keep an open mind, to try imaginatively and charitably to enter into the other's way of thinking and perception. It is difficult to persevere when apparently nothing is being achieved. The spiritual activity of conversation, therefore, must include a generosity of spirit that opens a space within us for welcoming challenges and other points of view. The spirituality of conversation calls for a change of heart—nothing short of the fullness of Christian conversion—in order to initiate a dialogue with others who may be quite different from us, who hold contrary positions, and who challenge our deeply held values, convictions, and beliefs. This conversion of heart creates an inner receptive charity that can become the space for the mutual exchange of gifts. *Kenosis* is the way of moving from contention and controversy to genuine dialogue. When understood as a face-to-face encounter, dialogue is not merely a way of speaking; it is also an exercise in charity. Dialogue is a spiritual engagement with the other, which can then, in turn, open us up to experiencing God.

The spirituality of conversation has a generative power in creating a community of reconciliation. Through mutuality, reciprocity, and intimacy, which are the fruits of a spirituality of conversation, a community can be formed. Hospitality, as expressed in conversation, has the ability to nurture communion among persons. Dialogue can nurture peace and understanding even among diverse cultures at odds with one another, prompting Theodore Zeldin to observe:

> Never has there been more need for conversation between civilizations, because never have they been able to inflict so much damage on each other. . . . Our education cannot be complete until we have had conversations with every continent, and every civilization. It is a humbling experience which makes one conscious of the enormous difficulty of living in peace when there is so much injustice, but which also gives one great hopes, every time one succeeds in having a conversation which establishes a sense of common humanity, a mutual respect.[23]

Conclusion

The metaphor of hospitality is helpful in theologically framing the questions of diversity and academic freedom on the campuses of Christian universities. By using this model of campus life, Christian universities can create an atmosphere that is rigorously intellectual, academically free, and even hospitable to the conflict and tension inherently part of the educational enterprise. Christian hospitality makes room for both the gifts and burdens of others and provides a means toward substantive and real community in a fragmented world. Hospitality can manifest itself in friendship and truthfulness alike. And this emphasis on truth is important because it helps counter a tendency toward the mere tolerance of other beliefs and ideas, which can slip into a well-intentioned but sloppy relativism and indifference that ignores claims of Christian revelation and objectivity.

As a practice, hospitality integrates Christian identity into the various dimensions of campus life, helping to establish the elusive quality of genuine community that the world vainly seeks apart from the church. James Fodor speaks in a related vein: "Ironically, it is the Christian virtue of humility and not the modern liberal democratic ideal of tolerance which is genuinely open to the otherness of the stranger."[24] Church-re-

---

23. Theodore Zeldin, *Conversation: How Talk Can Change Our Lives* (Mahwah, NJ: Hidden Spring, 2000), 91, 93–94.
24. James Fodor, *Christian Hermeneutics: Paul Ricoeur and the Refiguring of Theology* (Oxford: Clarendon, 1995), 20.

lated colleges and universities—grounded in faith, sustained by hope, and prompted by love—can through the practice of Christian hospitality come to embody vital, lively places of learning, all the stronger and more interesting than their secular peers, and precisely because and not in spite of their religious identity. For these reasons, Christian hospitality thereby gives fitting expression to one mode of Christian faith as a foundation for intellectual community.[25]

25. Of relevance but not otherwise mentioned in this chapter are Hans Boersma, *Violence, Hospitality, and the Cross: Reappropriating the Atonement Tradition* (Grand Rapids: Baker, 2004); Delia Halverson, *The Gift of Hospitality: In Church, in the Home, in All of Life* (St. Louis: Chalice, 1999); Daniel Homan and Lonni Collins Pratt, *Radical Hospitality* (Brewster, MA: Paraclete, 2002); Arland Hultgren, "The Johannine Footwashing (13:1–11) as a Symbol of Eschatological Hospitality," *New Testament Studies* 28 (1982): 539–46; David Kirk, "Hospitality: Essence of Eastern Christian Lifestyle," *Diakonia* 16, no. 2 (1981): 104–17; Eugene LaVerdiere, *Dining in the Kingdom of God* (Chicago: Liturgical Training Publications, 1994); Henri J. M. Nouwen, *On Hospitality and Other Matters*, Monastic Studies, no. 10 (Pine City, NY: Mount Saviour Monastery, 1974); and Ana Maria Pineda, "Hospitality," in *Practicing Our Faith*, ed. Dorothy C. Bass (San Francisco: Jossey-Bass, 1997), 38–56.

8

||||||||||||||||||||||||||||||||||||||||

COMMUNAL CONFLICT IN THE
POSTMODERN CHRISTIAN UNIVERSITY

||||||||||||||||||||||||||||||||||||||||

Steven R. Harmon

THE CURRENT ATTENTION TO THE integration of faith and learning in Christian universities may prove to be the most significant development in the history of Christian higher education in America. In many cases, institutions are having the first serious conversation since their founding about their distinctiveness as church-related schools, and about what that might mean for the teaching of all university disciplines. Yet discussions of the integration of faith and learning sometimes result in faculty uneasiness about such an enterprise, especially when someone suggests that theological reflection is integral to the pursuit of diverse academic disciplines in a Christian intellectual community. Conflict over Baylor University's "Baylor 2012" institutional vision and its call for the integration of faith and learning has recently received considerable public attention,[1] yet similar battles are being waged less publicly at numerous colleges with historic denominational ties. Many have

1. See Robert Benne, "Crisis of Identity: A Clash over Faith and Learning," *Christian Century* 121, no. 2 (January 27, 2004): 22–26; Ralph C. Wood, "The Heresy of Solitary Faith," *Christianity Today* 48, no. 1 (January 2004): 58–60; and Katherine S. Mangan, "Baylor President Faces the Test of His Tenure," *Chronicle of Higher Education*, September

surely had the experience of discussing religious matters at lunch with fellow faculty members from various departments and realizing, during a less-than-cordial turn in the conversation, that the cross-disciplinary integration of faith and learning in their own institution would be rough going indeed.

In some quarters, aversion to cross-disciplinary theological conversation threatens to paralyze encouraging steps toward the integration of faith and learning before the movement is fully underway. Institutions of Christian higher education must therefore recognize and address such aversion—and the paralysis that accompanies it—if they hope to make real progress toward intellectual community founded upon Christian faith. After identifying the sources of academic conflict avoidance that stifle interdisciplinary debate of matters of ultimate concern, I argue that constructive conflict, located within a tradition grounded in the practice of worship, is vital for the integration of faith and learning in the postmodern context of today's Christian university.

Giving Up the Contest

Faculty aversion to serious discussion of the integration of faith and learning may be attributed to at least three factors. First, many faculty members have personal experience of the theological controversies that have divided most American denominations in recent years. The real divisions in American Christianity today are not as much between denominations as within them.[2] My own experience has been of the theological-political controversy in the Southern Baptist Convention during the past three decades;[3] yet faculty from most other denominations can tell a similar story of bitter conflict over matters of faith and practice.[4]

19, 2003, A27. Documents articulating the Baylor 2012 vision are available at http://www
.baylor.edu/vision (accessed August 29, 2005).

2. These developments and their implications are explored in Robert Wuthnow, *The Restructuring of American Religion: Society and Faith since World War II*, ed. John F. Wilson, Studies in Church and State 1 (Princeton: Princeton University Press, 1988), esp. 71–99, 215–40.

3. Perhaps the most objectively written historical inquiry into this conflict is David T. Morgan, *The New Crusades, The New Holy Land: Conflict in the Southern Baptist Convention, 1969–1991* (Tuscaloosa: University of Alabama Press, 1996).

4. Consider, for instance, the current controversies over same-sex unions and the ordination of homosexual persons in the Episcopal Church in the USA, the Presbyterian Church (USA), the United Methodist Church, and the Evangelical Lutheran Church in America referenced in recent issues of *Christian Century*: John Dart, "Split Visions for Presbyterians, Episcopalians," *Christian Century* 120, no. 20 (October 4, 2003): 10; Stephen Bates, "Anglicans Warn U.S. Church," *Christian Century* 120, no. 22 (November 1, 2003): 12–13; Kevin Eckstrom, "Openly Gay Bishop Consecrated," *Christian Century* 120,

Consequently, many devoutly Christian professors are understandably uneasy about extending theological discussion, the source of so much divisiveness in their own Christian experience, beyond the classrooms of the religion department or divinity school.

Second, the politicization of most academic disciplines and professional fields in the wake of the American culture wars has been accompanied by diverse and conflicting Christian proposals as to the proper "Christian" positions in these conflicts. Influencing the outcome of the culture wars is not properly the concern of Christian higher education.[5] As Ralph Wood rightly urges, "It is ever so important not to confuse Christian education with taking a position within the culture wars"; rather, "our loyalty must always be to the transcendent and redeeming Lord who rules over all nations and all states."[6] Nevertheless, Christian faculty who hear sermons, listen to Christian radio programs, or read Christian publications have had their thinking shaped by Christian arguments for or against capital punishment, Christian arguments for or against egalitarian gender relationships or gender-inclusive language, Christian arguments for or against various economic paradigms—the list of examples could continue ad infinitum. If faith is proposed as a foundation for intellectual community, which version of faith will it be? And how will faith be connected to the issues dividing most academic and professional disciplines today, when possible Christian positions on the same issues cover the spectrum? A professor in the undergraduate religion department of my institution tells of having lunch with a professor in a nontheological discipline who is having a hard time fathoming how a relatively conservative Christian can be a straight-ticket

---

no. 23 (November 15, 2003): 12; John Dart, "Dissident Bishops Hold Defiant Service," *Christian Century* 121, no. 7 (April 6, 2004): 10; Les Fetchko (United Methodist News Service), "Methodist Bishops: Gay Clergy Ban Intact," *Christian Century* 121, no. 8 (April 20, 2004): 10–11; and John Dart, "Storm Clouds Gathering: Lutherans Face Sexuality Issues," *Christian Century* 121, no. 9 (May 4, 2004): 8–9.

5. This is not to suggest that Christians and Christian educators should refrain from taking definite stands on controversial issues or retreat from Christian involvement in the public square. Rather, Christian higher education must take great pains to avoid addressing such issues by lazily appropriating the assumptions, polarities, and rhetoric of the culture wars. We must be in this culture and its conflicts, but we must not belong to them (John 17:11–18).

6. Ralph C. Wood, "An Alternative Vision for the Christian University" (unpublished address to the faculty of Campbell University, Buies Creek, NC, March 30, 2004). This caveat is rooted in the perspective on the church relating to society as exemplified in Stanley Hauerwas and William H. Willimon, *Resident Aliens: Life in the Christian Colony* (Nashville: Abingdon, 1989); Stanley Hauerwas, *After Christendom: How the Church Is to Behave If Freedom, Justice, and a Christian Nation Are Bad Ideas* (Nashville: Abingdon, 1991); and Rodney Clapp, *A Peculiar People: The Church as Culture in a Post-Christian Society* (Downers Grove, IL: InterVarsity, 1996).

Democrat; my colleague in turn has a hard time understanding how his lunch partner's support of the Republican platform is compatible with Christian faith. Faculty members are well aware that any serious discussion of the integration of faith and learning must negotiate all sorts of sensitive political land mines.

Third, faculty members in religious and theological studies, theologically formed by an academic theological education as well as by the church, and faculty members in other disciplines, whose theological formation took place primarily in church and parachurch contexts— frequently are suspicious of one another's theologies. In the discourse of theological laypersons, theological professionals sometimes hear the fundamentalism they moved beyond during their academic theological educations; and in the discourse of theological professionals, theological laypersons sometimes hear the positions their ministers or popular Christian media had led them to believe were sub-Christian or heretical. Such mutual mistrust reinforces a two-spheres paradigm for faith and learning that from the outset precludes faith from becoming foundational for university-wide intellectual community, especially in the minds of theological professionals who would prefer that theological laypersons not introduce their "naive faith" into the teaching of university disciplines beyond the religion department or divinity school.[7]

The result of these combined factors is a fear, not of communal theological reflection per se, but rather of the intellectual conflict inevitably arising from this much-needed conversation. Nevertheless, the temptation to avoid or to retreat from theological conflict must be tempered, I argue, in light of three developments in philosophy, theology, and liturgy; each bears upon the recovery of faith as a foundation for intellectual community in a postmodern context. These developments include, first, the work of moral philosopher Alasdair MacIntyre regarding the contested character of a community's tradition; second, the insights of postliberal narrative theology regarding the Christian story as the ground of communal theological reflection; and third, contemporary efforts to recover the early church's understanding of the inseparability of theology and worship.

7. For case studies of the two-spheres paradigm and reflections on its instability as a long-term strategy for relating faith and learning, see Larry Lyon and Michael Beaty, "Integration, Secularization, and the Two-Spheres View at Religious Colleges: Comparing Baylor University with the University of Notre Dame and Georgetown College," *Christian Scholar's Review* 29, no. 1 (Fall 1999): 73–112; see also Michael Beaty, Todd Buras, and Larry Lyon, "Christian Higher Education: An Historical and Philosophical Perspective," *Perspectives in Religious Studies* 24, no. 2 (Summer 1997): 145–65.

Living Traditions and Vital Conflict

The work of Alasdair MacIntyre on the inescapably traditioned nature of rationality in general, and moral reasoning in particular, has received much attention in the twenty-five years since the publication of his book *After Virtue*. Therein he defines "a living tradition" as "an historically extended, socially embodied argument, and an argument precisely in part about the goods which constitute that tradition."[8] MacIntyre illustrates this understanding of tradition by suggesting that "when an institution—a university, say, or a farm, or a hospital—is the bearer of a tradition of practice or practices, its common life will be partly, but in a centrally important way, constituted by a continuous argument as to what a university is and ought to be or what good farming is or what good medicine is. Traditions, when vital, embody continuities of conflict."[9] If a tradition does not embody this continuity of conflict, he says, "it is always dying or dead."[10]

A MacIntyrean understanding of traditioned rationality has much potential for overcoming the aforementioned obstacles to engaging the theme of this book. Christian universities must reclaim the Christian tradition as the unifying center of Christian intellectual life, but they cannot do that without also embracing conflict about that tradition. If there is an absence of conflict about a Christian university's understanding of the Christian tradition and its vision for the integration of faith and learning, then, in MacIntyre's words, "it is always dying or dead." Yet it is precisely an aversion to conflict that threatens to keep many institutions from fully engaging the implications of their distinctiveness as Christian universities. At the outset of these discussions, if we recognize that they will necessitate conflict, that such conflict is a mark of vitality, and that constructive dissension is welcome, then we may be more successful in navigating stormy waters without the crew jumping ship or leading a mutiny along the way.[11]

8. Alasdair MacIntyre, *After Virtue: A Study in Moral Theory*, 2nd ed. (Notre Dame: University of Notre Dame Press, 1984), 222.

9. Ibid.

10. Ibid.

11. In "Reconceiving the University as an Institution and the Lecture as a Genre," the concluding lecture of his 1988 Gifford Lectures, MacIntyre envisions a university "as a place of constrained disagreement, of imposed participation in conflict, in which a central responsibility of higher education would be to initiate students into conflict" and "as an arena of conflict in which the most fundamental type of moral and theological disagreement was accorded recognition" (Alasdair MacIntyre, *Three Rival Versions of Moral Inquiry: Encyclopedia, Genealogy, and Tradition; Being Gifford Lectures Delivered in the University of Edinburgh in 1988* [Notre Dame: University of Notre Dame Press, 1990], 230–31). As Ralph Wood observed in a discussion of these matters, the ongoing conflict that constitutes the

To MacIntyre's affirmation of intellectual conflict as a mark of living traditions in general, we may add a twofold theological rationale for affirming a certain species of conflict in Christian institutions. First, because the matters to be contested within a Christian intellectual community are of ultimate concern, they are worth serious and spirited debate. Not debating them would allow penultimate concerns to replace them. Second, because of the noetic limitations of the earthly church between the two advents,[12] Christian scholars must cultivate the epistemological humility to submit their perspectives to the Christian intellectual community to which they belong, as well as to practice Christian hospitality toward those with whom they differ.[13] Neglecting either part of this theological rationale for conflict can easily allow it to degenerate into the petty disputes and personal attacks that demoralize those within far too many academic milieus.

Telling the Story

But what exactly is the "historically extended, socially embodied argument . . . about the goods" constitutive of the tradition that Christian universities must embrace? An institution might identify a generic "Christian worldview" as the common foundation of the university's intellectual life; sometimes this is expressed in terms of adherence to a few basic Christian doctrines or positions on specific moral issues.[14] Some institutions might emphasize a particular denominational tradition as a foundation for intellectual community, though few (if any) faculties will be drawn entirely or even mostly from a single denominational tradition. Neither approach to defining foundational faith will be adequate for the postmodern milieu of our Christian universities if it frames a Christian "worldview"[15] or a particular denominational perspective in terms of doc-

---

Christian tradition makes it immensely more interesting than secularism as a foundation for intellectual community.

12. Cf. the apostle Paul's rationale for the necessity of contested heresies in the life of the church this side of heaven: "so it will become clear who among you are genuine" (1 Cor. 11:19).

13. See chap. 7 in this book, Aurelie Hagstrom, "Christian Hospitality in the Intellectual Community," for an instructive rendering of essential differences between Christian hospitality and mere tolerance.

14. See, for example, the "Statement of Christian Affirmation" adopted by the board of trustees of the University of Mobile, as explained by the president of the institution: Mark Foley, "'Distinctively Christian': Higher Education for a Higher Purpose," http://umobile.edu/foley.asp (accessed August 29, 2005).

15. *Worldview* is a term laden with Enlightenment-era presuppositions about the capacity of human rationality to have what Hilary Putnam has called an "externalist perspective" or "God's-eye point of view" on the world (Hilary Putnam, *Reason, Truth,*

trinal or ethical propositions. Any understanding of the Christian tradition in its catholicity or of a particular denominational tradition—any such understanding that emphasizes a body of truly articulated propositions is liable to squelch healthy cross-disciplinary theological argumentation, especially within a denominationally and theologically diverse faculty. Some institutions, such as Calvin College, may succeed in recruiting and retaining whole faculties committed to confessional specificity without compromising intellectual openness or stifling debate, but many more Christian university faculties share in common mainly a commitment to support the Christian purposes of the institution. These more confessionally diverse faculties may find a more viable model of faith as a foundation for postmodern Christian intellectual community in the narrative theology proposals of "New Yale" postliberalism.[16]

George Lindbeck and others have proposed that the first-order stuff of Christian faith is the Christian story, which forms the identity of Christian community. Doctrine, in turn, is second-order reflection on the foundational narrative of the church. If we understand Lindbeck's observations on the nature of doctrine in MacIntyrean terms, doctrine is both the process and the product of second-order argumentation about the story we share in Christian community. Where do we find this story? It is told with rich particularity in the canonical Scriptures. Making faith the foundation of Christian intellectual community will therefore mean that in some manner the Christian university will identify the Bible as the normative expression of the Christian narrative. This story is also summarized[17] in the ancient

---

and History [Cambridge: Cambridge University Press, 1981], 49). According to Dan Stiver, "What virtually all postmodern thinkers would agree upon is that we do not have a transcendent, perspicuous vantage point, a God's-eye point-of-view. . . . God may have, but not us!" (Dan R. Stiver, "Baptists: Modern or Postmodern?" Review and Expositor 100, no. 4 [Fall 2003]: 536). Christian educators seeking to respond constructively to the postmodern context would do well to dispense with the modern phraseology of a "Christian worldview" in favor of an expressed commitment to "the Christian tradition." Fidelity to the Christian tradition in the postmodern Christian university must be accompanied by an epistemological humility that takes seriously the Christian understanding of the fallenness of human rationality, even the rationality of the Christian mind on its way toward conformity to the mind of Christ—a transformation that is not fully realized in this present life.

16. See, for example, George Lindbeck, The Nature of Doctrine: Religion and Theology in a Postliberal Age (London: SPCK, 1984); Hans Frei, Theology and Narrative: Selected Essays, ed. George Hunsinger and William C. Placher (Oxford: Oxford University Press, 1993); Stanley Hauerwas and L. Gregory Jones, eds., Why Narrative? Readings in Narrative Theology (Grand Rapids: Eerdmans, 1989); and Gerard Loughlin, Telling God's Story: Bible, Church, and Narrative Theology (Cambridge: Cambridge University Press, 1996). Although narrative theology has primarily developed within Anglo-American circles, there are exceptions. See Johann Baptist Metz, "A Short Apology of Narrative," in Why Narrative?, 251–62.

17. The ancient creeds were understood in the period of their origin as concise summaries of the story and teachings of the Bible, as is evident in Cyril of Jerusalem, Catecheses

rule of faith underlying the Apostles' Creed and the Nicene Creed.[18] These ancient confessions of communal faith did not originate as lists of doctrinal propositions but rather as narrative rehearsals of the acts of the Triune God in creation, reconciliation, and consummation, intended to serve as liturgical expressions and instruments of Christian education.[19] While many in my own Baptist tradition would balk at granting the ancient creeds an authority alongside the Bible,[20] Christian universities of all denominational traditions would do well to reclaim these concise summaries of the Christian narrative as foci for interdisciplinary theological reflection. The Christian tradition is fundamentally the Christian story, within which we understand ourselves and our world. Reclaiming this story as the first-order foundation of Christian intellectual community provides common ground on which faculty from multiple denominational traditions and theological perspectives may stand together while making their own distinctive contributions to the second-order argument that the integration of faith and learning entails.[21]

Lex Orandi, Lex Credendi

This narrative conception of the tradition that is to be contested by the Christian university community will function best when the tradi-

---

5.12: "For not according to [human] pleasure have the articles of faith been composed, but the most important parts collected from the Scriptures make up one complete teaching of the faith. And just as the mustard seed in a small grain contains in embryo many future branches, so also the creed embraces in a few words all the religious knowledge in both the Old and the New Testament" (Leo P. McCauley and Anthony A. Stephenson, trans., *The Works of Saint Cyril of Jerusalem*, Fathers of the Church 61 [Washington, DC: Catholic University of America Press, 1969], 1:146).

18. Properly, the Niceno-Constantinopolitan Creed, as the text of the creed received and confessed by the church, is the edition adopted at the Council of Constantinople in 381, with the expanded third-article affirmations about the person and work of the Holy Spirit.

19. On the narrative shape and function of the ancient creeds, see Paul M. Blowers, "The *Regula fidei* and the Narrative Character of Early Christian Faith," *Pro ecclesia* 6 (Spring 1997): 199–228.

20. Baptist theologian Barry Harvey, however, rejects the mantra that "Baptists have no creed but the Bible," arguing that "our time and effort would be better served if we attended to the question, What are the proper and improper uses of the ancient creeds and confessions, in worship and in the pedagogical responsibilities of the church?" (Barry Harvey, "Doctrinally Speaking: James McClendon on the Nature of Doctrine," *Perspectives in Religious Studies* 27, no. 1 [Spring 2000]: 56–57n82; cf. idem, "Where, Then, Do We Stand? Baptists, History, and Authority," *Perspectives in Religious Studies* 29, no. 4 [Winter 2002]: 359–80, especially 371–79).

21. Cf. Richard Hays's essay in this volume (chap. 1) in which he locates the ground of *koinōnia* in the story of God's gracious initiative in the incarnation of the Word.

tional narrative that forms Christian community, particularly Christian intellectual community, is given its proper locus: in the worship of the community. Few discussions of faith and learning in the Christian university have given attention to worship as the university's primary public expression of its foundational faith; Robert Benne's *Quality with Soul* is a notable exception.[22] If we are to recover faith as a foundation for intellectual community in our universities, we must recover the classical Christian context for the first-order narrative expression of that faith. Early Christianity understood doctrine and worship to be inseparable, an understanding expressed by the patristic axiom *lex orandi, lex credendi,* "the law of praying is the law of believing," or "the faith that is prayed is the faith that is believed."[23] Worship is formative and normative for theological reflection, and theological reflection informs worship. Geoffrey Wainwright among others has retrieved this principle in contemporary theological reflection;[24] at a popular level, Robert Webber's work on "ancient-future" worship has sought to implement the principle in the liturgical life of local congregations.[25]

If Christian universities are serious about initiating cross-disciplinary conversation on the integration of faith and learning, they ought first to seek ways to implement the *lex orandi, lex credendi* principle in the common life of the university community. This might be accomplished through weekly services of worship for faculty and students that tell the

22. Robert Benne, *Quality with Soul: How Six Premier Colleges and Universities Keep Faith with Their Religious Traditions* (Grand Rapids: Eerdmans, 2001), esp. 7, 11, 61–62, 145–46, 150, 155–57, 160–62, 165–66, 171, 193–94.

23. The influential formula seems to have originated with Prosper of Aquitaine (d. after 455) in a treatise formerly attributed to Celestine I, the *Capitula* or *Praeteritorum sedis apostolicae episcoporum auctoritates, de gratia Dei et libero voluntatis arbitrio*: "Let the rule of prayer lay down the rule of faith," *lex supplicandi statuat legem credendi* (Prosper of Aquitaine, "Official Pronouncements of the Apostolic See on Divine Grace and Free Will," 8, in *Defense of St. Augustine*, trans. P. de Letter, Ancient Christian Writers 32 [Westminster, MD: Newman Press, 1963], 183). In context, Prosper invokes this principle in an argument against semi-Pelagianism: the fact that during the liturgy Christian pastors throughout the world always pray that God may bring people to faith provides traditional grounds for attributing the entirety of the human experience of salvation to God's gracious work.

24. Geoffrey Wainwright, *Doxology: The Praise of God in Worship, Doctrine, and Life: A Systematic Theology* (New York: Oxford University Press, 1980).

25. Robert E. Webber, *Ancient-Future Faith: Rethinking Evangelicalism for a Post-modern World* (Grand Rapids: Baker, 1999); and idem, *Worship Old and New: A Biblical, Historical, and Practical Introduction*, rev. ed. (Grand Rapids: Zondervan, 1994) are good places to begin. Baptist patrologist Daniel H. Williams likewise has argued well the need of evangelicals to recover their roots in the ancient Christian tradition if they are to have the resources they need for the engagement of postmodernity. See D. H. Williams, *Retrieving the Tradition and Renewing Evangelicalism: A Primer for Suspicious Protestants* (Grand Rapids: Eerdmans, 1999); and D. H. Williams, ed., *The Free Church and the Early Church: Bridging the Historical and Theological Divide* (Grand Rapids: Eerdmans, 2002).

common Christian story through the systematic reading and proclamation of Scripture, the confession of the ancient ecumenical creeds, and where ecclesiologically feasible, eucharistic celebrations. With reference to the latter, a eucharistic narration of God's relation to the world is an essential foundation for the integration of Christian faith with the arts and sciences. As Robert Wilken has recently reminded us, a key feature of the spirit of early Christian thought is the notion that in light of the incarnation, we may experience the presence of God by means of things—audible things such as words and musical tones, tangible things such as water and bread and wine, and visible things such as icons and various media of the material and visual arts.[26]

Regular university-wide services of word and table would help foster a shared first-order foundation upon which faculty and students alike could build in the second-order task of relating their faith to scholarship across the university disciplines. Susan Wood has observed that "the Christian repeatedly participates in the liturgy in order to imprint that economy [of salvation-history] in his or her very being," so that "worship provides the parameters for thinking about Scripture and theology by keeping these reflections oriented toward their proper object, God, and within their proper context, the Christian community."[27] The primary setting for this liturgical formation of the Christian mind is certainly the local church community, but a complementary university-wide shared liturgical life will help the Christian university to become a Christian intellectual community in more than name only.[28] Our liturgical rehearsal of the foundational narrative of Christian intellectual community would be reinforced by furnishing our campuses with architecture and art that communicate the Christian story in image and symbol throughout the campus, but especially in a focal worship space that makes clear the university's identity as a worshipping community. It is not only with words that we tell the story of Christian faith.

The recovery of a common experience of worship would need to be preceded and supplemented by intentional interdisciplinary discussion, perhaps during faculty development workshops, of how the Christian

26. Robert Louis Wilken, *The Spirit of Early Christian Thought: Seeking the Face of God* (New Haven: Yale University Press, 2003), xxi, referencing chap. 9, "The Glorious Deeds of Christ," 212–36, and chap. 10, "Making This Thing Other," 237–61; see also chap. 2, "An Awesome and Unbloody Sacrifice," 25–49; and chap. 3, "The Face of God for Now," 50–79.

27. Susan K. Wood, "The Liturgy: Participatory Knowledge of God in the Liturgy," in *Knowing the Triune God: The Work of the Spirit in the Practices of the Church*, ed. James J. Buckley and David S. Yeago (Grand Rapids: Eerdmans, 2001), 109–10.

28. In his essay (chap. 5) in the present volume, David Lyle Jeffrey likewise calls for a common experience of worship among the faculty of the university as central to the full character of Christian intellectual community.

narrative might reframe disciplinary self-understandings in the context of a Christian university, and also of how the various university disciplines might make their own contributions to our understanding of the story. If this is to be a community-wide argument about the significance of our story, then the university faculty as a whole must become conversant with the biblical narrative, with the theological categories through which we reflect on this narrative and the faith and practices formed by it, with the story of the sponsoring denominational tradition, and with the stories of the other Christian traditions represented within the faculty and in the larger body of Christ. Faculty members in the department of religious studies or school of divinity will need to serve as instructional resources for including theological education in a larger program of faculty development; yet there are valuable resources for this work in the university community beyond the faculty in the explicitly theological disciplines. These resources include representatives of multiple denominational traditions throughout the faculty.

Most institutions that publicly accept the challenge to make faith foundational for intellectual community will either fit or aspire to the "critical-mass" category of Robert Benne's typology of church-related colleges.[29] Institutions of this type "insist that a critical mass of adherents from their [sponsoring] tradition inhabit all the constituencies of the educational enterprise," including the faculty, but they also value the presence of other traditions in these constituencies for the contributions they make to the pursuit of truth.[30] The presence of faculty from traditions other than the sponsoring tradition will ensure that the distinctive tellings of the Christian story in the multiple streams of the larger Christian tradition are heard. The faculty in a Baptist critical-mass university, for example, needs to hear from Presbyterian, Catholic, Orthodox, or Pentecostal colleagues in various disciplines regarding their perspectives on the significance of their own Christian traditions for the life of the mind. At the same time, the presence of a critical mass of faculty members from the sponsoring tradition will help the denominational college to offer a public account, displaying the unique contributions of a particular denominational telling of the Christian story, and thus contributing to the intellectual life of the larger body of Christ. The encounter, and even conflict, of multiple denominational traditions in the Christian university is beneficial both to the sponsoring tradition and to the church catholic: it requires that our story be genuinely contested.

29. Benne, *Quality with Soul*, 48–68, esp. 49, with the summary table comparing the characteristics of "Orthodox," "Critical-Mass," "Intentionally Pluralist," and "Accidentally Pluralist" institutions.
30. Ibid., 50.

The collapse of modern foundational metanarratives provides us with a wonderful opportunity for refounding the Christian university on Christian faith itself. A nonfoundational rationality need not mean a noncommittal relativism. Rather, it liberates Christian thought from bondage to alien rationalities that never were as universal as they pretended to be.[31] Christian faith is grounded in nothing other than the shared Christian story, a story that invites argument among those who are shaped by it in worship. This sort of conflict is necessary and welcome; it helps ensure the vitality of the tradition.[32] Perhaps these proposals will elicit some argument from readers of this chapter. May our disagreements concerning these proposals lead to a more robust contesting of the story we share in Christian intellectual community, through Jesus Christ our Lord.[33]

31. For a constructive Christian response to the opportunity presented by the postmodern situation from an evangelical perspective, see Stanley J. Grenz and John R. Franke, *Beyond Foundationalism: Shaping Theology in a Postmodern Context* (Louisville: Westminster John Knox, 2001).

32. Elsewhere, I more fully develop this understanding of tradition as the community's ongoing contesting of the story by which it is formed in worship; see Steven R. Harmon, "The Authority of the Community (of All the Saints): Toward a Postmodern Baptist Hermeneutic of Tradition," *Review and Expositor* 100, no. 4 (Fall 2003): 587–621.

33. I hereby thank Ralph C. Wood for reviewing an earlier draft of this essay and offering much helpful criticism.

9

Moral Imagination at a Christian Institution

Daniel Russ and Mark L. Sargent

PERHAPS THE FOREMOST ETHICAL CHALLENGE for Christians, as Richard Hays argues, is to live "in imaginative obedience" to the "moral vision" of the New Testament. As heirs to the great tradition of Christian witness, we are called to consider how the teachings of Christ and the apostles can edify the church, shape ethics and behavior, and transform modern culture. Such faithfulness requires imagination, not simple prescription or routine. As Hays observes, even the task of exegesis, so vital for Christian ethics, is not alone sufficient for moral discourse, since careful exegesis often increases our awareness of the diversity within Scripture and heightens our awareness of our "historical distance" from the "original communities . . . to whom these texts were addressed."[1]

To understand how the witnesses from the first-century Mediterranean world continue to speak to scientific, social, and geopolitical dimensions of the twenty-first century requires the constant renewing of our minds, cultivating the ability to hear the New Testament voices in both their

1. Richard Hays, *The Moral Vision of the New Testament: Community, Cross, New Creation* (San Francisco: HarperCollins, 1996), xi, 3.

145

historical context and their prophetic relevance. This task—the challenge of understanding the New Testament as a compelling moral vision and not simply a reductive behavioral code—requires the community of faith to have a full range of intellectual endeavors, from logical and historical reasoning to empathy, creativity, scholarly intuition, patience, and foresight. Fostering this "imaginative obedience" is one of the most precarious and compelling challenges facing the modern church—and certainly one that should define the soul of the Christian college and university seeking intellectual community grounded in faith.

Among American religious institutions, evangelical colleges and universities have been among the most persistent in maintaining their commitments to Christian faith and worship, but in general have been far less distinguished in cultivating a vital moral imagination. For the most part, evangelicals perceive moral vitality in terms of loyalty to various ideological positions and behavioral standards rather than as an imaginative endeavor to resolve social dilemmas or to discern ethical duties. Among modern evangelicals, aesthetics run toward the commercial and pragmatic, as modern technology and media are embraced widely as tools of utility for worship and witness; they are far less concerned about the philosophical and belletristic assessment of film, music, and the visual arts. Although evangelical churches have shed much of the separatist language of the fundamentalist past, sermons still routinely remind students of the dangerous lure of culture, encouraging avoidance rather than engagement, and offering occasional jeremiads on the debilitating state of postmodernity. Quite often, discussions of morality in public life among evangelicals have been captive to partisan politics, which often discourage students from thinking beyond the conventional rhetoric about social problems and possible remedies.

The primacy of moral ideology over moral imagination is evident in both James Davison Hunter's *Evangelicalism: The Coming Generation* and the recent rebuttal by James Penning and Corwin Smidt, in *Evangelicalism: The Next Generation*. Both forecast the evangelical future by measuring the fidelity of students to selected behavioral standards or political stances. In the early 1980s Hunter predicted a precipitous falling away from traditional mores. By contrast, Penning and Smidt conclude that today the moral boundary lines among evangelicals have not wavered much from those of the past couple decades, except for a wider vision about the freedom of women and possibilities for them.[2] At the level of survey design, both books offer the usual social-scientific

2. James D. Hunter, *Evangelicalism: The Coming Generation* (Chicago: University of Chicago Press, 1987), 203–4; and James M. Penning and Corwin E. Smidt, *Evangelicalism: The Next Generation* (Grand Rapids: Baker, 2002), 128–29, 165–66.

fare, measuring student responses to questions about what they believe and do. Questions that move beyond the level of ideology and behavior seldom enter the equation, so that the role of art, literature, music, narrative—in short, any of the resources of the moral imagination—are wholly absent.

The need for a more imaginative endeavor to resolve modern social and moral issues appears in the tensions that Penning and Smidt find in their data. For instance, they report that the vast majority of students in the Christian College Consortium believe that justice requires moral earnestness and changes of heart. However, considerably fewer affirm the importance of realigning social structures or creating new policies, concerns that demand the possibility of imagining life as other than it is. Furthermore, only 15 percent of Christian College Consortium students believe that the poor are responsible for their own poverty, but three-quarters of those same students believe that social problems are best addressed by changing people's hearts. For the most part, evangelical students contend that the church should focus on spiritual issues and be wary of becoming involved with changes to the social structures.[3] As the research of Michael Emerson and Christian Smith reveals, this emphasis on personal piety rather than social change is especially strong among white evangelicals, who are considerably less likely than members of African-American churches to acknowledge the need to address structural inequities in society.[4]

We believe that Christians need both moral integrity and moral imagination, first for the sake of a vital and rich interior life as Christians, and second for the development of socially attuned responsiveness to the moral demands that life in human community presents. For example, the deep piety and spiritual character of people like Augustine, Martin Luther, and Henri Nouwen led them to address the systemic corruptions and moral needs that they faced. Likewise, the social conscience of St. Francis, William Wilberforce, and Mother Teresa drove them to seek God's face and to seek to live lives of moral integrity. In short, one dimension of Christian faith as a foundation for intellectual community involves the capacity of faith to draw us up and beyond our narrow view of self and world, enlarging our vision of what we must be as bearers of God's image and in relation to others. Thus, we do well to ask how the university can nurture a larger conversation about what it means to live in "imaginative obedience" to the gospel. How can we shape our programs to prepare students to see people as images of the Creator

3. Penning and Smidt, *Evangelicalism*, 97–105.
4. See Michael O. Emerson and Christian Smith, *Divided by Faith: Evangelical Religion and the Problem of Race in America* (Oxford: Oxford University Press, 2000), especially 116–33.

and to understand the prospects for renewal and reconciliation? How do we cultivate not only a heart to serve but also a mind to imagine new possibilities for social hope?

Two Ways of Regarding Moral Imagination

The concept of a "moral imagination" concerns both the convictions of the heart and also the justice of social structures. These concerns constitute two general streams of thought about a moral imagination: the concern for personal integrity and moral discernment, and the concern for justice and redemptive action.

In the first stream, a vibrant moral imagination, especially among the young, is an antidote to modern skepticism about moral knowledge or action. Some writers, taking cues from Robert Coles's book on fairy tales and the moral imagination, have focused on the development of virtue and character in young persons, especially children.[5] They know that children have imaginations that are provoked and enriched by experience, yet they want to ensure that tradition and moral principles are entwined early in the imaginative life. In fact, they perceive a social crisis in a lack of attention to communicate faith, morality, and civic virtue, and argue that social reform begins with the effort to help balance the curiosity of children with the strength of tradition, spiritual purposefulness, and communal standards.

James Fowler asserts that this same power to cultivate a moral imagination is available throughout adult development by the reading of classics:

> A classic is an expression of the human spirit that seems to gather into a fitting unity something that is fundamental, recurring, and universal in our experience. It brings into irresistible focus some perennial nexus or knot, that, in every century, bedevils our species. . . . A classic brings to expression something that is fundamentally true about the human condition but does [so] in a way that respects the essential complexity, the stubborn persistence, and the honest opacity of its subject matter.[6]

Fowler claims that through such classical perspective one finds not only a personal calling that satisfies an inward sense of meaning, but also a vocation that serves God and his creation.

5. Robert Coles, *The Call of Stories: Teaching and the Moral Imagination* (Boston: Houghton Mifflin, 1989).

6. James Fowler, *Becoming Adult, Becoming Christian: Adult Development and Christian Faith* (San Francisco: Jossey-Bass, 2000), 64.

A second stream in the literature strives to balance the obsession with morality as private ethics and behavior with an expanded concern for social justice, responsible citizenship, and creative resolution of human conflict. "Moral imagination is energized and expanded," according to Thomas McCollough, "as we remember and reflect on those experiences in which we empathize with others and try to find ways to meet their needs and take action on their behalf. When such moments are shared by a group, they may become part of a community's moral heritage."[7] Patricia Werhane even contends that much of the "morally questionable behavior" of modern leaders and managers derives not simply from lapses in integrity but from a failure "to imagine a wider range of possible issues, consequences and remedies."[8] This link between imagination and social justice has roots in John Dewey's pragmatism—in Dewey's perception that moral contemplation is the envisioning of what is both probable and possible.[9]

Inasmuch as Christian colleges can falter in relation to both ways of regarding the moral imagination, we want to reflect on how to cultivate moral imaginations in two distinct but interpenetrating arenas of life in the academy: the intimate space of the classroom, and the public spaces of the community. The classroom is where the teacher is able to explore worlds through great texts and ideas, moving students beyond the boundaries of their own historical moment and the contemporary culture that many like to call "the real world." Here they are able to understand their real world in light of other real worlds, and to discern not only what is normal in their generation but also to understand such normality in light of historical and cultural norms. The teacher appeals to their conscious thoughts, challenges their personal biases, and invites them to enlarge their vision of reality. Likewise, the formal and informal gatherings of the larger academic community afford opportunities to enlarge, enrich, and deepen the moral vision of students and faculty through language and symbol, through art and argument, and through public expression of deep institutional values.

7. Thomas E. McCollough, *The Moral Imagination and Public Life: Raising the Ethical Question* (Chatham, NJ: Chatham, 1991), xiii.

8. Patricia H. Werhane, *Moral Imagination and Management Decision-Making* (New York: Oxford University Press, 1999), 45.

9. The link between the moral imagination and the tradition of John Dewey is most overtly made in Steven Fesmire, *John Dewey and Moral Imagination: Pragmatism in Ethics* (Bloomington: University of Indiana Press, 2003). Mark Johnson's *Moral Imagination: Implications of Cognitive Science for Ethics* (Chicago: University of Chicago Press, 1993) also explores the connections between the imaginative and the pragmatic.

Moral Imagination in the Academic Disciplines

The classroom is certainly at the heart of the academic enterprise, comprising what Donald Cowan has suggested is a sacred space, a place set apart from the mundane, where teacher and student enter into the covenant of the curriculum.[10] The curriculum is the course of studies that is the liturgy, so to speak, enacted in that space. Shaped by past tradition, current thought, and future challenges, both faculty and students enter into the course of studies to be formed and transformed, to enjoy the renewal of their minds, to borrow St. Paul's phrase.

The alpha and omega of such an education in the Christian academy is the study of Scripture. Students need a richer understanding of the biblical imagination. That is vital for all Christians who teach, and not least among them the professors whose discipline is the teaching of Scripture. In what sense do we approach the Bible imaginatively, and in what ways does the Bible form and reform our imaginations? Actually, without imagination one cannot read the story of creation in Genesis. Even those of us who are evangelicals and believe that God created the world in the beginning often approach this seminal narrative as if it were a modern scientific description. We have done so in reaction to Enlightenment science and its "demythologizing" of Scripture. But if we attempt to read contemporary scientific theories into Genesis 1–2, we will not hear the word of God. Whatever it means that the Spirit of God hovered over the face of the deep requires an appreciation for the metaphorical. When we start trying to force these chapters to answer the question about when dinosaurs became extinct, and whom Cain married, our intellects often fail to imagine what God is revealing about Godself, humanity, and the whole of creation.

Nor can we properly approach the remainder of the Bible without a disciplined imagination. How else do we understand Melchizedek, who comes to Abraham (Gen. 14) and is memorialized in Psalm 110 and the Epistle to the Hebrews (chaps. 5–7) as the founder of a priesthood from which the Messiah would arise? Or are we to try to explain all the sacrifices and purification laws in the Law by suggesting that God wanted Israel to eat well and have good hygiene? In short, the modern reductionistic skepticism practiced by secular thinkers has too often been mirrored by the modern reductionistic literalism of many evangelical minds.

The greatest single cause of this reductionism may be the evangelical's sanctification of the inductive method of Bible study. There is noth-

10. Donald Cowan, *Classic Texts and the Nature of Authority* (Dallas: Dallas Institute Publications, 1993), 264–65.

ing wrong with the inductive method of study in itself, as long as we understand its origins and limits. The method arose in the seventeenth century with the growth of modern science and was especially advocated by Bacon and Newton. Its genius is its danger: analysis that takes things apart but tends not to put them back together again, to recover the larger perspective. It makes the Bible accessible, verse-by-verse, but has little to say about how the verses cohere as Epistles, Gospels, histories, prophecies, and poetry. This fragmented reading should disturb us, since the division of the Bible into chapters and verses only began in the medieval era. The mentality that such study creates is more inclined to proof-texting and ignoring contexts than to showing how the great sweep of biblical revelation, in context, speaks to the great issues of life. And we modern American Christians are very attracted to induction, because we can quickly access the Bible and package or decoupage its "truths." The actual Scriptures, and the moral teaching that follows from them, are neither that simple nor so neatly packaged.

This attraction to the simple and easy is not peculiar to Christians in America. Thinkers as diverse as Alexis de Tocqueville, Joseph Wood Krutch, R. W. B. Lewis, Jacques Barzun, and more recently Christopher Lasch and Robert Bellah have pointed out the historical, cultural, sociological, psychological, and spiritual character of the American myth that inclines us toward the transient and the simple. Historians such as Mark Noll and George Marsden have described how the church has participated in this aspect of the American myth.[11] They largely agree that this propensity to the simple, the singular, and the common is the dark side of the American vision for the plain truth, the individual, and the egalitarian.

The Scriptures, however, are not simple, and often their truths are anything but plain. Not only does the content of Scripture—the rituals, the history, the psalms, the prophecies, the parables, the theology—demand an imaginative understanding, but the very form of Scripture also demands and cultivates imagination. First, the scope of the biblical books demands what Dante called a polysemous understanding of reality. The simplest example is the Eucharist. All over the world every week Chris-

11. See Jacques Barzun, *The House of Intellect* (New York: Harper, 1959); Robert N. Bellah, *Habits of the Heart: Individualism and Commitment in American Life* (Berkeley: University of California Press, 1985); Joseph Wood Krutch, *The Modern Temper* (New York: Harcourt, Brace, 1929); R. W. B. Lewis, *The American Adam: Innocence, Tragedy, and Tradition in the Nineteenth Century* (Chicago: University of Chicago Press, 1955); George M. Marsden, *Reforming Fundamentalism: Fuller Seminary and the New Evangelicalism* (Grand Rapids: Eerdmans, 1987); Mark A. Noll, *The Scandal of the Evangelical Mind* (Grand Rapids: Eerdmans, 1994); and Alexis de Tocqueville, *Democracy in America*, trans. and ed. Harvey C. Mansfield and Delba Winthrop (Chicago: University of Chicago Press, 2002).

tians partake of the bread and cup. To believers who know Scripture, this is at once bread and wine, the body and blood of Christ, the last Passover, the first Holy Communion, and the promise of the marriage feast of the Lamb. The Gospel narrative is simple, its metaphorical layers rich and deep. The lamb on the rural hillside becomes the "Lamb of God who takes away the sin of the world!" (John 1:29), the Old Testament sacrifice, the "Lamb slain from the foundation of the world" (Rev. 13:8 KJV), and the Lamb who stands on the throne at the end of time, surrounded by the twenty-four elders and the angelic creatures who cry out, "Holy, holy, holy!" (Rev. 5). All waters, including the morning bath or shower, are potentially the waters of baptism, the Red Sea, the rivers that ran through the Garden of Eden and that will run through the new Jerusalem, and the river Jordan, which we all must cross to enter his presence. Taking the Bible seriously as it is written deepens, complicates, and profoundly enriches our image of God, the wonders of creation, and the symbolic language and vision for each successive generation. If we can learn not to reduce the Torah to the Ten Commandments, acknowledging instead their rich and complex historical, poetic, and theological context, then we can understand how to live those commandments in our own rich and complex historical, cultural, and personal stories in this place and time. After all, the Ten Commandments are surrounded by statutes and ordinances that address matters of worship and hygiene, justice and diet. They give us a way of imagining that the Creator of the universe might be concerned to let the poor and the alien eat from the edges of the fields, and also interested in the rotation of crops, so that the land can rest.

Cultivating the imagination inevitably leads to words and to stories—the literary imagination as well as the linguistic imagination that precedes it. Not only does language set human beings apart from the rest of creation, it also mysteriously connects humanity with the Word himself, and language becomes the medium through which all academic disciplines are understood. We must learn to understand and use language as such before we can tell, listen to, write, or read stories. The learning of language is both natural and cultural. We are born linguistic creatures, but we do not learn to use language effectively without endless hours of parents informally and teachers formally repeating words, correcting pronunciation, and refining our expressions. And the teacher can never forget that all this repetition of letters, sounds, phrases, vocabulary, correct spelling, grammar, and syntax is not simply about dictating to students; it also is about unlocking a capacity for which they were created—to be creators themselves. As such, learning is not only by rote but also by heart. One can never forget that the linguistic imagination probes the mysteries of the law of God written on the hearts of humankind, as well as the Word becoming flesh and dwelling among us. It is the key that unlocks the world of intimate relationships, effective leadership, eloquent speech, and beautiful letters, as well as the proclamation of the gospel. When done without imagination, it becomes drudgery and drill, making students unable to mine the treasures God has created in them. Done with rigor and joy, the linguistic imagination opens up the joy of learning for a lifetime, both in our native tongue and in the tongues of all those other natives. Finally, the study of language instills in us the *habitus* of paying attention to the nuances of words, the source of many of the moral conflicts and diplomatic resolutions that life presents.

Perhaps the greatest joy and gift opened up by the linguistic imagination is the gift of story, for story is the seminal way we express and discover who we are, whether around the dinner table, in leisure reading, or in formal study of the great histories, biographies, epics, plays, and novels that are our legacy. Whether historical narrative or fiction, literature is a mode of knowledge that tells the truth in a unique way, for which there is no substitute. It is no accident, after all, that most of the Bible is historical narrative and that our Lord taught the deepest truths of his kingdom in parables—little fictions. Properly understood and properly taught, the literary imagination combines pleasure and discipline that serves every person for a lifetime of worship, leisure, work, and civic engagement, thereby both enabling and partly constituting the good human life.

Students need encouragement to appreciate the imaginative in the study and writing of history. As Aristotle instructs us in the ninth chapter of his *Poetics*, poetry can be about what might have been or should have been, while history must be bound by what, to our knowledge, actually occurred.[12] But the historian engages the imagination in at least two ways. First, the connections between past and present are not self-evident. People, events, wars, proclamations, and speeches spanning many cultures and centuries may or may not be connected. The historical imagination attempts to discover these connections, not impose them, so that human beings can gain wisdom and human cultures can acquire some sense of understanding, if not control, over the events that formed them and may shape their future. Second, having discovered such connections, historians must, like the sculptor or the novelist, decide what to include and exclude from their voluminous research in order to make their theses factual, convincing, and engaging. Certainly, as Walter Brueggemann has argued in *The Bible Makes Sense*, the term

---

12. Aristotle, *Poetics* (New York: Hill & Wang, 1961), 68–69 (1451b).

"historical imagination" aptly describes the vision and style found in most of the books of the Bible.[13]

And again, let it be clear that the exercise of historical imagination, just as for other forms of artfully rethinking the way things are, redounds to the more generally important and morally imaginative capacity to consider the multiplicity of ways in which persons and cultures may be virtuous or vicious, dull or interesting, a little lower than the angels or merely the top of the food chain.

It is easier for most of us to associate imagination with language, literature, and history than with mathematics and science. And yet few human endeavors engage the imagination more than mathematical and scientific learning. The mathematical imagination discovers in the messy reality of things an abstract order that enables human beings to see and make an order in the world that we cannot see on the surface of things. Even the most elementary math—arithmetic—quickly moves a person beyond fingers and toes, enabling one to envision numberless stars, grains of sand, trees, lakes, and living creatures in the universe, what we can never see but can imagine. And each subdiscipline of mathematics—algebra, geometry, calculus, and so on—opens a new angle on reality and new possibilities for organizing reality, including the Internet. In an era of microchips and space exploration, we must engage the imagination of young people who live in a mathematized "virtual world." We should do so not only in order to turn out mathematicians, but also because in a world that appears to be chaotic, politically and morally, young people need to grasp this invisible order of God's creation. Moreover, given the tremendous power discovered and unleashed by mathematical minds in the twentieth century, we cannot afford to educate mathematicians who do not understand the moral implications of that power.

While the mathematician looks for the invisible order of things, scientific inquiry attempts to order creation in light of that invisible order. Jacques Maritain describes physics and the natural sciences as "mainly concerned with the mathematical reading of natural phenomena, and [they] insure in this way the domination of the human spirit over the world of matter."[14] Beginning with Adam naming the animals, God has created human beings to bring order to creation out of the order of the human mind. While we certainly can teach science in a hands-on way, the real work of science begins and ends in the human imagination, as it discovers the hidden order of things and then transforms realities to conform to once-invisible principles. Just as the goal of math is not

13. Walter Brueggemann, *The Bible Makes Sense* (Atlanta: John Knox, 1977), 29–36.
14. Jacques Maritain, *Education at the Crossroads* (New Haven: Yale University Press, 1964), 69.

merely to make mathematicians, the goal of science is not primarily to train engineers and doctors. Science should remind human beings that we are truly "a little lower than the angels" (Ps. 8:5 KJV) and are stewards of creation. Not many of us will make computers, research DNA, or cure diseases, but all of us live in a world where science transforms the way we live every day. We must understand how the moral imagination can inform the scientific imagination so that we can discern the difference between using our God-given wisdom to shape the world and playing god with our world.

Two other ways of imagining the world, perhaps, give the fullest and most common expression to pure creativity: art and athletics. Many of us think of these two disciplines as opposites, the former dealing purely with aesthetic creativity, and the latter dealing purely with physical activity. Indeed, some academics would not grant that athletics involves any intellectual discipline at all. And certainly the current business of athletics is a far cry from what Plato describes as gymnastics. But we would argue that both the arts and athletics bring to human culture an artificial order, one that educates through beauty and pleasure. The artistic imagination, whether in the visual or performing arts, gives order through the senses. The artist takes sound, color, and sight, then reorders them in forms that are like nature but which nature would never have produced. The artistic imagination transforms the way we see and experience everything from the human body to human dwellings to nature itself. We can never again see the body in the same way after viewing ancient Greek sculpture. We can never again see light the same way after seeing it wash through medieval stained-glass windows. We can never again see the dignity of people in the same way after gazing upon Renaissance portraits. Nor can we ever again see nature in the same way after observing an impressionist landscape. And the sounds of the world have been forever changed by the chants, madrigals, symphonies, gospel songs, blues, jazz, and rock music that resonate through history and our communal imagination. Many of us, moreover, first discovered the meaning of our own personal experience while lost in the dramatic portrayal of someone else's story on stage or in film. Plainly enough, artists do not always render their visions of reality with the explicit purpose of changing human beings and culture; sometimes they fulfill their vocation simply and only for the sake of giving form to their vision. However, we must educate students to understand that the artistic imagination does not merely decorate life, but indeed also informs and transforms the way we sense and, finally, the way we live and shape reality.

Like the arts, athletics bring to the human enterprise a gift, one of pure play. This is more than simply physical education, which serves to ground students in the grammar of disciplining the body so that later they will be free to enjoy its fullness. In the case of athletics, game or play *is* the fullness. For we easily forget that games are an artifice: they are a fiction developed by human beings in order to play out actions for which the human spirit longs but which are not readily available in ordinary life. Like other fictions, games teach virtue, but they do so indirectly through the pleasure of leisure work. For the essence of games—of play—is that they serve no obvious practical purposes. Perhaps this is why professional sports can never be true play. The athletic imagination teaches us to know life in and through our bodies. It enables us to understand the deep connection between pain and pleasure, sweat and beauty. Even the games that mimic war—the so-called contact sports—teach us to turn fighting into a fiction where victors honor losers and no one dies. Is it not intriguing that the epics of Homer and Virgil tell us of warriors who long for athletic games as preludes, interludes, and postludes to battle? At their best, athletic contests contain moments of beauty when the body performs at such a level that the opposing fans become one humanity, celebrating the human spirit. Is this, perhaps, the reason why athletic contests are surrounded by such pageantry: chanting, music, banners, and food? Athletic competition is first and finally a metaphor for life.

But then, life is metaphorical. In *The Mind of the Maker*, Dorothy Sayers reminds us: "All language about everything is analogical; we think in a series of metaphors. . . . We can explain nothing in terms of itself, but only in terms of other things. . . . In particular, when we speak about something of which we have no direct experience, we must think by analogy or refrain from thought. It may be perilous," she disclaims, "as it must be inadequate, to interpret God by analogy with ourselves, but we are compelled to do so; we have no other means of interpreting anything."[15] This God-given ability to make the real connections between apparently disconnected realities constitutes the imagination, which John Bolt defines as the "capacity to make present to our consciousness that which is either spatially, temporally, or logically absent."[16] This capacity distinguishes humanity as God-imaged creatures from all other creatures. As images ourselves, we cannot help but imagine, because we know from infancy and we know in our bones that we are profoundly connected to the invisible Creator and deeply connected to the rest of creation, most of which we will never see.

From infancy, the child's imagination is necessarily primitive, self-centered, and naive. From birth, children learn by analogy: me/not me, mommy/not mommy, daddy/not daddy, and so on. They usually begin

15. Dorothy L. Sayers, *The Mind of the Maker* (San Francisco: Harper & Row, 1987), 23.

16. John Bolt, *The Christian Story and the Christian School* (Grand Rapids: Christian Schools International, 1993), 202.

by thinking metaphorically, although to them they are thinking literally. For example, after discovering that there are more females in the world than mommy, they at first may call all women "Mommy." Later they learn that such creatures are like mommy, but not mommy. What we suggest is that from infancy, parents and later teachers should cultivate in the child a disciplined imagination that no longer makes naive and self-centered connections, but instead understands all the differences and distinctions among the endless variety of people, things, and ideas—an imagination that yet can apprehend and comprehend within that variety the essential unity of all creation.

God, in commanding Israel to establish memorials in the land, tells them that when the children ask, "'What is the meaning of the testimonies and the statutes and the ordinances which the LORD our God has commanded you?' then you shall say to your son, 'We were Pharaoh's slaves in Egypt; and the LORD brought us out of Egypt with a mighty hand'" (Deut. 6:20–21 RSV). In other words, the "catechism" revealed through Moses explains the laws first in the context of the great story of emancipation, not through abstract definitions and propositions. The purpose of the curriculum in the Christian academy is to cultivate this God-given capacity to see the invisible but real connections between the Creator and the creation, among all human beings, and with the rest of creation. If we can imagine these profound and complex relationships, we can imagine the ways in which we must be morally responsible to the Creator, to our fellow human beings, and to all creation.

Moral Imagination in the Academic Community

Most faculty cherish the occasion to nurture the moral imagination in their own classrooms, but there is generally less confidence that the institutional message will be conveyed with imagination and nuance. But colleges must think more about how our institutional rhetoric—as especially evident in public forums and ceremonial occasions, all those community moments outside the scope of the classroom, yet which we often undervalue as learning opportunities—signals an imaginative obedience to the challenges of Christian faith. There are countless rhetorical moments—chapels, convocations, commissioning services, alumni newsletters, building dedications, student retreats, trustee meetings—when we need to present the boldest and most imaginative expression of our Christian mission. Doing so reminds us of and brings us nearer to the true and good community to which Christian faith beckons us.

What must we do better? We might start by reinvigorating a more imaginative conversation about tradition—the great Christian and biblical tradition as well as our specific theological traditions. One factor that will keep an imaginative and coherent intellectual life is a greater fluency among students, faculty, and trustees in the traditions of greatest relevance to the institution—the broad Christian traditions as well as the particulars of denominational or theological strain. As thoughtful believers, students and faculty need to enter what Alasdair MacIntyre calls "an historically extended, socially embodied argument . . . about the goods which constitute that tradition."[17] They need to perceive their own tradition not simply as a weathered orthodoxy, vulnerable to the winds of postmodernism, but as a morally complex heritage, full of moments of both prophetic courage and ethical failure. In evangelicalism are plenty of currents that resist tradition—a personal and privatized "relationship" with God that exists separate from the community of faith, a heritage of distrust toward Catholicism, and a sense that spiritual authenticity breaks away from liturgy and tradition. And modern media do not help. As each new half-life of technology turns over more rapidly, students' sense of distance from the past becomes exponentially more remote. There is always the danger of condescending toward the past—based on a naive, economically or technologically oriented faith in human progress, or on a postmodern deconstruction of the ideological blindness of the past. Or especially in recent years, there is a new tendency to overreact the other way—to venerate the past, embracing church tradition, liturgy, and ceremony as a more stable and intellectually sustaining experience than the affective tendencies of contemporary evangelical worship. Yet traditions thrive or falter, according to MacIntyre, not merely by veneration, but also in response to the "exercise or the lack of exercise of the relevant virtues."[18]

Our challenge is to balance respect for our Christian heritage with our concern for the gospel to thrive in a contemporary idiom. That balance may require us to speak of our own denominational or institutional traditions with greater courage and honesty. We have done better at crafting and reinforcing mission statements and discussing marketing and branding, but all mission statements and brands run a risk of silencing the past in safe platitudes. We can lose the narratives of faith and failure. Perhaps we need to consider tradition as a heritage of morally courageous and imaginative action—as well as ethical pratfalls and detours. For most of our denominations and institutions, the

17. Alasdair MacIntyre, *After Virtue: A Study in Moral Theory*, 2nd ed. (Notre Dame: University of Notre Dame Press, 1984), 222. Also see Steven Harmon's chapter (8) in this volume, "Communal Conflict in the Postmodern Christian University," in which he discusses the importance of self-reflective argument about the nature and goods of Christian tradition within the context of church-related higher education.

18. MacIntyre, *After Virtue*, 223.

past is a mixed report. In some cases, there were progressive stances on freedom for slaves and equality for women that became mixed with an anti-intellectual resistance to scientific inquiry or reaffirmation of cruel stereotypes. In other cases, a revival of Christian devotion and moral accountability flourished in a subculture that vilified Jews, Catholics, or Muslims. How the institution presents this past to its students—its alertness to the promises and virtues of Christian predecessors, even with candor about the frailties of the past—may do much to encourage the discernment, honesty, and empathy necessary to address ethical complexities in social contexts.

In presenting our past, we might take more cues from Scripture: the Chronicler's ability to linger over failures, the psalmist's unease or anger, the disciples' naïveté or doubt, the Pauline Epistles' frank confrontation of signs of communal friction. Evangelical Christianity has been nervous about hagiography or saints, though our students are not especially fluent when it comes to understanding the ideological or theological junctures in the road (what Mark Noll called "turning points") that shaped our doctrines, our ideologies, or our departures from the past. This does not have to emerge out of a hypercritical condescension toward the past. Again, the marvel of Scripture is how often it blends devotional words of praise with starkly lit moments of fear, sinfulness, and confession. At Gordon College, we have tried to address some of these needs with the theme of "critical loyalty"—our label for a current venture in Christian vocation. We have tried to delve into that double entendre—prompting faculty, on various public occasions, to discuss the critical factors that have encouraged their relationship or loyalty to our institution, even as they discuss the criticisms that compel them to remain loyally connected to the institution and to evangelical tradition in order to reform them.

Second, we need to consider more imaginative strategies for civic engagement and service. Long prone to separatist impulses, the evangelical movement has frequently set itself against culture, at times with justice, but far too often with fear. As a general rule, evangelical institutions have tried to be good neighbors in their communities, yet all the while working with the eagerness of a New England farmer to keep our ideological fences intact. As a result, our participation within our communities tends to be less philosophical than commercial. While we are anxious to help our students find places in the marketplace and the "real world" of generating capital, we have been less successful in engaging civic leaders about the moral contours of public policy and the marketplace. If our students are going to cultivate and live by the light of a vital moral imagination, they need to see how Christian values and biblical precepts are not only separate from culture, but also how they find their place in a pluralistic culture. When honest with ourselves, we should admit that many students, even some of the most devout, remain skeptical about our own confidence that Christianity can engage the culture without being simply adversarial, insulated, or triumphalist. Is there respect for our intellectual capital—our faculties, students, ethos, traditions—as a vital resource for social action and civic deliberation?

At the soul of our universities, therefore, must be the conviction that we can do more imaginative work to promote social hope. With the particularly fevered pitch of political discourse today, so many social issues—the bioethical debates over what it means to be human, the economic quarrels about distribution of wealth, the high rates of incarceration, the care for the environment—remain caught in familiar partisan logjams. It will take creative leadership to resolve them. That creativity can draw deeply from the polysemous understanding of reality that Dante saw in the biblical narrative. Those with experience in reading the biblical text—its rich resources of metaphor, its balance of story and precept, its courage in voicing human sorrow and prophetic hope—can enrich public reflection and discourse about social need and change. That requires a rehabilitation of the Christian thinker's public image as one who contributes with empathy and generosity to address social need.

Such public perceptions will not come easily; the image of evangelicals as antagonists to the public welfare is still prevalent. But Christian higher education can exercise greater imagination in how it seeks a place in the public square. It may begin by thinking locally—gathering regional activists, policy makers, community leaders, and intellectuals into dialogues about the environment, school policy, social work, small business, and ecumenical issues. We need more boldly to consider how to transform our campuses into hospitable spaces for the consideration and resolution of civic issues. At least, we need to provide space—through forums, shared readings, sustained collaborations, and so on—that provides a basis for faithfully and morally imaginative deliberation as Christian intellectual communities. In many respects, we still strive to create a liberal-arts campus ethos that is insulated, allowing students to enjoy a sense of community, coherence, and personal contemplation during their college years. There is a level of incubation in the college experience that is necessary for risk taking, community building, and reflection. But too often engagement with the culture—a vital expression of the mission of many of our institutions—remains a road trip, so to speak, or even a postseason affair. Faculty members serve as ambassadors to their disciplines, and students are engaged in internships—or essentially find entry into a marketplace. Yet students and colleagues are given little opportunity to see faculty, visitors, scholars, and civic leaders engage in ongoing, patient, and respectful collaborative discussion and consideration, often with individuals with whom they disagree. Without witnessing and participating in such discussions, students will not develop a strong sense of their own possibilities for vocation and calling. Students do not need simple reminders about engaging the culture; they also need practice and discipline in civic dialogue.

Finally, we have been drawn to the need for civic engagement and the language of moral imagination as a means of seasoning our current ideas about "the integration of faith and learning"—a phrase in Christian higher education that has become a little shopworn. At its best, the "project" of integration has stepped into the void created by the poles of anti-intellectualism and secularism and has sought to close the Enlightenment gap between the spiritual and the rational. At its best, the project of integration has been about first principles, the relationship between biblical teachings and values and disciplinary methodologies. At its weak point, however, the project of integration has prompted a dialogue that has remained contained within Christian higher education, with considerably less impact on the academy, the media, the marketplace of ideas, and the church, especially the global church. Its strength has been helping students to construct a coherent, biblically oriented worldview; its weakness has been in demonstrating how one lives in a world where worldviews collide. Among alumni of Christian colleges, that remains one of the most prevalent complaints—that they are ill prepared to find their way as firm believers in a more pluralistic culture.

These sketches about moral imagination in the disciplines and in the academic community do not begin to probe the reaches of our vision of educating the young in knowledge, skill, and wisdom. But they suggest some of the depths that may be plumbed to educate students toward a moral imagination grounded in Christian faith. Combined with more robust rhetoric in the public forums and ceremonial occasions in the institutional life outside the classroom, students in a Christian college or university can dwell in a faithful intellectual community that instills moral conviction and imaginative hope. They thereby can enrich the soul of the university—and awaken the heart of the communities—in which many seek and find their Christian calling.

10

American Protestantism and Vocation in Higher Education

Daniel H. Williams

OVER THE LAST DECADE OR SO, select colleges and universities have benefited from generous grants provided by the Lilly Endowment for studying the concept and role of vocation within higher education. Geared especially to students, the grants are intended to encourage young people to consider basic questions of faith and commitment as they think about careers. It is a worthy undertaking, and I have yet to hear about the university that has not benefited from implementing such a program.[1] Yet there is nothing new about emphasizing the place of calling within American Protestantism. Vocation has been the driving force, often implicitly, behind the Protestant imperative during the nineteenth and twentieth centuries to orchestrate a moral, spiritual, and educational climate within our culture. The very idea of possessing a calling, especially if this is regarded as a providential calling, is what once fueled commitment for such efforts as reforming the social order,

1. As underscored by a meeting of universities involved in the Lilly-sponsored Programs for the Theological Exploration of Vocation (PTEV) initiative, held in Indianapolis on October 10–12, 2004, and attended by more than two hundred professors and administrators representing almost one hundred participating institutions.

strengthening moral responsibility, and founding institutions of higher learning. What characterized that "calling" and how its obligatory nature slipped away from Protestant hands into near oblivion is a story that needs to be told and acknowledged. For it is chiefly a story, not of the forces of secularization versus religion, but of the predominance of antitraditionalist religious ideals over other religious ideals.

In relating this story, I argue that Christian confessionalism (subscription to a priori norms of religious belief and morality)—shunned in principle by many universities as an embarrassing vestige of social and religious intolerance—should be accorded legitimacy if we hope to avoid the complete deterioration, except nominally, of any distinctive Christian character within church-originated universities. Now that the potential value of discovering vocation for the shaping of the academic agenda has reemerged, it is possible also to take up the religious dynamics of vocation within the academy and to avoid former mistakes. For it is no secret that religiously founded institutions have been so fearful of association with authoritarianism and confessional indoctrination that they have moved in the opposite direction, only to find that the majority of faculty and students no longer recognize, much less subscribe to, the religious principles that were vital to their institutions' foundation. In the process, the notion of "calling" in academic culture has been radically redefined, not abandoned.

"Calling" Redefined

Dwight Bradley's lead article in a 1932 issue of the *Christian Century* extols the blessings and responsibilities of Protestantism in America. Supremely confident of Protestantism's well-defined course and normative cultural status, "What's Coming in Protestantism?" reads more like a manifesto than an analysis of religious trends. Bradley locates the Protestant achievement, ostensibly begun by the sixteenth-century Reformation, in its "irresistible desire to regain the lost simplicity and immediacy of religious experience,"[2] which resulted in a return to the Bible and freedom from the Roman ecclesiastical establishment.

While Bradley acknowledges that individualism easily leads to sectarianism and denominationalism, perceived as undesirable, he believes the risks are outweighed by the benefits of "a new emphasis upon education and a tremendous growth of general intelligence,"[3] which naturally lends itself to democratic principles. In fact, American democracy and Protes-

---

2. Dwight Bradley, "What's Coming in Protestantism?" *Christian Century* 49, no. 1 (January 6, 1932): 10.
    3. Ibid.

tantism share a marvelous alignment of purpose because democracy too is essentially individualistic and yet progressive, best thriving without the pressures of any external authority imposed upon it.[4] Protestantism is de facto a religious and moral extension of democratic principles.

> To Protestantism, as well as to all liberal religion with an ethical passion, is left the responsibility for putting back into individualism its proper meaning. What, then, is the proper meaning of individualism? Is it not the meaning implied by the designation "free man"? Does it not carry with it a meaning that penetrates every nook and corner of life? Does it not mean freedom to think independently and the responsibility to think intelligently? Does it not mean the freedom to act independently and the responsibility to act uprightly? . . . Protestantism at this moment is presented with its supreme opportunity.[5]

To secure the future, Bradley adjures Protestants to take an aggressive stand on the key points of their identity: the centrality of direct religious experience, which ought "to go even beyond the limits reached by past tradition,"[6] allowing the Holy Spirit to direct one's path rather than human authority; and the reclaiming of a prophetic and ethical faith that eschews mysticism or sacramentalism.[7] No less important for liberal or free religion is the acknowledgment that "the *really* Protestant church" is "bound up intimately with the development of science in every field."[8] Herein is said to lie the future for theology and the church as Protestantism becomes the leading interpreter of scientific data in terms of spiritual experience. Bradley bestows a sacred status upon scientific inquiry as a means of fulfilling the divine calling. Spiritual intensity, moral passion, and progressive attitudes are the new canons of personal freedom of faith and the possibility for unity on a democratic basis. Even if we remove the optimistic tone typical of liberal amillennial attitudes and the platitudes of democratic idealism, the writer is proclaiming nothing less than the conjunction of providential operation with the agenda of American Protestantism.

Particularly noteworthy is Bradley's negative assessment of the ecclesiastical establishment and its tradition—"wholly archaic"—as irrelevant

---

4. Ibid. "Catholicism on the one hand, and facism or communism on the other, threaten the individual with unreasonable restraints; while Protestantism offers to the individual an opportunity to think, to speak, and to conduct his affairs with the maximum of liberty" (ibid.).

5. Ibid., 12.

6. Ibid., 10.

7. Ibid., 11.

8. Ibid., 13.

to the present and future vitality of Christian faith.[9] Society can realize human rational and moral potential once it is freed from external constraints such as religious standards specific to church affiliations. Scientific, political, and ethical progress is thus attained as all enlightened individuals agree about the great value of this progress. Inherent to this ideology we find what one historian has identified as the three persistent elements of modernist thought in Protestantism: (1) a conscious adaptation of religious ideas to modern culture, (2) the belief in the immanence of God in human nature and cultural development, and (3) an optimistic assumption that society is being formed as a kingdom of God on earth.[10]

At least in the earlier stages of the American Protestant program of reform, this combination of ideas replaced the alleged constrictions of confessional theology and thereby came to govern educational perspectives. One cannot fail to hear the voices of academic freedom within this sentiment, by this time in vogue. It was not merely a freedom from dictatorial powers of university trustees or pressure from political agencies for which the American Association of University Professors (AAUP) had so forcefully advocated in the beginning of the century, but a freedom from religious tradition(s) as the more serious threat.[11] Ironically, liberal Protestantism, diligently seeking to be a Christianity freed from all sectarian prejudices or forms of confessionalism, became quite sectarian in practice by censuring doctrinaire forms of Protestantism and Roman Catholicism as inimical to rational inquiry and the exercise of personal freedom. In its own reaction to fundamentalist evangelicalism, which by the 1930s had the reputation of hostility toward modern science and cultural and intellectual freedom, liberal religion was proving itself to be no less fundamentalist in attitude and approach. The reality of divine revelation and the intersection of the supranatural and natural orders are routinely marginalized or discounted altogether as reliable sources of knowledge.

The central issue here is this: in what ways has the modernist Protestant "calling" helped to create an educational philosophy formed in its own antisectarian image? Alasdair MacIntyre has argued that

9. Throughout this essay, I will be using "tradition" in two distinguishable ways: in the broad or categorical sense of the term, wherein tradition is that which expresses how a past system of rationality provides operating guidelines for present experience, and in the specific sense, a definitive qualification of the Christian faith that entails normative beliefs and practices.

10. William R. Hutchinson, *The Modernist Impulse in American Protestantism* (Cambridge: Harvard University Press, 1976), 32.

11. See "General Declaration of Principles" of the AAUP (1915), in *American Higher Education: A Documentary History*, ed. Richard Hofstadter and Wilson Smith, vol. 2 (Chicago: University of Chicago Press, 1961), 860–78.

"liberalism" successfully imposed unstated policies of enforced exclusion of any parties that did not conform to its particular platform of rationality. Such a platform was constructed on the broad thesis that human rationality and the methods with which it embodied itself are such that, if freed from external constraints such as religious and moral tests, they would produce not only progress in inquiry but also agreement among all rational persons about the nature of rationally justifiable arguments.[12] Thus, often in the academic context we have seen the illusory appearance of unconstrained rational agreement. We can recognize part of this as post-Enlightenment philosophy's effect in that only certain kinds of conversations and statements about what constitutes knowledge are permitted to coinhabit the classrooms of the modern university.

The notion of a calling, so pervasive in American Protestantism's program for social and pedagogical reform in the early twentieth century, became slowly and yet utterly redefined by Protestantism's quest for a latitudinarian religion. Once this agenda was in place, the religious character of a call, and eventually the need for maintaining any sort of specific calling within much of higher education, became superfluous.

Generally, the only remaining vestige of the older enterprise today is the belief that higher education ought somehow also to address moral formation. Despite the ejection of religious or ecclesiastical confessions, there has remained the nagging sense among many colleges and universities that the intellectual enterprise cannot afford completely to neglect the impartation of an ethical consciousness. Education should, inter alia, prepare young men and women to take responsible places in society for the civic good.

Built into liberal educational models is the principle that responsible inquiry should include some formation of self-understanding—a principle derived from classical epistemological theory about the process of human rationality. Cultivation of the intellect depends upon a moral formation of the knowing self. But this too has become an impossible task to maintain given the absence of agreement on what is good, beautiful, or just. As concrete notions of morality became ephemeral and even accidental to the goals of higher education, it was still assumed that students would somehow construct for themselves a practical and compatible ethical code through intellectual discipline and social integration within the university community. Such an assumption was and is obviously unfounded: institutions are constantly searching for ways

12. Alasdair MacIntyre, *Three Rival Versions of Moral Enquiry: Encyclopaedia, Genealogy, and Tradition; Being Gifford Lectures Delivered in the University of Edinburgh in 1988* (Notre Dame: University of Notre Dame Press, 1990), 225.

to provide a "core" of instruction in the arts and sciences that meaningfully imparts "values."

Indeed, the process underway since the 1960s has been to discount normative claims as nothing more than statements of personal preference. In *The Closing of the American Mind*, Allan Bloom elucidates the contradictory nature of the situation by arguing that every educational system has moral goals that inform its curriculum and are used to produce a particular kind of human being. On the postmodern American university campus, the prevailing moral code is based on the relativity of moral judgments. Relativism, supposedly the proper condition of a free society, is necessary to openness and "is the virtue, the only virtue, which all primary education for more than fifty years has dedicated itself to inculcating."[13] If absolutism is still teaching students just one danger to avoid, Bloom says, it is intolerance, not error.

Fundamental to the liberal project is the opening of political and intellectual space where all substantive agendas have an equal chance to compete. That "space" is necessarily circumscribed, as all political orders are, on specific principles of exclusion. Attempts to reshape public life according to a specific vision of the good are outside acceptable bounds.[14] Systems that suggest moral intolerance cannot be tolerated. Values proposed as normative or absolute are perceived as tyrannical. We are thus left with the view that the adoption of a particular set of traditional norms is not an acknowledgment reflecting transcendent or a priori standards, but an individual act of choosing a preference.

Every two years for the last decade, in an attempt to awaken institutions of higher education to the necessity of values, the John M. Templeton Foundation has published an "honor role" of universities and colleges that seek to foster in some programmatic way the development of virtue and moral character.[15] The foundation never exactly identifies the sources for "character," and at once we see that a Dewey-type civic idealism is apparent in the Templeton project.[16] Yet there is a difference:

13. Allan Bloom, *The Closing of the American Mind: How Higher Education Has Failed Democracy and Impoverished the Souls of Today's Students* (New York: Simon & Schuster, 1987), 26.

14. See Peter Leithart's review of Stanley Fish's *The Trouble with Principle* (Cambridge: Harvard University Press, 1999), in *First Things* 102 (April 2000): 55–58, esp. 56.

15. "Those habits of mind, heart and spirit that help young people to know, desire and do what is good . . . [are] a primary goal of educators" (*Honor Roll for Character-Building Colleges 1997–1998* [Radnor, PA: John Templeton Foundation, 1997], xi–xii).

16. For John Dewey, the formation of values is inherent to the process of democracy, as is faith in the capacities of human nature and the call for its liberation from all external and organizational coercion. See John Dewey, "Democracy Is Radical" (1937), in *The Essential Dewey: Pragmatism, Education Democracy*, ed. Larry Hickman and Thomas M. Alexander, vol. 1 (Bloomington: Indiana University Press, 1998), 337–39. Dewey valued the

the latter does not assume that a thoroughgoing democracy will produce the virtue and moral character needed to sustain itself. Something more definitive is needed. Employing the goad of an "honor roll" as a means to urge schools toward higher aims in their educational mission reveals the concern that the ultimate triumph of humanism cannot be taken for granted. One might ask whether or not a noble ideology, having replaced theology, can produce the desiderata of virtue and character in the university.

Freedom and Tradition at Odds

The new task of discerning the role of vocation within colleges and universities of Protestant origins is in fact a toned-down return to old byways and well-trod paths. The religious origins and early vocational mission of these institutions have been mostly forgotten; it obviously is much too late for a return to these vocational ideals, nor perhaps is such a return desirable. I do not want to argue that we should return to a lost golden age, if there ever was one. In any case, it is the very nature of Protestantism's sense of calling that serves as the major source of antagonism between advocates of cultural pluralism and defenders of religious foundationalism in the culture wars over truth claims. In hindsight, it is not difficult to see how the liberal Protestant agenda for education provided support for both of these positions.

It is far too simplistic to say that secularism was and is the cause of the tendencies within the academy that seek to ban or relativize absolutist concepts of morality or religious doctrinal norms. The story is not simply how secularism overpowered the church, for Protestant-originated and -operated universities of their own accord often embraced a nonconfessional and nondenominational platform as the most fruitful for achieving academic respectability. In his book *The Soul of the American University*, George Marsden has convincingly documented how the theology of nineteenth-century and early-twentieth-century Protestantism was itself as much the source for the widespread reception of pragmatic and positivist approaches to pedagogy as the rising forces of scientific methodology. Although Protestantism was not the only factor shaping the intellectual heritage of those who founded and governed the major universities, those educational ideals that may not seem especially religious—scientific and progressive ideals growing out of the Enlightenment, democratic moral and populist ideals, and

---

freedom of the individual but not as its own end and only as it contributed to the maintenance of liberty within society.

romantic principles of individual development—were mediated through the American Protestant context. Likewise, the liberal Protestantism that came to dominate American education was shaped by these ideals and perceived them as completely indigenous to sound biblical interpretation and to the essence of the Christian calling.

Again, the irony in this situation is that a Protestant establishment, motivated by virtues of freedom, democracy, reform, and inclusiveness, was determined to create a standardized system of higher education, excluding all but liberal Protestant or "nonsectarian" perspectives and forcing the alternatives (Protestant evangelical and Roman Catholic institutions) to a marginal existence on the educational periphery. But the real irony became manifest when the same nonsectarian logic, set in motion by liberalism and having successfully rooted out evangelical convictions from mainstream university education, eventually turned against the liberal Protestant establishment itself. The result, according to Marsden, was a so-called inclusive higher education that virtually excluded all religious perspectives from academic life.[17]

The Protestant outlook that lay behind so much of these educational perspectives cannot be adequately explained without discerning its free-church or believers-church roots. What Marsden also calls "low-church" Protestantism was the key reason why American universities acquired their characteristic traits. In fact, he observes, the United States is the only modern nation in which the dominant culture was substantially shaped by low-church Protestantism:

> So with respect to American universities, their pragmatism, their traditionlessness, their competitiveness, . . . their emphasis on freedom as free enterprise for professors and individual choice for students, their anti-Catholicism, their scientific spirit, . . . their tendency to equate Christianity with democracy and service to the nation, all reflect substantial ties to their low-church Protestant past.[18]

By way of one example, Marsden points to the educational vision of William Rainey Harper, a Baptist and the first president of the University of Chicago.[19] Harper had a passion for cultural reform through Bible study. It was a biblicism reminiscent of the previous century and fueled by the notion that sanctification of mind and heart consisted of a return

---

17. George M. Marsden, *The Soul of the American University: From Protestant Establishment to Established Nonbelief* (New York: Oxford University Press, 1994), 4–6.

18. Ibid., 239.

19. The University of Chicago, which Marsden styles as "a quintessential Protestant institution," was organized by the Chicago Baptists of the American Educational Society and initially funded by John D. Rockefeller Sr., himself a Baptist layman.

to the purity and simplicity of the primitive faith. Essential to primitivistic ideals, typical of free-church theology, was an emphasis on freedom
from ecclesial and traditional intellectual authority, a general disdain
for tradition, along with a focus on individual moral responsibility.[20]
Harper's goals in restoring the centrality of the Bible and placing it in a
prominent role within higher education stem from his conviction that
American democratic and individualistic values were derived from the
Bible, just as the Bible was also a firm foundation for science and the
investigation of truth. This program of restoration was not concerned
with Christianizing pagan America but was aimed against Christian
"superstition" (meaning fundamentalist Christians, whose prescientific
reading of Scripture and pessimistic views of culture brought discredit
to Christianity). One of Harper's most frequently reiterated themes was
that traditional Bible teaching was unworthy of the faith of enlightened
and modern persons, and it certainly had no place in an institution of
higher learning. In effect, the Protestant calling to enable the sacralization
of a nation was being jeopardized by the narrow vision of obscurantist
Christian churches.

Marsden tracks quite similar movements of "progressive Christianity"
in a number of universities—Chicago (Baptist), Vanderbilt (Methodist), Syracuse (Methodist), Johns Hopkins (Quaker), Boston University
(Methodist)—all in one way or another seeking to elevate their academic
stature and become eligible for funding from the Carnegie Foundation
by eschewing their denominational positions. Religiousness, while still
relevant for training in liberal arts, needed to be freed from confessional
moorings in order to be the most pliable for the academic identity that
was emerging. But there was a high and unexpected price to be paid for
the dismissal of doctrine. In the ousting of a specified Christian tradition
through purging religion from sectarian biases, modernist Protestantism
did not ultimately achieve a more objective and culturally amenable faith,
as was its original intention. Instead, it found itself confronted by a new
hostility toward the legitimacy of *any* Christian norms. The liberal Protestant "virtue" of freedom had become so critical to the faith that there
was absolutely no way for the distinctive aspects of that faith to survive
in the academic institutions of a free society.[21] Even the reduction of
doctrine into ethical ideology became an impediment to the progressive
attitudes that now reigned in the once-Protestant universities. By the
early twentieth century, the quest for nonsectarian religion had become
translated as "nonreligious."

20. Marsden, *Soul of the American University*, 243–44.
21. Ibid., 398.

Over the last century and a half, the Protestant attempt to establish a kind of impartial and unbiased religion, one that does not offend the sensibilities of the academy, has backfired. There is no such thing as a truly latitudinarian perspective of religion, which in reality is an exhibition of modernity's own quest for the objective based on scientific means. The reduction of religious particularities and uniqueness produced not a broader base of agreement, but a pious insipidity that is neither compelling for satisfying intellectual acumen nor for offering guidance to the believing community.

At the heart of the liberal Protestant experiment with education lay ideological assumptions about the nature of freedom. Freedom guaranteed an authentic faith because it allowed for the exercise of self-awareness and self-criticism, a view structured according to liberal notions of divine immanence: the presence and working of God *within* the world rather than upon it. This freedom assumed that humanity was essentially capable of discovering and conforming to the divine plan, thus placing an emphasis on human dignity rather than its corruption, and on the potential for human achievement rather than its weakness and vulnerability. Through its authoritative nature, dogmatic Christianity, as represented in its historic creeds and doctrines, seemed opposed to the call to freedom. The traditional character of its creeds and doctrines either prohibited or stunted the religious freedom inherent to the Protestant view because it undermined the perspective necessary for uniting faith and culture. A few, however, have made serious criticisms about the uncritical exaltation of freedom in liberal Protestant circles. Reinhold Niebuhr once warned against what he called "extravagant estimates of freedom," which provide the illusion that humanity's increasing freedom first emancipates itself from subjection to natural necessity, then makes humanity the master of historical destiny.[22] Indeed, intellectual freedom becomes a self-evident virtue that begets its own sense of calling, whereas religious tradition confronts the modern mind with the unacceptable proposition of its own impotence and decadency.

As long as academic freedom and tradition are arraigned in competition with one another, each with its own separate vision of what constitutes the cardinal principles and goals of higher learning, the misguided paradigm of the rational versus the confessional will continue. The AAUP has its origins in just such a paradigm. Largely the creation of Protestant liberal academics, the AAUP's interpretation of religion is grounded on antisectarianism; and not unexpectedly, the relationship between the parameters of religious commitment and academic inquiry is mostly a

---

22. Reinhold Niebuhr, *Faith and History: A Comparison of Christian and Modern Views of History* (New York: Scribner, 1949), 79.

negative one. At first glance, this may seem to be an unfair appraisal of the organization. For it is acknowledged in the AAUP's "General Declaration of Principles of 1915" that there are fields of human endeavor about which our knowledge is only at a beginning: natural science, social science, and philosophy and religion. These areas of knowledge constitute the relations of humanity to outer nature, to one's fellow human beings, and to ultimate realities and values. Regarding the latter, the document gives credence to the epistemological value of "spiritual life" and discovery of the "general meaning and ends of human existence."[23] The sentiment expressed here is not antireligious, provided that we understand "religion" in its broadest possible sense. In this document the AAUP does not make clear what tangible forms such "religion" might actually take, except as it concerns "the general meaning and ends of human existence." Perhaps it cannot make "religion" clear in any concrete way since the very same paragraph stipulates that progress in any field of knowledge, including religion or spirituality, must be conditioned by "complete and unlimited freedom to pursue inquiry."

While religious knowledge may be said to constitute a legitimate form of understanding, it must not infringe on the greater good of unlimited academic freedom. The statement's declaration on academic freedom articulates where religion infringes on this greater good: "In the early period of university development in America the chief menace to academic freedom was ecclesiastical."[24]

The reworking of the 1915 resolution in "The Statement of Principles on Academic Freedom and Tenure" (1940) sounds a more negative tone about religion, although it is also clearer. This 1940 statement is less helpful because it simply states that religion poses limitations on academic freedom without ever explaining how.[25] It deems any sort of governing tradition to be problematic and says that a college or university is "a marketplace of ideas, and it cannot fulfill its purposes of transmitting, evaluating and extending knowledge if it requires conformity with any orthodoxy of content and method." This statement claims that erecting boundaries or whatever it is that comprises "orthodoxy" prevents effective production and transmission of knowledge. For this reason, the AAUP in 1915 denied to church-affiliated institutions of higher learning the name of "university." It claims that such institutions have not accepted principles of freedom and inquiry because they assert the truth of the incarnation or resurrection of Christ, convictions not subject to

23. Hofstadter and Smith, *American Higher Education*, 2:867.
24. Ibid., 868.
25. Section b under "Academic Freedom," http://www.aaup.org/statements/Redbook/1940stat.htm (accessed August 29, 2005).

the test of deliberative reason.[26] And yet, the AAUP also says that faculty members are completely free to engage in political activities, and that institutions ought to give leaves of absence for a reasonable period if a faculty member serves in a political campaign or term of office.[27] The AAUP thus apparently counts politics as somehow free—in a way that religion is not free—from indoctrinating influences on academic inquiry. Whatever the AAUP means for academic freedom to protect, its definition of freedom clearly protects the academy from confronting its own blind spots and biases.

There can be no doubt that much of the antagonism between academic freedom and the heavy hand of "tradition" results from modern educators' confusion and uncertainty about the concept and function of tradition. When Jaroslav Pelikan delivered the Jefferson lectures in 1983 (sponsored by the National Endowment for the Humanities) on the subject of tradition, he began with the assumption that none of his listeners knew what tradition really was.[28] There is no point in talking about the loss of tradition in modern scholarship, he said, if no one knows its identity, either as a category of research or as possessing a specific content. The very idea of tradition suffers largely from constructed and influential caricatures that have become and have been an indissoluble, though not necessary, part of the Protestant rationality and religious epistemology since the late sixteenth century.

It is important to recognize that for Protestant thinking, the axiom on which the sixteenth-century Reformation turned was upon making a sharp distinction between gospel and tradition. Protestants equated gospel with the timeless and divine truths exhibited in the New Testament; they regarded tradition as an artificial accumulation of human machination and religious practices. The gospel is the primitive and simple message of fundamental religious experience; tradition is derived from doctrinal systems, political institutions, and ceremonial rituals that arose during the late first and second centuries—during the emergence of Catholicism.

Perhaps in this dichotomous version of early Christian history, Protestant liberalism and conservativism come closest together. For completely

26. Cf. Stanley Fish, "One University under God?" *Chronicle of Higher Education*, January 7, 2005, C4.

27. Section 12 of the AAUP's "Recommended Institutional Regulations on Academic Freedom and Tenure" (revised in 1999), http://www.aaup.org/statements/Redbook/Rbrir.htm (accessed August 29, 2005).

28. See Jaroslav Pelikan, *The Vindication of Tradition* (New Haven: Yale University Press, 1984), chap. 1, "The Rediscovery of Tradition," esp. 19: "For even if—or especially if—the tradition of our past is a burden that the next generation must finally drop, it will not be able to drop it, or understand why it must drop it, unless it has some sense of what its content is and of how and why it has persisted for so long."

different reasons, both share a view of relative discontinuity when it comes to a historically applied understanding of doctrine. Although the Protestant liberal model denies the existence of a narrative linking present faith experiences with the concrete expressions of that faith in the past,[29] evangelical Protestantism nullifies a tangible connection by its tendency to embrace the "true" faith through an immediate (and often ahistorical) appropriation of the New Testament era.[30] In both cases, antitraditionalist and antidogmatic perspectives are built into the Protestant religious ethos, liberal or conservative, implicitly or explicitly, and these have determined what should be included and excluded for a responsible educational pedagogy. Both are stamped by the influences of romantic modernism (with its roots in the Enlightenment), as witnessed in their emphasis on individualism, egalitarianism, and low tolerance for honoring practices or beliefs in accordance with the classical principles of antiquity. Epistemological principles—such as the right of private judgment, and personal experience as an arbiter of ultimate meaning—have become definitive: for the liberal, because experience is the chief, if not the only, means left for securing knowledge; and for the conservative, because the priority of every believer's individual judgment or conscience ultimately guarantees freedom of the spirit and mind.

Essentialist Catholicism and the Reunion of Calling, Freedom, and Tradition

If the Protestant American experience has taught leaders of higher education anything, it is that church-related institutions must maintain their confessionalism if they wish to preserve any sense of Christian vocation within the current pluralist context. A specifically Christian institution—Protestant or Roman Catholic—cannot succeed unless it unapologetically sets forth certain points of tangible belief as the philo-

29. Historian Frances Young, for example, has argued for the problematic nature of ascertaining "orthodoxy" because all doctrinal development is environmentally conditioned and determined by such factors as politics, philosophical presuppositions, and the chances of history. The disjunction between present forms of faith and the earliest Christians is an undeniable, if regrettable, fact of reality. See Frances Young, "A Cloud of Witnesses," in *The Myth of God Incarnate*, ed. John Hick (Philadelphia: Westminster, 1977), 23.

30. A primitivistic or restitutionist view of history underlies the belief that a connection between the apostolic and present church exists, but largely in a spiritual sense. Since most of church history is "fallen" or corrupt, it is necessary that the "true church" of the present age find its own predecessors in select instances or figures of the past, while rejecting the main body of the historical narrative. The rise of the episcopacy, dependency on tradition rather than the Bible or the Holy Spirit, the use of creeds, and so on, all bespeak of a faith that had become misaligned and detached from the pristine and simple spirituality of the Bible.

sophical cornerstone of the school's identity. To do otherwise risks repeating the failure of religiously liberal or latitudinarian approaches,
whose reduction of theology amounted to little more than "a *supply* of
the wants of human nature," as Newman once characterized it.[31]

At least, universities whose heritage is founded in the Christian tradition ought to retain what I call an "essentialist catholicism": basic
transdenominational propositions that pertain to the (historical) core
of the Christian identity. A working definition of "essentialist catholicism," for example, can be found in the recent restatement of *Ex corde
ecclesiae*, which argues for

> a shared baptismal belief in the truths that are rooted in Scripture and tra-
> dition, as interpreted by the church, concerning the mystery of the Trinity:
> God the Father and Creator, who works even until now; God the Son and
> incarnate Redeemer, who is the way and the truth and the life; and God
> the Holy Spirit, the Paraclete, whom the Father and the Son send.[32]

Virtually every church-originated institution, regardless of denominational affiliation,[33] can espouse these truths about God and his unique
revelation, along with truths that also insist on the importance of religion
or theology when it comes to determining emphases in the university
curriculum. Or one might equally point to the Apostles' Creed, which
has functioned throughout the church's history in a way similar to the
Rule of Faith used in the second and third centuries.

Herein may be found discernable and important implications for
how one should construct reality: the creation has meaning inherent
in itself as ultimately accountable to its Creator; the incarnation of the
Word tells us that the natural and the supranatural are not closed off
to each other (and so on). In whatever way the diversity of the human
response is conveyed (and it should be conveyed) in an educational curriculum, an essentialist catholicism preserves a broad but not hopelessly
vague Christian ontology within the realms of knowledge. Essentialist
catholicism thus presents studies of theology and religion as legitimate
parts of studies within liberal arts, being no less practical and functional
to the understanding of the human person and society than the other
disciplines. Moreover, the maintenance of an essentialist catholicism

31. John Henry Newman, *The Idea of the University* (Notre Dame: University of Notre
Dame Press, 1982), 28–29.

32. "*Ex corde ecclesiae*: An Application to the United States," *Origins* 29 (1999): 404.

33. As illustrated in the ecumenical concord achieved in *Baptism, Eucharist, and Ministry* (Geneva: World Council of Churches, 1982), which represented the input from virtually all the major church traditions as it sought to express a common understanding of the
apostolic faith.

prevents the study of theology from being reduced to a phenomenology of religion that has little toleration for confessional Christianity, or conversely, prone to an individualistic piety that evades critically confronting the intellectual content of the Christian faith.

In practice within the university context, the role of Christian tradition in its specific confessional sense need not be antithetical to rational inquiry and freedom of the intellect. The latter has always operated in dependency on some kind of intellectual tradition or set of norms, spoken or unspoken, which has enabled discovery and an ordering of reality. Just as no discipline can achieve complete objectivity, so also total freedom from all forms of tradition or authority does not exist. Part of the modern myth is the simple replacement of religious tradition with methods of rationality, a myth that has had the effect of making contemporary culture susceptible to the influence of seemingly normless norms and traditionless traditions. Thus the question—to repeat—always needs to be asked: to what context of traditions or antitraditional traditions are we submitting our inquiries?[34]

In its broad or specific senses, tradition is not opposed to the freedom of rational inquiry; instead, it understands freedom as the creative exercise of the will within an acknowledged circle of governing first principles because such principles enable the very process of rational inquiry. A rationality of tradition, as MacIntyre insists, is always subject to correction and change, since tradition is itself a dynamic of self-reflection as it becomes aware of new needs for greater internal coherency or responds to inadequacies raised by new situations. But it is important that a core belief remains, surviving and holding together the identity of the tradition so that we can make corrections.[35]

If we are going to be consistent with a broad-minded notion of academic freedom, then it must include the freedom to be religious, including confessionally or traditionally Christian, within academic dialogue. A religious posture does not and should not ipso facto rule out participation in enlightened and critical inquiry. To take this a step further via MacIntyre's argument for the rationality of tradition, we can reasonably argue that religious tradition provides a cohesive framework such that rational arguments for and against a viewpoint are even possible. Even if one does not agree with all the data within a certain confessional position, at least meaningful dialogue over such issues is possible. Antagonists who work from completely disparate sets of conceptions about reality or who believe that there is no unifying conception of rationality

34. See Mark Schwehn, *Exiles from Eden: Religion and the Academic Vocation in America* (New York: Oxford University Press, 1993), 58–64.

35. See J. Herdt, "Alasdair MacIntyre's 'Rationality of Traditions' and Tradition-Transcendental Standards of Justification," *Journal of Religion* 78 (1998): 528.

are unable to engage in a concerted dispute about their conflict. Since tradition is itself the formation of a dialectical process, it offers the greatest potential for situating radically conflicting views on a common plane of rationality, so that progress or even some agreement about what constitutes progress may be achieved.[36]

Conclusion

A lesson for future discussion about vocation in the academy presents itself. The vision of American liberal Protestantism for higher education has not come to pass in the way that it was intended, nor was its vision as self-evident as proponents declared it to be. It had strong biases against confessional or doctrinal theology, biases masked as commitments to academic freedom and progressive thinking. But in time these biases became unmasked, shown up as ideals of intellectual freedom and rationality that were erected on an anticonfessional platform that remains intact today. To claim that the alleged synthesis of science and Protestant theology, which once inspired the reform of American higher learning, is largely moribund[37] does not adequately explain the almost total alienation between the two. Not only has the older liberal vision *not* resulted in a unified and harmonized approach to learning within the arts and sciences, in addition, progressive Protestantism, by means of its sacralization of culture and scientific method, has also been displaced by a secular ideology of progress through technology and the "values" of pragmatic strategies. With this displacement, secular ideology no longer accepts any need for a "call" (religious or otherwise) that would imply (1) that the ultimate telos of learning and intellectual formation lies in a source outside of itself, and (2) that pragmatic ideology and the use of technology are not conceptually neutral practices but exist within a definite framework of conceptions often contrary to (religious) higher goods.[38]

The liberal Protestant educational experience has shown us that Protestantism's absorption of the national culture, with the aim of shaping and unifying it, led to the loss of distinctive confessional parameters as

36. MacIntyre, *Three Rival Versions*, 10–12.

37. Edward Schaffer, "The Protestant Ideology of the American University: Past and Future Prospects," *Educational Theology* 40 (1990): 20.

38. In part, this is what Neil Postman warns us against as the rise of a cultural technopoly eschews moral and religious commitments for efficiency, interest, and economic advance. "It [the technopoly story] casts aside all traditional narratives and symbols that suggest stability and orderliness, and tells instead of a life of skills, technical expertise and the ecstasy of consumption, . . . saying that the story of Western civilization is irrelevant" (Neil Postman, *Technopoly: The Surrender of Culture to Technology* [New York: Knopf, 1992], 179).

Protestantism was demoted to play a supporting role in that culture. Religion is still regarded as useful for maintaining an ethos of civility, but commitments to religious doctrine too easily interfere with cultural and intellectual freedom. The notion of "calling" thereby devolved into vague moral idealism and flabby pietism that, devoid of doctrinal identity, could not ultimately sustain itself. Out of the chaos of the undefined (but much applauded) benefits of "diversity," the core credenda of the Christian tradition keep before us the imperative of the call to seek the Good, the True, and the Beautiful. As the dialogue about the role of church-originated institutions of higher learning takes new steps forward into the mainstream of the academy, we must give confessionalism a new hearing for redressing the balance in academic opinion, for only therein can vocation be reclaimed as constitutive of the Christian intellectual community that stands at the heart of the university that is church-related.

CONTRIBUTORS

Michael D. Beaty is professor of philosophy at Baylor University, where he has served since 1987. Currently chair of the department, he has previously held posts at Baylor as vice provost for faculty development and director of the Institute for Faith and Learning. A specialist in moral and social philosophy, and the philosophy of religion and Christianity and higher education, he is the author of numerous articles and is the editor or coeditor of three books: *Christian Theism and the Problems of Philosophy*; *Christian Theism and Moral Philosophy*; and *Cultivating Citizens: Essay on Soulcraft and Contemporary Citizenship*.

Joel A. Carpenter is currently the provost of Calvin College, a post he has held since 1996, and is the director of Calvin's new Nagel Institute for the Study of World Christianity. He is the former director of the Religion Program at Pew Charitable Trusts, a position he assumed after a dozen years in teaching posts at Calvin College, Trinity College (Illinois), and Wheaton College. A scholar of American religious history, he has published many articles and chapters and is the author or coeditor of several books, including *Making Higher Education Christian*; *Twentieth-Century Evangelicalism: A Guide to the Sources*; *Earthen Vessels: American Evangelicals and Foreign Missions*; and the award-winning study *Revive Us Again: The Reawakening of American Fundamentalism*. Carpenter's latest work, coedited with Lamin Sanneh, is *The Changing Face of Christianity: Africa, the West, and the World*.

Jean Bethke Elshtain is the Laura Spelman Rockefeller Professor of Social and Political Ethics at the University of Chicago Divinity School. She is the author of many books, including *Just War against Terror: The Burden of American Power in a Violent World*; *The Jane Addams Reader*; *Jane Addams and the Dream of American Democracy*; *Who Are We? Critical Reflections and Hopeful Possibilities*; *Augustine and the Limits of Poli-*

tics; *Democracy on Trial*; *Women and War*; and *Meditations on Modern Political Thought*. In addition to other books for which she has been an author, editor, or contributor, Elshtain is also the author of more than five hundred articles and essays in scholarly journals and journals of civic opinion. In 1996, she was elected a fellow of the American Academy of Arts and Sciences. She is the recipient of seven honorary degrees and is cochair of the Pew Forum on Religion and American Public Life.

Susan M. Felch is professor of English at Calvin College and the past director of the Calvin Seminars in Christian Scholarship (1997–2003). She is author of numerous articles on sixteenth-century British literature and literary theory, and she is the editor or coeditor of *The Collected Works of Anne Vaughan Lock*; *Bakhtin and Religion: A Feeling for Faith*; *The Self: Beyond the Postmodern Crisis*; Elizabeth Tyrwhit's *Morning and Evening Prayers*; and three volumes on winter, autumn, and summer, each subtitled *A Spiritual Biography of the Season*.

Aurelie A. Hagstrom is associate professor of theology at Providence College in Providence, Rhode Island. She was formerly chair of the department of theology/philosophy at the University of St. Francis in Joliet, Illinois. Hagstrom is a former consultant to the U.S. Catholic Bishops' Committee on the Laity, and her main area of research is the theology of the laity. She has taught in formation programs for the permanent deaconate and ecclesial lay ministry, and she is a popular speaker for adult education and parish renewal programs. Among her publications are *The Concepts of the Vocation and Mission of the Laity* and *A Pilgrim's Guide to Rome and the Holy Land for the Third Millennium*.

Steven R. Harmon is associate professor of Christian theology at Campbell University Divinity School in Buies Creek, North Carolina. A specialist in patristic theology, he is the author of *Every Knee Should Bow: Biblical Rationales for Universal Salvation in Early Christian Thought*, along with a forthcoming book, *Towards Baptist Catholicity: Essays on Tradition and the Baptist Vision*. In addition, Harmon is associate editor of the Baptist theological journal *Review and Expositor* and is an ordained Baptist minister.

Richard B. Hays, George Washington Ivey Professor of New Testament at Duke Divinity School, is internationally recognized for his work on the letters of Paul and on New Testament ethics. His book *The Moral Vision of the New Testament: Community, Cross, New Creation* was selected by *Christianity Today* as one of the one hundred most important religious books of the twentieth century. Hays has lectured widely worldwide, and as an ordained minister, he has preached in settings ranging from rural Oklahoma churches to London's Westminster Abbey. Hays has chaired the Pauline Epistles section of the Society of Biblical Literature, as well as the seminar on New Testament Ethics for the Society for New Testament Studies. He convened the Consultation on Teaching the Bible in the Twenty-First Century and was coconvener of the Scripture Project, a research initiative sponsored by the Center of Theological Inquiry at Princeton.

Douglas V. Henry serves as director of the Institute for Faith and Learning and assistant professor of philosophy in the Honors College at Baylor University. In addition to work in ancient philosophy and ethics, his research interests include the history, philosophy, and theology of Christian higher education. Coeditor of *Faithful Learning and the Christian Scholarly Vocation*, he is currently at work on two other volumes: *The Schooled Heart: Moral Formation in American Higher Education* and *For Freedom, For Love: Liberal Education and the Baptist Vision*.

David Lyle Jeffrey is provost and distinguished professor of literature and the humanities at Baylor University. He was elected fellow of the Royal Society of Canada in 1996. Named Inaugural Professor of the Year at the University of Ottawa in 1995, he has also been a guest professor at Peking University (Beijing) since 1996. He served as department chair of English both at the University of Victoria and the University of Ottawa and has also taught at the University of Rochester, the University of Hull (UK), and Regent College. Besides being the general editor and coauthor of *A Dictionary of Biblical Tradition in English Literature* and coauthor of *Rethinking the Future of the University*, Jeffrey is also the author of *English Spirituality in the Age of Wesley*; *English Spirituality in the Age of Wyclif*; *People of the Book: Christian Identity and Literary Culture*; and most recently, *Houses of the Interpreter: Reading Scripture, Reading Culture*.

John C. Polkinghorne is president emeritus and fellow of Queen's College and former professor of mathematical physics at Cambridge University. An ordained Anglican priest, he was elected fellow of the Royal Society in 1974, appointed knight commander of the Order of the British Empire in 1997, and selected to receive the Templeton Prize for Progress toward Research or Discoveries about Spiritual Realities in 2002. His latest books include *Living with Hope: A Scientist Looks at Advent, Christmas, and Epiphany* and *Science and The Trinity: The Christian Encounter with Reality*. Among his other books are *Quarks, Chaos, and Christianity: Questions to Science and Religion*; *The Faith of* *a Physicist: Reflections of a Bottom-up Thinker; Belief in God in an Age of Science; Faith, Science, and Understanding; Quantum Theory: A Very Short Introduction; The God of Hope and the End of the World*; and *Science and Theology: An Introduction.*

Daniel Russ is the director of the Center for Christian Studies and a faculty member at Gordon College in Wenham, Massachusetts. From 2002 to 2003, he was the executive director of Christians in the Visual Arts at Gordon College, where the CIVA office is housed. Russ serves as a moderator and academic consultant for the Trinity Forum and has contributed to a number of books on classics, biblical studies, and cultural leadership, including *The Terrain of Comedy; The Epic Cosmos; Classic Texts and the Nature of Authority; Invitation to the Classics*; and *The Tragic Abyss.*

Mark L. Sargent serves as the provost of Gordon College in Wenham, Massachusetts, a post he has held since 1996. Previously he served as the academic vice president at Spring Arbor College (Michigan), and he has also taught at Biola University and the University of Utrecht (Netherlands). He is a contributor to several books and journals on American history and culture, including most recently *Lives out of Letters: Essays in American Literary Biography and Documentation.* For his work on William Bradford, he was awarded the Walter Muir Whitehill Prize in Colonial History.

Daniel H. Williams is professor of religion in patristics and historical theology at Baylor University. Before going to Baylor in 2002, he served on the theology faculty at Loyola University Chicago, and he has twice served as a pastor of American Baptist churches. Williams is the author or editor of five books, including *Evangelicals and Tradition: The Formative Influence of the Early Church; Retrieving the Tradition and Renewing Evangelicalism: A Primer for Suspicious Protestants*; and *The Free Church and the Early Church: Bridging the Historical and Theological Divide.*

Index